Readings in Education
a sequence

J. M. Longbridge

October 19th, 1968

Readings in Education

a sequence

edited by

W. KENNETH RICHMOND

M.A., M.ED.
Senior Lecturer in Education
Glasgow University

Methuen & Co Ltd

11 NEW FETTER LANE · LONDON · EC4

First published 1968 by Methuen & Co Ltd
11 New Fetter Lane, London EC4
© 1968 by W. Kenneth Richmond
Printed in Great Britain by
Richard Clay (The Chaucer Press) Ltd,
Bungay, Suffolk

Distributed in the U.S.A.
by Barnes & Noble Inc.

Contents

	Acknowledgements	*page* vii
1	Words, Words, Words	1
2	The Relationship between Theory and Practice	11
3	The Aims of Education	25
4	General and Special Education	37
5	The Concept of Educability	55
6	The Nature and Nurture of Human Abilities	68
7	Punishment	99
8	Discipline	119
9	Moral Education	134
10	Character Training	154
11	Examinations, Tests, Evaluation	173
12	Curriculum	194
13	Methods	218
	Index	239

Acknowledgements

The editor and publishers wish to thank the following for permission to reproduce extracts from the books listed below: Allman & Sons Ltd. for *The Psychology of Punishment* by A. B. Allen; Allen & Unwin Ltd. for *Branch Street: A Sociological Study* by Marie Paneth, *Ethics and Education* by R. S. Peters, *Training for Teaching* by J. E. Sadler & A. N. Gillett, *Introduction to Modern Genetics* by C. H. Waddington and *Homer Lane* by W. David Wills; Allen & Unwin Ltd. and Paul S. Eriksson, Inc. for *Authority, Responsibility and Education* by R. S. Peters; Allen & Unwin Ltd. and Ohio State University Press for *Bertrand Russell on Education* by J. Park; Edward Arnold Ltd. for *Education: Its Data and First Principles* by Sir Percy Nunn; Asia Publishing House for *Education from Dewey to Gandhi* by G. Ramanathan; Association of Teachers in Colleges and Departments of Education for *Education for Teaching*; Ernest Benn Ltd. for *The Aims of Education* by A. N. Whitehead; A. & C. Black Ltd. for *Secondary Modern Discipline* by Richard Farley and *The Great Didactic of John Amos Comenius* trans. by M. W. Keatinge; The Brookings Institution for *The Effects of Federal Programs on Higher Education* by Harold Orlans; Cambridge University Press for *Religion in the Making* by A. N. Whitehead; Chatto & Windus Ltd. for *In Spite of the Alphabet* by Hunter Diack; Wm. Collins Sons & Co. Ltd. for *Teachers and Machines* by W. Kenneth Richmond; The Cornmarket Press for *New Education*; J. M. Dent & Sons Ltd. and E. P. Dutton & Co. Inc. for *A New View of Society and Other Writings* (E.M.L.) by Robert Owen; Professor James Drever for *Data for Edinburgh*; E. M. Eppel for *The Adolescent and Changing Moral Standards* published by Faber & Faber Ltd. in *Moral Education in a Changing Society* edited by W. R. Niblett; Faber & Faber Ltd. for *Education and Values* by G. H. Bantock and *Good Enough for the Children?* by J. E. H. Blackie; Fearon Publishers Inc. for *Preparing Instructional Objectives* by R. F. Mager; Victor Gollancz Ltd. for *The Teacher and his World* by Walter James and *Talking of Summerhill* by A. S. Neill; Harper & Row Inc. for *New Curricula* edited by Robert W. Heath; Harrap & Co. Ltd. for *Groundwork of Educational Theory* by James S. Ross; Harvard Educational Review for *The Science of*

Learning and the Art of Teaching by B. F. Skinner; Harvard University Press for *Toward a Theory of Instruction* by Jerome S. Bruner, *General Education in a Free Society* by the Harvard Committee and *Three Thousand Years of Educational Wisdom* edited by R. Ulich; William Heinemann Ltd. and A. P. Watt & Son for *Dr Moberley's Mint Mark* by Christopher Dilke; H.M.S.O. for the *Newsom Report*, the *Plowden Report*, *Statistics of Education* 1962, the *Robbins Report*, the *Norwood Report*, the *Hadow Report* and the *Brunton Report*; David Higham Associates Ltd. for *Examinations: The End of Education* by Lord David Cecil and *One Rat in Twenty is a Leader* by Colin Wilson; Hutchinson & Co. Ltd. for *An Experimental Study of Mathematics Learning* by Z. P. Dienes; Hutchinson & Co. Ltd. and Barnes & Noble Inc. for *The Concept of Mind* by Gilbert Ryle; Incorporated Association of Assistant Masters in Secondary Schools for *The A.M.A.* (November 1958); The Loeb Classical Library (Heinemann and Harvard University Press) for their translations of Aristotle's *Nichomachean Ethics* and *Politics* and Plato's *Letters*; Longmans, Green & Co. Ltd. for *Linking Home and School* edited by Maurice Croft, John Raynor & Louis Cohen, *Education and the Training of Teachers* by P. Gurrey, *Learning and Teaching* by A. G. & E. H. Hughes, *The Public Schools* by G. Kalton and *Sir Fred Clarke: Master Teacher* by F. W. Mitchell; Longmans Green & Co. Ltd. and Penguin Books for *Nuffield Physics – Teachers Guide*; Maclellan for *Being a Headmaster* by Norman Tosh; McGraw-Hill Book Company for *Realms of Meaning* by Philip H. Phenix and *Principles of Genetics* by E. W. Sinnott, C. Dunn and T. Dobzhansky; Macmillan & Co. Ltd. for *The Evolution of Educational Theory* by Sir John Adams, *Technology and the Academics* by Sir Eric Ashby, *A Teacher's Story* by Guy Boas and *The Examination of Examination* by Hartog and Rhodes; Robert F. Mager for the transcript of a lecture; Manchester University Press for *Aims in Education* edited by T. H. B. Hollins and *Education and Environment* by S. Wiseman; Methuen & Co. Ltd. for *The Greek Philosophers from Thales to Aristotle* by W. K. C. Guthrie, *Contrary Imaginations* by Liam Hudson, *The Sociology of Education* by P. W. Musgrave, *Culture and General Education* by W. Kenneth Richmond, *The Teaching Revolution* by W. Kenneth Richmond and *Georg Kerschensteiner* by Diane Simons; John Murray (Publishers) Ltd. for *Landmarks in the History of Education* by T. L. Jarman; National Education Association of the United States for *Programmed Instruction: Breakthrough in Air Force Training* by J. E. Briggs; National Foundation for Educational Research in England and Wales for *A Survey of Rewards and Punishments in Schools*; W. R. Niblett for *Some Problems in Moral Education Today* published by Faber & Faber Ltd. in *Moral Education in a Changing Society* edited by W. R. Niblett; Oldbourne Press for *The Nature of Education* by Brogan and *Technical Teaching and Instruction* by Alexander Maclennan; Oliver & Boyd Ltd. for *The Borders and Beyond* by Abel Chapman, *The Scaling of Teachers Marks and Estimates* by D. M. McIntoch *et al.*, *Genetic and Environmental Factors in Human Ability* edited by J. E. Meade & A. S. Parkes; Oxford at the Clarendon Press for Plato's *Republic* trans. by F. M.

Cornford; Penguin Books Ltd. for *The Comprehensive School* by R. Pedley and *Education for Tomorrow* by John Vaizey; Pergamon Press Ltd. for *Society Schools and Progress in France* by W. D. Halls and *Introduction to Techniques of Teaching* by A. D. C. Peterson; A. D. Peters & Co. for *Pavlov in Retreat* by Arthur Koestler; R. S. Peters for *Reason and Habit* published by Faber & Faber Ltd. in *Moral Education in a Changing Society* edited by W. R. Niblett; The Philosophical Library Inc. for *Moral Principles in Education* by John Dewey; Sir Isaac Pitman & Sons Ltd. for *Glaucon* by M. V. C. Jeffreys; PSW (Educational) Publications for *Non-Streaming in the Junior School* by B. Simon; Alvin Redman Ltd. for *The Measure of Man* by J. W. Krutch; Routledge & Kegan Paul Ltd. for *Unfolding Character* by Arnold Brown, *Education and the Working Class* by Brian Jackson and Denis Marsden; Routledge & Kegan Paul Ltd. and Philosophical Library for *An Introduction to the Philosophy of Education* by D. J. O'Connor; Routledge & Kegan Paul and Humanities Press Inc. for *Philosophical Analysis and Education* edited by R. D. Archaumbault and *Tractatus* by Wittgenstein; Routledge and Kegan Paul Ltd. for *The Philosophy of Education* by R. S. Peters and *The History of Education* by Brian Simon from *The Study of Education* edited by J. W. Tibble; Routledge & Kegan Paul Ltd. and McGraw-Hill Book Company for *Understanding Media* by Marshall McLuhan; Routledge & Kegan Paul Ltd. and The Macmillan Company for *The Moral Judgement of the Child* by J. Piaget; Routledge and Kegan Paul Ltd. and The Shoe String Press Inc. for *Latin and Greek* by R. M. Ogilvie; S.C.M. Press Ltd. and The Westminster Press for *Augustine: Earlier Writings* trans. by J. H. S. Burleigh; Sidgwick & Jackson Ltd. for *Eton Microcosm* edited by A. Cheetham and E. Parfit; Souvenir Press Ltd. for *Mechanization in the Classroom* edited by Goldsmith; A. H. D. Tozer and Mrs Gwen Larwood, widow of H. J. C. Larwood, for *Data for Liverpool*; The University of Hull Institute of Education for *Moral Values in a Mixed Society* (Aspects of Education No. 1) by Lionel Elvin; University of London Press Ltd. for *Purpose in the Curriculum* by Stanley Nisbet; University of London Press Ltd. and Philosophical Library for *The Measurement of Abilities* by P. E. Vernon; A. P. Watt & Son and Hart Publishing Co. for *Summerhill* by A. S. Neill; John Wiley & Sons, Inc. for *Creativity and Intelligence* by J. W. Getzels & P. W. Jackson, *Educational Anthropology* by G. F. Kneller, *Applied Programed Instruction* by S. Margulies and L. D. Eigen, *The Psychology of Character Development* by Peck and Havighurst and *Philosophies of Education* edited by P. H. Phenix.

I

Words, Words, Words

In discussing educational topics we constantly use words such as 'ability', 'intelligence', 'learning', 'instruction', 'discipline' and so on. At a somewhat higher level of discourse we are accustomed to basing our arguments on such abstract concepts as 'equality of opportunity', 'the democratic way of life', 'liberal education', 'specialization' and others which are only too familiar. The assumption is that, because it enjoys a common currency, this kind of language can be trusted.

Can it? A great deal of the confusion and misunderstanding which arises in discussions about educational problems might be avoided if the participants were first alerted to the dangers of supposing that the meaning attached to this or that word or term by one individual is the same for all. Without going so far as to say that informed, critical thinking is virtually impossible unless the person concerned has undertaken a thorough study of semantics and linguistic analysis, we certainly need to be on our guard against the dangers of 'talking past' each other – and of double-thinking. The trouble about Education is that it is one of those fields in which each of us feels entitled to express his own opinion. In exercising this right, we owe it to ourselves and to others to be as sure as we can that the terms we use are clearly understood.

1 Plato's disclaimer

One statement at any rate I can make in regard to all who have written, or who may write with a claim to knowledge of the subjects to which I devote myself – no matter how they pretend to have acquired it, whether from instruction, or from others or by their own discovery. Such writers can in my opinion have no real acquaintance with the subject. I certainly have composed no work in regard to it, nor shall I ever do so in the future, for *there is no way of putting it into words like other studies*. Acquaintance with it must come rather after a long period of attendance or instruction in the subject itself and of close companionship when, suddenly, like a blaze kindled by a living spark, it is generated in the soul and at once becomes self-sustaining . . .

There is a true doctrine which I have often stated before, which stands in the way of the man who would dare to write even the least thing on such matters, and which it seems I am now called upon to repeat. (At this point in his letter to Dionysius, Plato outlines four progressive stages of knowledge – naming, describing, imagining, understanding. Of these, only the last approaches the fifth stage, which alone represents true knowledge, while the others are correspondingly remote from it.) Now if in the case of any of these a man does not somehow or other get hold of the first four, he will never gain a complete understanding of the fifth. Furthermore, these four – names, descriptions, bodily forms, concepts – do as much to illustrate the *particular quality* of any object as they do to illustrate its *essential reality* because of the inadequacy of language. Hence no intelligent man will ever be so bold as to put into language those things which his reason has contemplated, especially in a form which is unalterable – which must be the case with what is expressed in written symbols.

PLATO, *Letters*, Loeb Classical Library

For discussion

1 If it is true that 'there is no way of putting it into words' why did Plato bother to write his letters in the first place, you may ask? It's a fair question. In considering your answer it may help if you bear in mind these alternative questions: (*i*) Is all thinking necessarily verbal? (*ii*) Is it not the case that the kind of thinking which finds its expression in the written (or printed) word is 'unalterable', whereas private thinking and discussion ('thinking aloud') are essentially fluid? (*iii*) In what kind of situations are you forced to acknowledge that, 'words fail me?', and (*iv*) When it comes to communicating the deeper meanings, are not music, painting, sculpture and other art forms just as effective as literature?

2 According to Plato, knowledge is hierarchical. How do you imagine a Christian would arrange the following sentences, in which the word 'know' has different levels of meaning, according to the five stages outlined in the above passage?

I know that Pekin is in China.
I'd know Smith anywhere – he has a scar on his left cheek.
I know that my Redeemer liveth.
In the equation $E = mc^2$ I know that c stands for the speed of light.
I know the difference between tea and coffee.
I know that my husband is innocent, but I can't prove it.

Which, if any, of these statements can be verified in terms of verbal reasoning alone?

2 A caveat from the Dark Ages

What happens when we teach? Is it simply a case of someone-who-knows telling those who don't? St Augustine thinks not. Just as the eye sees through the medium of light waves which come from the sun, so the inner eye of the mind perceives meaning through a Divine Illumination which comes from God. Sun is to seeing as God is to knowing, he maintains. The following extract is taken from Augustine's short dialogue *De Magistro* (*The Teacher*), written c. A.D. 389.

The utmost value I can attribute to words is this. They bid us look for things, but they do not show them to us so that we may know them. He alone teaches me anything who sets before my eyes, or one of my bodily senses, or my mind, the things which I desire to know. From words we can learn only words. Indeed we can learn only their sound and noise. Even if words, in order to be words really, must also be signs, I do not know that any sound I may hear is a word until I know what it means. Knowledge of words is completed by knowledge of things, and by the hearing of words not even words are learned. We learn nothing new when we know the words already, and when we don't know them we cannot say we have learned anything unless we also learn their meaning. And their meaning we learn not from hearing their sound when they are uttered, but from getting to know the things they signify. It is sound reasoning and truly said that when words are spoken we either know or do not know what they mean. If we know, we do not learn, but are rather reminded of what we know. If we do not know already, we are not even reminded, but are perhaps urged to inquire.

On the one hand we need light that we may see colours and the elements of this world, and sentient bodies that we may perceive things of sense, and the senses themselves which the mind uses as interpreters in its search for sense-knowledge. On the other hand, to know intelligible things with our reason we pay attention to the interior truth. How, then, can it be shown that words teach us anything besides the sound that strikes the ear? Everything we perceive we perceive either by bodily sense or by the mind. The former we call 'sensible things', the latter 'intelligible things'. . . .

But when we have to do with things which we behold with the mind, that is, with the intelligence and with reason, we speak of things which we look upon directly in the inner light of truth which illumines the inner man and is inwardly enjoyed. There again if my hearer sees these things himself with his inward eye, he comes to know what I say not as a result of my words but as a result of his own contemplation. Even when I speak what is true and he sees what is true, it is not I who teach him. He is taught not by my words but by the things themselves which inwardly God has made manifest to him. Accordingly, if asked he can make answer regarding these things. What could be more absurd than that he should suppose that by my speaking I have taught him, when, if asked, he could himself have explained these things before I spoke? It often happens that a man, when asked a question, gives a negative answer, but by further questioning can be brought to answer in the affirmative. The reason lies in his own weakness. He is unable to let the light illumine the whole problem.

> ST AUGUSTINE, *De Magistro*,
> 36–40, from *Augustine: Earlier Writings*, L.C.C., vol. VI,
> (ed.) J. S. BURLEIGH, S.C.M. Press.
> Published in the U.S.A. by The Westminster Press, 1953

For discussion

1 Nowadays we associate words first and foremost with printed symbols. 'We can learn only their sound and noise,' says Augustine. How do you account for the change in viewpoint between A.D. 389 and the present day?

2 'It is not I who teach him.' Examine the implications of this statement.

3 'It often happens that a man, when asked a question, gives a negative answer, but by further questioning can be brought to answer in the affirmative.' YOU HAVE BEEN WARNED!

3 The advent of the printed word

With the invention of movable type, books became the principal means of disseminating information and ideas. The enthusiasm of Reformation educators is reflected in this passage from Comenius, *The Great Didactic* (1632).

Specially prepared books should be supplied to each class, and these should contain the whole subject matter of the literary, moral and religious instruction prescribed for the class. Within these limits no other books should be needed, and by their aid the desired results should infallibly be obtained. . . .

We might adapt the term 'typography' and call the new method of teaching 'didachography'. Instead of paper, we have pupils whose minds have to be impressed with the symbols of knowledge. Instead of type, we have the class-books and the rest of the apparatus. The ink is replaced by the voice of the master, since this it is that conveys information from the books to the minds of the listener, while the press is school-discipline, which keeps the pupils up to their work and compels them to learn. . . .

As soon as we have succeeded in finding the proper method it will be no harder to teach schoolboys, in any number desired, than with the help of the printing press to cover a thousand sheets daily with the neatest writing, or with Archimedes' machine to move houses, towers and immense weights, or to cross the ocean in a ship and journey to the New World. The whole process, too, will be as free from friction as is the movement of a clock whose motive power is supplied by weights. It will be as pleasant to see education carried out on my plan as to look at an automatic machine of this kind, and the process will be as free from failure as are these mechanical contrivances when skilfully made.

For discussion

In fairness, it should be pointed out that the passage is not altogether typical of the educational theory of Comenius, which is usually credited with being pre-eminently child-centred. Here, the comparison between pupils and sheets of paper is reminiscent of Locke's *tabula rasa*; and Comenius's faith in the self-sufficiency of the printed word now strikes us as more than a little naïve. At the same time, his enthusiasm for the Gutenberg technology is understandable. Without books, would mass education have been possible?

4 An eighteenth-century protest

I hate books – they only teach us to talk about things we know nothing about. . . .

Since we must have books, there is one book which, in my opinion, supplies the best treatise on an education according to nature. This is the first book Émile will read; for a long time it will form his entire library, and will always retain an honoured place. It will be the text to which all our lessons on natural science are but a commentary. It will serve to test our progress towards a right judgment, and it will invariably be read with delight so long as our taste remains unspoilt. What is this wonderful book? Is it Aristotle? Pliny? Buffon? No: it is *Robinson Crusoe*.

ROUSSEAU, *Émile*, Book 3 (1762)

For discussion

1 'I hate books!' Then why write them, you ask? As an author, Rousseau is nothing if not paradoxical. How far, if at all, do you agree that books only purvey second-hand information and encourage us 'to talk about things we know nothing about'?

2 Keep the young child dependent on things, not words, is the gist of Rousseau's advice. What *are* 'things', and how can we be sure that first-hand experience of them is more real than information derived from 'words'?

3 Forcing the child to read at an early age is unnatural and harmful, Rousseau insists: 'Nature would have them be children before they become men. If we try to invert this order we shall produce forced fruit that is immature and flavourless, fruit which turns rotten before it is ripe: we shall have young professors and old children. Childhood has its own ways of seeing, thinking and feeling; nothing could be more foolish than to try to substitute our grown-up ways – I should no more expect judgment in a ten-year-old child

than I should expect him to be five feet high.' And again, 'Give your scholar no verbal lessons; he should be taught by experience alone.'

Yet most of us have been brought up on a diet of verbal lessons from an early age. Books have played an enormously important part in our education, and the pressure on the learner to acquire more and more information is increasing all the time. Was Rousseau a voice crying in the wilderness? Are we 'the hollow men, headpiece stuffed with straw', as T. S. Eliot inferred?

5 The need for analysis: a twentieth-century view

66. Consider for example the proceedings that we call 'games'. I mean board-games, card-games, ball-games, Olympic games, and so on. What is common to them all? – Don't say: 'There *must* be something common, or they would not be called "games" ' – but *look and see* whether there is anything common to all. – For if you look at them you will not see something that is common to *all*, but similarities, relationships, and a whole series of them at that. To repeat: don't think, but look! – Look for example at board-games, with their multifarious relationships. Now pass to card-games; here you find many correspondences with the first group, but many common features drop out, and others appear. When we pass next to ball-games, much that is common is retained, but much is lost. Are they all 'amusing'? Compare chess with noughts and crosses. Or is there always winning and losing, or competition between players? Think of patience. In ball-games there is winning and losing; but when a child throws his ball at the wall and catches it again, this feature has disappeared. Look at the parts played by skill and luck; and at the difference between skill in chess and skill in tennis. Think now of games like ring-a-ring-a-roses; here is the element of amusement, but how many other characteristic features have disappeared! And we can go through the many, many other groups of games in the same way; can see how similarities crop up and disappear.

And the result of this examination is: we see a complicated network of similarities overlapping and criss-crossing: sometimes overall similarities, sometimes similarities of detail.

67. I can think of no better expression to characterize these similarities than 'family resemblances'; for the various resemblances between members of a family: build, features, colour of eyes, gait, temperament, etc. etc., overlap and criss-cross in the same way. – And I shall say: 'games' form a family. . . .

In such a difficulty always ask yourself: How did we *learn* the meaning of this word ('good' for instance)? From what sort of examples? in what language-games? Then it will be easier for you to see that the word must have a family of meanings.

LUDWIG WITTGENSTEIN, *Tractatus,*
Routledge & Kegan Paul and Humanities Press

For discussion

1 As we said, many of the words we use in speaking or writing about educational topics stand for concepts which are decidedly blurred at the edges. When in doubt, says Wittgenstein, always ask yourself, 'From what sort of examples did I learn the meaning of this word?' (To repeat: don't think, but look!) He illustrates his advice by taking the word 'game', and concludes that the most that can be deduced from an examination of its various uses is a vague family resemblance rather than a common core.

We suggest that you follow his advice and see what emerges from a close scrutiny of the words 'education', 'learning', 'intelligence' and 'theory'. In each case make your list as exhaustive as possible.

To start you off, here are a few items which might be included in the lists:

education: Department of Education and Science, Driver Education, Education Committee, sex education, co-education, Master of Education, Adult Education, etc., etc.

learning: learning to walk, a man of learning, learning theory, learning the latest news, learning bad habits, etc., etc.

intelligence: military intelligence, intelligence test, a higher intelligence, etc.

2 Can you discern any sort of 'family resemblance' between the following words?:

education – instruction – training – teaching – learning – scholarship – character-formation – discipline – indoctrination – conditioning – schooling – brain-washing – acculturation.

6 After literacy – what?

As an intensification and extension of the visual function, the phonetic alphabet diminishes the role of the other senses of sound and touch and taste in any literate culture. The fact that this does not happen in cultures such as the Chinese, which use nonphonetic scripts, enables them to retain a rich store of inclusive perception in depth of experience that tends to become eroded in civilized cultures of the phonetic alphabet. For the ideogram is an inclusive *gestalt*, not an analytic dissociation of senses and functions like phonetic writing.

The achievements of the Western world, it is obvious, are testimony to the tremendous values of literacy. But many people are also disposed to object that we have purchased our structure of specialist technology and values at too high a price. Certainly the lineal structuring of rational life by phonetic literacy has involved us in an interlocking set of consistencies that are striking enough to justify a much more extensive inquiry than that of the present chapter. Perhaps there are better approaches along quite different lines; for example, consciousness is regarded as the mark of a rational being, yet there is nothing lineal or

B

sequential about the total field of awareness that exists in any moment of consciousness. Consciousness is not a verbal process. Yet during all our centuries
of phonetic literacy we have favored the chain of inference as the mark of logic
and reason. Chinese writing, in contrast, invests each ideogram with a total
intuition of being and reason that allows only a small role to visual sequence as a
mark of mental effort and organization. In Western literate society it is still
plausible and acceptable to say that something 'follows' from something, as if
there were some cause at work that makes such a sequence. It was David Hume
who, in the eighteenth century, demonstrated that there is no causality indicated
in any sequence, natural or logical. The sequential is merely additive, not
causative. Hume's argument, said Immanuel Kant, 'awoke me from my dogmatic
slumber'. Neither Hume nor Kant, however, detected the hidden cause of our
Western bias toward sequence as 'logic' in the all-pervasive technology of the
alphabet. Today in the electric age we feel as free to invent nonlineal logics as
we do to make non-Euclidean geometries. Even the assembly line, as the method
of analytic sequence for mechanizing every kind of making and production, is
nowadays yielding to new forms.

> MARSHALL MCLUHAN, *Understanding Media*, p. 84,
> Routledge & Kegan Paul and McGraw-Hill

The Medium is the Message. C. P. Snow, reviewing a book of A. L. Rowse (*The
New York Times Book Review*, December 24, 1961) on *Appeasement* and the
road to Munich, describes the top level of British brains and experience in the
1930s. 'Their I.Q.s were much higher than usual among political bosses. Why
were they such a disaster?' The view of Rowse, Snow approves: 'They would
not listen to warnings because they did not wish to hear.' Being anti-Red made
it impossible for them to read the message of Hitler. But their failure was as
nothing compared to our present one. The American stake in literacy as a technology or uniformity applied to every level of education, government, industry,
and social life is totally threatened by the electric technology. The threat of
Stalin or Hitler was external. The electric technology is within the gates, and we
are numb, deaf, blind, and mute about its encounter with the Gutenberg
technology, on and through which the American way of life was formed. It is,
however, no time to suggest strategies when the threat has not even been
acknowledged to exist. I am in the position of Louis Pasteur telling doctors that
their greatest enemy was quite invisible, and quite unrecognized by them. Our
conventional response to all media, namely that it is how they are used that
counts, is the numb stance of the technological idiot. For the 'content' of a
medium is like the juicy piece of meat carried by the burglar to distract the
watch-dog of the mind. The effect of the medium is made strong and intense
just because it is given another medium as 'content'. The content of a movie is a
novel or a play or an opera. The effect of the movie form is not related to its

program content. The 'content' of writing or print is speech, but the reader is almost entirely unaware either of print or of speech.

MARSHALL MCLUHAN, *Understanding Media*, p. 17–18,
Routledge & Kegan Paul and McGraw-Hill

For discussion

1 McLuhan's argument is not easy to follow. What he is saying, in effect, is that ours is a print-dominated culture. Ever since the invention of movable type, our modes of thinking (and feeling) have been conditioned by reading and writing, with the result that we have become slaves to the 'technology of the alphabet'. The cult of literacy, concentrating as it does on visual symbols to the exclusion of the other senses, has made nationalism, industrialism and other features of modern civilized life possible and changed the ratio between man's senses in subtle ways in the process. With the arrival of an electric technology, he thinks, we face an entirely new situation.

What evidence can you adduce from your own experience in support of this argument?

2 Television, radio, language laboratories, teaching machines – these and other examples of mechanization in the classroom are standing proof that 'the electric technology is within the gates'. As teachers, how do we respond to the accusation that we are numb, deaf, blind and mute about its encounter with the Gutenberg technology which has been our stock in trade for the past four centuries?

The medium is the message, says McLuhan. Have we got the message?

3 Students who have worked through this section of 'Readings in Education' sometimes complain that 'It makes you think, I suppose, but it leaves me not knowing *what* to think'. Fair criticism?

7 What's the use?

QUESTIONER: So you are a budding philosopher, are you? Please tell me what use there is in studying philosophy.

PHILOSOPHER: I am not sure what sense of 'use' you are employing. Are you asking me whether philosophy has a use in the sense in which, shall we say, engineering has a use?

QUESTIONER: Yes; that is the sort of thing that I mean. Engineering enables us to build roads, houses and hospitals. Surely philosophy is pretty useless when compared with something like that.

PHILOSOPHER: Perhaps. But let us pursue this matter a bit further. Engineering, you say, is useful because it enables us to build houses, to warm them properly, to provide drains for them and so on. But what use is that? What are houses for?

QUESTIONER: To live in, of course, with some kind of comfort. Surely even philosophers do that nowadays!

PHILOSOPHER: And by 'live' you don't mean just keeping your heart beating, or taking in nutriment and getting rid of its waste-products?

QUESTIONER: Of course I don't. I mean enjoying life as well.

PHILOSOPHER: By doing what? Playing Bingo? Making love to your wife? Discussing Plato's views about love with her. . . ?

QUESTIONER: Oh, don't be ridiculous! You know what I mean. Doing what everyone else does in their houses. . . .

PHILOSOPHER: But people do different things and perhaps some things are more worth doing than others. All really worthwhile things are absolutely useless in your sense of 'use'. For things which are useful in your sense are only so because they make possible things like philosophy, art and literature, which also have the function of transforming how things which are 'useful' in your sense are conceived.

QUESTIONER: Tell that to Lord Bowden!!

R. S. PETERS, 'The Philosophy of Education',
pp. 78–9, in *The Study of Education*, (ed.) J. W. TIBBLE,
Routledge & Kegan Paul, 1967

For discussion

The point of this dialogue, says Professor Peters, is to exhibit the logical incompleteness of questions about 'use'. One of the purposes of these readings is to provide practice in critical thinking. Is this a 'useful' purpose? Would it still be a 'useful' purpose if it left you not knowing what to think?

2

The Relationship between Theory and Practice

To the speculative genius of Hellenic thought the search for absolute principles – *theoria* – was of primary concern, sustained by the conviction that such principles not only existed but could be discovered. By contrast, the modern mood is more inclined to be pragmatic. It is no accident that textbooks entitled 'Principles of Education' are no longer in favour. Practice comes first, we are often told; and there is a widespread distrust of 'theory' – a distrust which is by no means confined to students training to become teachers. In the following passages you will find educational theory variously described as 'waffle', 'a rag-bag', 'all talk', 'a soft centre' and 'unsubstantiated conjectures' – none of which sounds like a promising introduction to the subject. Possibly these are the descriptions which you would yourself be tempted to use (at any rate in private!) regarding courses on 'Theory and Principles of Education'.

How far, if at all, is this sceptical attitude justified? What, precisely do we have in mind when we speak of 'educational theory'? How is 'educational theory' related to classroom practice? Is 'educational theory' undergoing a process of transition – and if so what is happening to it?

The readings are arranged with these questions in mind, *and in that order*. They are offered as a basis for discussion and, needless to say, they disclaim any intention of giving cut and dried answers.

1 The multiplication of theories

The tendency to propound Theories follows almost as a logical corollary upon the conditions outlined above. The absence of fresh field-observations and of facts – which can only be gathered in the field (and which, if gathered, would often place the said 'theories' in a different light) – is atoned – or ought to be atoned – by the propagation in all directions of 'fascinating theories' whereby almost each cryptic or recondite problem in Nature receives a sort of quasi-official explanation. The system is a negation of 'Science' – since science imparts

Knowledge: while 'Theory' is obviously an excursion beyond the bounds of knowledge. It is, moreover, fraught with danger: the very 'fascination' of a theory oft proves a fatal temptation to trespass afar into the unknown. In the first instance, it is the semi-hypnotised originator who is the worst 'criminal', for he, not unnaturally, glories in the beauty of his own creation: but the net result is tenfold worse, for to-day a popular topic is promptly appropriated by legion ready-writers of facile pen and brilliant imagination (not limited), who, masters of 'embroidery' and skilled word-play, speedily transform what was originally but a fugitive idea into an institution, apparently as stable as granite rock.

Thus there come to be erected these hosts of nebulous superstructures resting on no solid foundations and serving no good purpose (unless that of gratifying vanity – or misleading the outer world! – be so regarded). For, as each theory in turn is exploded and abandoned, no single 'originator' ever comes penitentially forward in a white sheet to recant his errors!

ABEL CHAPMAN, *The Borders and Beyond*,
pp. 444–5, Oliver & Boyd, 1924

For discussion

1 When asked how he came to formulate his General Theory of Relativity Einstein replied, 'I did it by refusing to accept an axiom.' Can science advance without making 'an excursion beyond the bounds of knowledge'?

2 Would you agree that educational theory is a 'nebulous superstructure resting on no solid foundation'?

2

I now wish to offer three grounds for the belief that, as matters stand at the moment in psychology, elaborate theory-building is out of place. The first is strategic: that precisely formulated theories give rise to long-drawn-out battles, for and against, which are finally unproductive.

Research designed with respect to theory is also likely to be wasteful. That a theory generates research does not prove its value unless the research is valuable. Much useless experimentation results from theories, and much energy and skill are absorbed by them. Most theories are eventually overthrown, and the greater part of the associated research is discarded.[1]

Theories (Hull's theory of learning, to take an example) make claims which other workers immediately try to test. This process of testing seems, on the face of it, relatively straightforward. A rat is claimed to learn when his primary drives are satisfied: satisfy his primary drives, and see whether he learns or not. How-

[1] Skinner (1959), p. 41.

ever, the design of an experiment which will test such predictions is a subtle affair, and the literature concerned with Hull's theory is a large one.[1] What usually happens in the end is that the dispute peters out inconclusively. Experimenters realize either that the theory is not sufficiently precise to test; or that it is too simple to be true. Once this stage is reached, there follows a period of patching up. Then, almost invariably, the theory is allowed to languish, and most of the research aimed to support or refute it is written off as lost.

It seems that this method of organizing psychology around a number of precisely formulated but simple theories must be a poor one:

> If undue emphasis is placed on formal theories before successful research strategies have been evolved, there is a clear danger that experimental results may be regarded as evidence for or against rival theories (and nearly all of them are certain to be wrong) instead of letting the data suggest new experiments and new research strategies.[2]

Human beings, it seems, are multifarious; and we achieve little by speculating about them without first finding out what they are like. There is, after all, little merit (and no point) in proposing general ideas about human beings if these are largely or completely mistaken. Nor is there any virtue in claiming that our idea is 'basically right' although obscured by the welter of people's individuality. It is the welter that we must observe and measure; and if we do observe, we are invariably forced to modify our initial hunches out of all recognition. It seems a matter of common prudence, therefore, if theories must be adapted continually to meet new facts, that we should not define any one theory too closely.

Some may say this criticism is glib; that the work promoted by Hull's theory is solid, empirical research, and is therefore invaluable, either as a springboard for the next theorizer, or simply as natural history. Whether this defence is justified in any given case, it is hard to tell. In general, though, it is unpersuasive. The back numbers of the journals of experimental psychology bulge with detailed, highly artificial studies of learning, memory and perception, which few psychologists now consult. Where an experiment is designed to test a specific prediction from a given theory, the chances of its having any readily intelligible value to later generations of psychologists is slight.

This first, strategic objection to precise theories seems to me a powerful one, and damning in itself. There are however two more, both arising from the mesmeric fascination which webs of ideas seem to exert over those who spin them. The first is that theories tend to be 'blind' leading their begetters to discover only what they expect to discover. The second is that they tend to be unsinkable – they are theories which cannot be proved wrong.

LIAM HUDSON, Contrary Imaginations,
pp. 6–7, Methuen, 1966

[1] Hull (1943). See, e.g., Osgood (1953), Hilgard (1956), Bugelski (1956), for discussion of this literature.   [2] Gregory (1960).

For discussion

Can science advance without making 'an excursion beyond the bounds of knowledge', we asked? The question was, of course, a loaded one, being prefaced by the mention of Einstein's Theory of Relativity. Because of this, presumably, your answer was in the negative. But here we have a distinguished psychologist warning us against the mesmeric fascination of theory-building.

So let us put the question again '*Is* a good deal of educational theory a "nebulous superstructure resting on no solid foundation"?'

3

The prejudice against teacher training dies hard and with it the prejudice against educational theory dies equally hard. Admittedly, the prejudice has some justification. A highly intelligent and highly trained young man or woman is bound to waste a good deal of time in teacher training. Education and Sociology are the two bastard disciplines of the century. Under their top dressing of diagrams and statistics they have less that is solid to say than the descriptive Natural History of Buffon's day. . . .

In spite of the waffle, Training Colleges have some valuable knowledge to impart, though they take too long in imparting it. Oskar Spiel of Vienna had apparently had striking success in teaching children who were enormously 'underprivileged' and therefore presumably recalcitrant. Yet the practical advice he gives in his book *Discipline without Punishment* is no more than the pragmatic counsel that would be given by any sensible master or mistress of Method.

No doubt that counsel could be given in a much shorter space of time, and no doubt the natural teacher would learn it all for himself. But if the natural teachers start with some knowledge of what experience and even psychology has to impart, his earlier years of teaching will be easier and the pupils he takes in those earlier years will be rather better taught.

COLM BROGAN, *The Nature of Education*,
pp. 106–7, Oldbourne, 1962

For discussion

Brogan seems to damn educational theory with faint praise. The inference is that the 'born' teacher can do without it, and that the others could acquire it in less time than they normally take during their period of professional teaching. How do you respond to this line of argument?

4

The influence of educational reformers like Pestalozzi, Froebel and Montessori is due more to their precepts and their practical achievements than to their theoretical writings. A new practical approach to teaching is more influential than a new theory about teaching. Ideally, of course, a new technique should be capable of being justified by theoretical considerations as it usually is in engineering or medicine, just as a new theory, if it is genuinely a theory, should result in practical advantages when it is applied in the classroom. But we do not find the connection between most educational theories and their practice is as close as this. It is rather similar in this respect to the present state of psychotherapy where there are a number of different therapeutic techniques in use, each with its theoretical background. It is found that although the theories are incompatible with one another, the techniques as used by skilled practitioners all seem to produce sufficient results to justify their continued use. And this would be impossible if the techniques were in fact tied as closely to their supposed theoretical foundations as is the case with physical or chemical theory and its applications. We must rather suppose that the theories of the psychiatrists are rationalizations of their practice rather than genuine reasons for them.

The same seems to be true of much of the so-called theory underlying established educational practice. The fact that a well conducted school using the Dalton plan or Montessori or Froebel methods produces good results is, of itself, no justification whatever of the supposed theoretical background of these practices. If indeed a representative group of schools using, say, project methods of teaching consistently got better results than a comparable group of schools using other methods, that would be some evidence in favour of Dewey's educational theories which the project method was designed to apply. But no very convincing evidence of this sort seems available at present. The cumulative effect of new proposals for teaching is, of course, considerable over long periods of time. The teaching practice and curriculum of a present day primary school is very different from those of a similar school of seventy years ago. And these differences are due to the ingenuity and hard work of many educational reformers. But the adoption of these different improvements in the art of teaching does not commit anyone to adopting the often elaborate 'theoretical' justifications of the new methods. The introduction of a new teaching method has often been more like the empirical insight of a herbalist in the early stages of medicine. Practice comes first; but its theoretical justification has to wait for the scientific development that can explain its success. Thus educational theories which preceded the rise of scientific psychology (when they were not metaphysical speculations or ethical judgments) were more or less acute guesses at explaining successful practice. Some of them were acute and systematic but misleading like the psychology of Herbart. Some were unsubstantiated conjectures, like Montessori's views on the training of the senses. Some, like Pestalozzi's doctrine of Anschauung, were unintelligible adaptations of metaphysical concepts. Many of such theorists indeed seem to have taken to heart the rule of method by which Rousseau attempted to explain the nature of man: 'Let us then begin by laying facts aside, as they do not affect the question.' It is not therefore surprising that the results were unsatisfactory. Usually, however, these abortive theories were just glosses on fruitful innovations in educational practice. It was the practice that mattered.

But the development of a scientific psychology has put us in the position where we no longer have to rely on practice to suggest theory. It may, of course, still do so but it is *experiment* rather than practice which now suggests theory. The relationship between theory and practice has become a reciprocal one. Theory directs practice and practice corrects theory. Present day knowledge of perception, learning, motivation, the nature of 'intelligence' and its distribution and development, the causes of educational backwardness, and many other matters of this kind enable us to amend educational practice in the expectation of improved results. We have, in other words, a body of established hypotheses that have been confirmed to a reliable degree. They enable us to predict the outcome of their application and to explain the processes that we are trying to control. They are, to that extent, genuine theories in the standard scientific sense of the word. Even so, they do not approach the theories of the physical sciences in their explanatory power. For example, learning theory is one of the best developed fields of psychology. The processes of human and animal learning have been very thoroughly studied by experimental methods for over fifty years. The great mass of accumulated results has greatly improved our understanding of how we learn but it has not yet been condensed into a single overall theory. There are several theories of learning all of which seem to be compatible with most of the known facts without being necessitated by them. Not one of them fits the facts so perfectly as to exclude all its rivals. What are still needed are crucial experiments which will enable psychologists to decide between one theory and another. Thus even the best examples of theories in the sciences of man are less closely tied to their supporting facts than in theories in the sciences of nature.

We can summarize this discussion by saying that the word 'theory' as it is used in educational contexts is generally a courtesy title. It is justified only where we are applying well-established experimental findings in psychology or sociology to the practice of education. And even here we should be aware that the conjectural gap between our theories and the facts on which they rest is sufficiently wide to make our logical consciences uneasy. We can hope that the future development of the social sciences will narrow this gap and this hope gives an incentive for developing these sciences.

D. J. O'CONNOR,
An Introduction to the Philosophy of Education,
pp. 107–10, Routledge & Kegan Paul,
paperback edition 1966

For discussion

1 Do you accept O'Connor's criticisms of the theories put forward by the Great Educators of the past? If not, how would you rebut them?
2 How would you distinguish between an 'acute guess' and a 'scientific hypothesis'?

5 The historical aspect

The student of educational theory, for example, is sometimes surprised and even annoyed at the frequency with which reference is made to Plato and Aristotle in all treatises that deal with his subject. There is a natural pedantry that leads writers in such a new branch of university study as education to support the dignity of their subject by appealing to the highly respected authorities of antiquity. But there is another and a more worthy explanation. The fifth century B.C. formed one of the two great educational maximal points of the past. Very many of our modern ideas on education are to be found implicit in Plato and Aristotle. In succeeding chapters abundant illustration of these anticipations will be found. It does not follow that these old writers were fully aware of all the implications of their own writings. No doubt we read into Plato and his fellows a great deal more than quite entered into their consciousness. This line of argument always has the unpleasant effect of making us moderns appear condescending towards the master minds of the past; and we need to keep reminding ourselves that we see farther than the men of old merely because we are standing upon their shoulders. We must humbly acknowledge the lift they give us; but it is folly to blink the fact that we do see farther.

But not everybody thinks that Herbert Spencer marks an advance on Plato. This raises the important question: in what does educational progress consist? Was Dr Johnson right after all when he maintained that all there is to be known about education was known long ago? It is a disquieting but necessary thing to ask point blank: Is our ordinary intelligent educator of to-day in possession of a better theory to enable him to carry on his life work than was his prototype among the contemporaries of Plato? A great deal depends on the view taken on the question of the progress of the world as a whole. Those who believe that the race has made no progress since Plato's time will certainly not admit any advance in educational method. But those who believe that the idea of evolution in its modern form has given a new point of view, that has profoundly modified our attitude to all matters involving life, will admit that we have got beyond the best that was available in the fifth century B.C. Even the men of the Renaissance had got ahead of Plato and Aristotle in the matter of the relation between the state and the individual. What is implicit in Aristotle becomes explicit at the Renaissance, thanks partly to Christianity and partly to the greater range of experience.

SIR JOHN ADAMS,
The Evolution of Educational Theory, Macmillan

For discussion

According to O'Connor the doctrines of the Great Educators are a load of old rubbish. According to Sir John Adams, 'we are standing on their shoulders'.

Which of the two metaphors is to be preferred?

6

The assertion that theory comes closer to truth or reality than practice is characteristically Platonic. In [*The Republic*], Socrates outlines an ideal state, claiming that an ideal is none the worse for not being realizable on earth. Glaucon's query – what is to happen supposing it turns out that the theory won't work – is first brushed aside, but in Book V, 471c, Glaucon raises the objection again.

The more you talk like that, he said, the less we shall be willing to let you off from telling us how this constitution can come into existence; so you had better waste no more time.

Well, said I, let me begin by reminding you that what brought us to this point was our inquiry into the nature of justice and injustice.

True; but what of that?

Merely this: suppose we do find out what justice is, are we going to demand that a man who is just shall have a character which exactly corresponds in respect to the ideal of justice? Or shall we be satisfied if he comes as near to the ideal as possible and has in him a larger measure of that quality than the rest of the world?

That will satisfy me.

If so, when we set out to discover the essential nature of justice and injustice and what a perfectly just and unjust man would be like, supposing them to exist, our purpose was to use them as ideal patterns: we were to observe the degree of happiness or unhappiness that each exhibited, and to draw the necessary inference that our own destiny would be like that of the one we most resembled. We did not set out to show that these ideals could exist in fact.

That is true.

Then suppose a painter had drawn an ideally beautiful figure complete to the last touch, would you think any the worse of him, if he could not show that a person as beautiful as that could exist?

No, I should not.

Well, we have been constructing in discourse the pattern of an ideal state. Is our theory any the worse if we cannot prove it possible that a state so organized should be actually founded?

Surely not.

That, then, is the truth of the matter. But if, for your satisfaction, I am to do my best to show under what conditions our ideal would have the best chance of being realized, I must ask you once again to admit that the same principle applies here. Can theory ever be fully realized in practice? Is it not in the nature of things that action should come less close to truth than thought? People may not think so; but do you agree or not?

I do.

Then you must not insist upon my showing that this construction we have traced in thought could be reproduced in fact down to the last detail. You must admit that we shall have found a way to meet your demand for realization if we can discover how a state might be constituted in the closest accordance with our description. Will not that content you? It would be enough for me.

F. M. CORNFORD's translation – Oxford: Clarendon Press, 1941

'And for me too,' says Glaucon.

M. V. C. JEFFREYS, *Glaucon*, Pitman

For discussion

Is Glaucon merely a stooge, allowing Socrates to pull the wool over his (and our eyes)? Scrutinize the argument carefully. Does it satisfy you, or can you detect loopholes in it? How about the painter analogy for a start? (After all, the imaginary portrait of an ideally beautifully person could only be based on *observable*, *actual* features.)

7 Common confusions in educational theory

Students in university departments of education study such topics as educational psychology, educational statistics, the history of education, comparative education, educational hygiene, etc., and for understandable economy of speech people have thrown a cordon around the lot and called it 'education'. Perhaps because this name is too vague, experts in England and elsewhere have devised the term 'educational theory' to distinguish those studies which have a more obvious bearing on the actual practice of teaching children.

Along with the growth of these special studies that form the core of teacher-training has spread the illusion that they comprise a unified body of expert knowledge by means of which problems of education can be appropriately tackled and solved. This illusion has been cherished most, perhaps, among those school teachers who so often tell us that the skill of teaching rests upon a precise and expert knowledge akin to that of the dentist, and that without this knowledge one cannot teach properly. In fact, the untrained teacher – that is, someone who lacks this knowledge – is to be compared with a quack, except that whereas the one merely causes physical mishap, the other plays havoc more seriously with the child's mind.

Many examples can be cited to show that the word 'theory' is used in several different ways. Perhaps the widest difference in the use of the word is seen when we contrast the terms 'physical theory' and 'educational theory'. The problem of the status of any theory is one that can hardly be treated competently in a few lines. It can be shown fairly easily, however, that the presentation of an *educational* theory must necessarily use a kind of language which would be quite out of place in any presentation of the other. We can make this clearer by saying something first about a physical theory. A simple example will suffice. By the middle of the last century it was universally accepted that the behaviour of gases was to be accounted for by the existence of molecules. It was put forward by Clausius, therefore, that owing to chance collisions which are occurring with perfect elasticity at any instant, the molecules of a gas are moving with all velocities in all directions. From these premises it was deduced mathematically that the pressure of a gas is equal to one third of the average value of the square of the speed of the molecules multiplied by the density of the gas. The elementary theory of gases thus described may be expressed by a mathematical formula, from which the observable facts witnessed in the behaviour of gases may be deduced. Such a theory, as an empirically testable hypothesis, must stand or fall on whether statements which we deduce from it are true.

Now a mere glance at any of the historically famous educational theories will convince the reader that in certain critical respects the mode of address is quite different from anything to be found in text-books of physical science. For whatever linguistic subtleties lie hidden in the statement of a scientific theory it is obvious that its purpose can never be to advise or commend a course of action. On the other hand, it would be wholly impossible to give a faithful version of one of the well-known educational theories without implying advice or, in more general terms, a prescription. For instance. In writing *Some Thoughts Concerning Education* John Locke had as his aim the production of the Christian squire, the prototype of England's late 17th century gentry, and, however one appraises the logic involved, it was from this that he reached such prescriptive conclusions as these:

The great thing to be minded about Education is what Habits you settle.

Playing and childish actions are to be left perfectly free and untrained.

Now although lack of rigour may occur within an educational theory – as when, for instance, the writer invites us to infer a duty to act in a certain way from apparently descriptive premises, there is no lack of agreement that educational theories are meant to guide and advise teachers in their educational activities, and this is true whatever explanation we give of the language of advice. Unhappily, however, the educational theories whose language is obviously advisory and prescriptive can be contrasted with educational theories in which the advice mingles with the statements and even the theories of the particular sciences. Thus an educational writer in advocating a new method of teaching may account for the supposed result of his method by the psychological explanation known as 'gestalt theory', so that he gives within one and the same account

two disparate theories: a scientific theory, which we may assume to be empirically verifiable, and an educational theory, of which it makes no sense to
talk of verifiability. One source of confusion to which we refer lies in the failure
to disentangle these two senses of the word 'theory'.

EDWARD BEST, in *Philosophical Analysis and Education*,
(ed.) R. D. ARCHAMBAULT, pp. 39–41,
Routledge & Kegan Paul, 1965

For discussion
1 Is it true that a scientific theory can never advise or commend a course of
   action? If you think it is true, what do you mean when you say that a scientific
   theory is 'prescriptive'?
2 According to the writer, a scientific theory is verifiable, whereas an educational
   theory is not. In that case, how is an educational theory to be validated?

8 The construction, possession and utilization of theories

Although there are plenty of avocations, both games and work which we describe
as intellectual without implying that their purpose is to discover truths, there
are good reasons for giving early consideration to that special family of avocations
in which we are concerned to discover truths. I say 'family of avocations', since
nothing is to be gained by pretending that Euclid, Thucydides, Columbus,
Adam Smith, Newton, Linnaeus, Porson and Bishop Butler were all in partner-
ship.

The work for which each of these men got his reputation can be called the
work of 'theory building' though the word 'theory' has widely different senses.
Sherlock Holmes' theories were not built by the same methods as those of Marx,
nor were the uses or applications of them similar to those of Marx. But both
were alike in delivering their theories in didactic prose.

Before we say anything more specific about the operations or processes of
building theories we should consider what it means to say that someone has a
theory. Building a theory is trying to get a theory, and to have a theory is to
have got and not forgotten it. Building a theory is travelling; having a theory is
being at one's destination.

To have a theory or a plan is not itself to be doing or saying anything, any
more than to have a pen is to be writing with it. To have a pen is to be in a
position to write with it, if occasion arises to do so; and to have a theory or plan
is to be prepared either to tell it or to apply it, if occasion arises to do so. The
work of building a theory or plan is the work of getting oneself so prepared.

I say that the possessor of a theory is prepared to state it or otherwise apply it.
What is this distinction? To be in a position to tell a theory is to be able to give
a good answer to someone, the theorist himself maybe, who wants or needs to

learn, or learn better what the theory is, i.e. to deliver, by word of mouth or in writing, an intelligible statement of the conclusions of the theory, the problems which they solve and perhaps also the reasons for accepting these and rejecting rival answers. Having a theory involves being able to deliver lessons or refresher-lessons in it. The intelligent recipient of such lessons comes himself to have the theory or else, if he is sophisticated enough, to grasp without adopting it. But we do not build theories, any more than we build plans, merely or primarily in order to be equipped to tell them. The chief point of giving didactic exercises to oneself, or to other pupils, is to prepare them to use these lessons for other than further didactic ends. Columbus did not explore only to add to what was recited in geography lessons. Having a theory or plan is not merely being able to tell what one's theory or plan is. Being able to tell a theory is, in fact, being able to make just one, namely the didactic exploitation of it. Mastery of Euclid's theorems is not merely ability to cite them; it is also ability to solve riders to them, meet objections to them and find out the dimensions of fields with their aid.

GILBERT RYLE, *The Concept of Mind*,
pp. 286–7, Hutchinson, 1949

For discussion

1 Ryle differentiates between having a theory, using a theory, and building a theory. 'Building a theory is travelling,' he affirms. That being so, would it not be true to say that the job of building theories is part and parcel of the teacher's daily practice? (It's a nice thought, but in the event of your approving it you had better explain just how this building of theories differs from muddling through.)

2 To build a theory is to be in the dark, in the position of Euclid *before* he solved his theorem. In other words, the task of creating paths where none as yet exist is inescapable. Are you so sure that 'practice comes first'? Is it not rather the case that theory (if only in the sense of thinking about what we are trying to do) invariably precedes, and accompanies, sound practice?

9

Without necessarily accepting the gravamen of Professor D. J. O'Connor's charge which is, bluntly, that most, if not all, of the literature purporting to deal with educational theory is mere windbaggery, it is evident that this literature must have been lacking in several important respects, otherwise it could not have given rise to the mood of dissatisfaction now prevailing. In what respects? While there can be no agreeing with O'Connor that the only acceptable model for an education theory must be a scientific one if, by 'scientific', we mean a model based exclusively on the natural sciences, we are surely entitled to expect that any theory worth the name will serve three functions. First, it will be prescriptive, laying down in general terms a course of action and the conditions under which it has to be followed. Second, it will be predictive, indicating the outcome of that course of action. Third, it will be explanatory, capable of verifying the hypotheses on which its prescriptions and predictions rely.

If, now, we ask what has been chiefly lacking in traditional theory the short answer must be that it was too content to remain descriptive. In considering its stock topics – 'discipline', 'Nature and Nurture', 'Transfer of training', 'general and special aims' and the rest – it offered no firm guidelines for the practitioner to follow. Its hypotheses were rarely working hypotheses, its precepts too tenuous to be serviceable.

In any profession, practice must find its eventual justification in some body of established, organised and coherent body or theory. In this respect it may be thought that teachers suffer from a certain disadvantage in that the theories at their disposal are neither very well organised or particularly coherent. At the highest level of discourse these theories tend to lose themselves in philosophical abstruseness: at the lowest, they degenerate into small-talk about the tricks of the trade. The disadvantage arises not so much from the diversity of many different educational theories (and their failure to agree among themselves) as from the lack of definition in the middle sections of their spectrum. It is as though they had little or nothing to offer the broad mass of teachers who are not content to think of themselves merely as honest journeymen – the glass-blowers of the profession – and who have no pretensions to the role of the philosopher-king and the creative genius – the symphony writers. The rank and file, therefore, can hardly be blamed if at times they feel envious of members of their professions whose work is conducted on more clear-cut lines. As they see it, theory is the soft centre, not the hard core around which their everyday practice revolves.

Plainly, we do not have such a hard core. At the same time we know what the requirements are, and here and there we can point to fragments of the theory which are already in place. Assembling them into a coherent whole is not going to be easy, and any verbal enunciation of the theory must, as yet, be in the nature of a raid on the inarticulate. To see in them the outlines of a new pedagogy may seem pretentious and would certainly be over-presumptuous were it not for the urgency of the need.

What we are groping towards is the kind of theory which will be capable of satisfying the threefold criteria of prescription, prediction and explanatoriness. As a guide to teaching and curriculum-planning it will accordingly be quite distinct from any so-called learning theory. The latter is essentially interpretive, being chiefly concerned to investigate and explain what happens *during* the act of learning. By contrast, a theory of instruction would be concerned with the prerequisite conditions and causes which ensure that learning takes place. To that extent, while it would not be above drawing on the findings of the learning theorists, it would not make the mistake of supposing that the solution of pedagogical problems can be left to the psychologists.

C

Such a theory, again, would be comprehensive, embracing far more than the techniques of imparting information and skills; it would have something to say about the affective, as well as the cognitive, domain, and might, indeed, be more appropriately dubbed a theory of pedagogy. So to designate it seems both apt and timely, for one of the useful purposes the theory would serve would be to discriminate between those aspects of the total culture which can and need to be transmitted via the formal agency of schooling and those which either cannot or do not need to be transmitted in this way. Another purpose would be to indicate the ways in which the apparent conflict between 'child-centred' and 'subject-centred' methods of teaching can be resolved, and to demonstrate just how, when and why the two approaches can be combined. Above all, the theory would be in keeping with the enlarged concept of educability which recent developments have thrust upon us, and would help to validate it by underlining the crucial importance of environmental influences and by indicating the ways in which these can be brought under rational control in the shaping of behaviour. The theory would be normative in the sense that it laid down established criteria and stated the conditions for satisfying them.

All of which, advisedly, is written in the future conditional. As its leading proponent, Bruner takes the position that the kind of theory that is needed is, at best, putative; and that the most that can be done in our present state of knowledge is to offer short notes towards its definition.

W. KENNETH RICHMOND, *The Teaching Revolution*,
Methuen, 1967

For discussion

It seems that we are left darkling. But, then, we have already agreed that to build a theory is to be in the dark. Those who wish to discern the outlines of a new pedagogy should read Jerome Bruner's essay 'Toward a Theory of Instruction' in which its main elements are listed under the headings of

[1] Predispositions (i.e. the attitudes, skills, etc., which the pupil brings to the learning situation).

[2] Structure (i.e. the conceptual framework of the course of instruction to be followed).

[3] Sequence (i.e. the order in which the instruction has to be presented).

[4] Consequences (i.e. the pacing and reinforcing of the learning process).

We shall be returning to these in the sections dealing with Curriculum and Methods, and referring to them incidentally in others. For the moment, the point which needs to be underlined is that theorizing is very much the concern of any practice which deserves to be called professional. As teachers, we cannot expect all our problems to be solved by learning theorists, whose expertise has not so far been conspicuously helpful anyway.

Agreed?

3

The Aims of Education

If educational theory means thinking about what one is doing, or trying to do, then the definition of aims claims prior consideration. Unfortunately, this business of stating clearly just what one *is* trying to do is beset with difficulties, not least the danger of self-deception. Too often the teacher's professed aim conceals his real intention, with the result that there is a gap between his theory and his practice – what he does gives the lie to what he says!

Easy enough to decide that educational aims can be stated either in general, long-range terms or in specific, short-range terms. Typical of the former are 'the education of the whole man', 'the nurture of personal growth', 'self-fulfilment', 'the responsible human being and the citizen', etc., etc. The trouble about such aims is simply that they are so generalized that it is never easy to decide how, when, or whether they are attained. This is not to disparage them, but no doubt their very amorphousness explains why most teachers prefer to settle for more immediate, tangible, and instrumental aims – e.g. explaining the ablative absolute before 4 p.m.

General and special aims are, indeed, related in the same way as ends and means. If anything, the tendency nowadays seems to be to concentrate on the special aim, or rather, to insist that it comes first. Some of the high-sounding general aims, e.g. 'the transmission of culture', are not really aims at all and might more correctly be described as *functions* of education. Others, like the Hellenic ideal of 'the good life', are held to be so metaphysical that to ask the teacher to aim at them seems as futile as asking an artillery expert to train his gun on an invisible (and possibly non-existent) target.

Another significant trend in contemporary educational theory may be noted in the following passages. The modern teacher can no longer afford the luxury of aims which remain pious intentions: they may flatter his ego – but the path to educational Hell is paved with them. To be meaningful, aims must be disclosed to the learner from the start!

What ought I to do? What am I trying to do – and why – and how do I know that what I intend to do is, in fact, accomplished? For that matter, am I sure that what I propose is practicable: in other words, is it merely a case of saying that I intend to do such and such when in reality what I *can* do falls short of the requirements of the task? Are my professed aims based on nothing better than vague hopes and fated on that account to end up in the limbo of lost causes?

These are uncomfortable questions and ones which no teacher can evade. The professional attitudes we bring to the classroom, the methods we adopt there, and the values we live by both inside school and outside, will be reflected in the kinds of answer we make.

What sort of a teacher am I going to be? Before studying the extracts in this section we suggest that you first read the following passage and then answer the question at the end of it as honestly as you can!

I

Education has aims – general and particular, great and small. If they are to be of any value these aims must be worthwhile in the eyes of the thinker, but also dynamic in their practical operation. And there, right at the beginning of our discussion, we encounter the major difficulty. It is comparatively easy for a teacher to set up for himself a set of specific practical aims – to get more than three-quarters of a particular class through an examination; to co-operate with parents; to produce Macbeth; to make first-year Latin interesting; to reconcile classroom order with freedom for the pupils; to operate a Social Studies pro-gramme which unites geography and history; to give a school a 'rural bias'; and so on.

It is again comparatively easy for a teacher to compose an aim, or a set of aims, at a high level of generality – to facilitate 'complete living'; to promote the highest intellectual and moral development of the pupil; to adjust him to his environment; to train democratic citizens to provide the vision of greatness; to liberate the human spirit; to transmit our cultural heritage to the rising generation. These, and a score of others, have become so familiar to our ears that we tend to accept them without critical analysis. They are produced in fair quantity every time there is in any educational establishment a ceremonial occasion which includes an 'address'. We are not belittling these aims; most of them are quite irreproachable and potentially valuable. All we are saying at the moment is that they are easy to formulate.

What, then, is the major difficulty we mentioned? It is simply the difficulty of finding aims which combine the advantages and avoid the faults of both of the above types. To do this it is necessary to explore the extensive but ill-charted intermediate area of thought which lies between general or abstract aims on the one hand and highly specific aims on the other.

Suppose we ask two teachers for their educational aims. One gives us a long list of particular aims; the other prefers to profess one or two abstract or general aims. Some days later we interrupt the first teacher without warning, present the list of aims he gave us, and ask what progress he has made towards achieving these aims during the last half hour. He will probably be able to give a good account of himself, showing that most of what has happened within the last half-hour has a direct bearing on at least one, and possibly two or three, of his stated aims, and that these aims were exerting a real and continuous driving force in motivating the work. If, however, we now proceed to question the significance of the particular aims themselves – to ask what the value is of the Latin he seeks to make interesting; or why the pupils should act Macbeth at all – he is quite likely to falter. He has been unable or unwilling to 'work upwards' by combining his particular aims or principles until he reaches a point at which their connection with the most fundamental human (or divine) values and aims is evident.

We now approach the second teacher in the same way. He shines where the other failed. Now, as always, he can connect his aims with the deepest and most significant statements about the purpose of life – not a very difficult task, since the two are in his case scarcely distinguishable. But when we come to the question of what he has been doing during the last half-hour it is his turn to fumble. His answers tend to be weak and unconvincing, and the fact that he has to grope about for them suggests that his high-sounding aims have not been exerting much influence, even at the back of his mind, on the day to day conduct of his work. His failure consists in being unable or unwilling to 'work downwards' by thinking out the practical implications and applications of his otherwise laudable aims.

Each of these teachers has successfully accomplished one of the two comparatively easy tasks, as we called them, but neither has made much progress in the more laborious task – that of integrating a worthy educational theory with workaday practice. Indeed, most of us must confess that we jib at the latter. Some of us even perform *both* the easier tasks well and yet leave the laborious task alone: we may pride ourselves on being both good theorists and good practitioners, without worrying unduly about the fact that the two are operating in separate mental compartments, and that we are, at best, suffering from split minds, and, at worst, guilty of chronic hypocrisy.

S. NISBET, Purpose in the Curriculum,
pp. 9–11, University of London Press, 1957

Question Two types of teacher are described in the passage. On the understanding that you *must* choose between them, which of the two would you say characterized your own position as regards the statement of aims?

2a

Suppose I offered to sell you an automobile for five hundred dollars, and suppose I claimed that this auto was in 'excellent condition' but refused to let you take a look at it. Would you buy it?

Suppose I offered to teach your children to be LOGICAL THINKERS for a thousand dollars. Now if I could do it, you would be getting a real bargain. But would you agree to such a bargain unless I told you beforehand more explicitly what I intended to accomplish and how we would measure my success? I hope not.

In a sense, a teacher makes a contract with his students. The students agree to pay a certain sum of money and effort in return for certain skills and knowledge. But most of the time they are expected to pay for something which is never carefully defined or described. They are asked to buy (with effort) a product which they are not allowed to see and which is only vaguely described. The teacher who doesn't clearly specify his instructional objectives, who doesn't describe to the best of his ability how he intends the learner to be different after his instruction, is certainly taking unfair advantage of his students.

2b

A meaningfully stated objective, then, is one that succeeds in communicating your intent: the best statement is the one that excludes the greatest number of possible alternatives to your goal. Unfortunately there are many 'loaded' words, words open to a wide range of interpretation. To the extent that we use ONLY such words, we leave ourselves open to *mis*interpretation.

Consider the following examples of words in this light.

Words open to many interpretations	Words open to fewer interpretations
to know	to write
to understand	to recite
to *really* understand	to identify
to appreciate	to differentiate
to *fully* appreciate	to solve
to grasp the significance of	to construct
to enjoy	to list
to believe	to compare
to have faith in	to contrast

What do we mean when we say we want a learner to 'know' something? Do we mean that we want him to be able to recite, or to solve, or to construct? Just to tell him we want him to 'know' tells him little – the word can mean many things.

Though it is all right to include such words as 'understand' and 'appreciate' in a statement of an objective, the statement is not explicit enough to be useful until it indicates how you intend to sample the 'understanding' and 'appreciating'. Until you describe what the learner will be DOING when demonstrating that he 'understands' and 'appreciates', you have described very little at all.

2c

1 A statement of instructional objectives is a collection of words or symbols describing one of your educational *intents*.
2 An objective will communicate your intent to the degree you have described what the learner will be DOING when demonstrating his achievement and how you will know when he is doing it.
3 To describe terminal behavior (what the learner will be DOING):

  a Identify and name the over-all behavior act.
  b Define the important conditions under which the behavior is to occur (givens and/or restrictions and limitations).
  c Define the criterion of acceptable performance.

4 Write a separate statement for each objective; the more statements you have, the better the chance of making clear your intent.
5 If you give each learner a copy of your objectives, you may not have to do much else.

R. F. MAGER,
Preparing Objectives for Programmed Instruction,
Fearon, 1962

For discussion
1 How far do statements about general aims suffer from ambiguity because they use words which are open to too many interpretations?
2 Mager's main concern is to ensure that the teacher's objectives are written in terms which leave the learner in no doubt as to what he will be capable of doing at the end of the course. This recalls Whitehead's insistence that education should turn out people who know something well and can *do* something well. Do you agree that clearly stated objectives are a *sine qua non*? If so, how does the teacher set about the task of making them clear to *himself* and his pupils?
3 Mager hints that once pupils have been given the objectives the teacher may not have to do much else. Is he being wildly over-optimistic? (Mager's own 'pupils', one gathers, have been mainly adult students. On the other hand, before jumping to conclusions, bear in mind what Froebel and others have said about the importance of 'self-activity' in the learning process.)

3

497. When we asked our witnesses for their views on the aims of primary education we found a wide general measure of agreement, though many of the replies seemed to have as much relevance to other phases of education as to primary. The heads of junior and infant schools laid emphasis upon the all round development of the individual and upon the acquisition of the basic skills necessary in contemporary society. Many added a third aim, that of the religious and moral development of the child and some a fourth, that of the child's physical development and acquisition of motor skills. Phrases such as 'whole personality', 'happy atmosphere', 'full and satisfying life', 'full development of powers', 'satisfaction of curiosity', 'confidence', 'perseverance', and 'alertness' occurred again and again. This list shows that general statements of aims, even by those engaged in teaching, tend to be little more than expressions of benevolent aspiration which may provide a rough guide to the general climate of a school, but which may have a rather tenuous relationship to the educational practices that actually go on there. It was interesting that some of the head teachers who were considered by H.M. inspectors to be most successful in practice were least able to formulate their aims clearly and convincingly.

Children and Their Primary Schools
(Plowden Report)

For discussion

1 Comment on the last sentence in the light of Mager's arguments regarding the need for clearly specified objectives.
2 According to John Dewey, 'Any aim is of value insofar as it assists observation, choice and planning, from moment to moment and hour to hour.' Is this a necessary criterion – and how do you respond to the suggestion that while it may be a necessary criterion it is not the only one which should decide the value of a teacher's aim?

4

In all we teach, what we teach and *how* we teach are controlled consciously or unconsciously by our *aims*, by the outcomes we expect. Suppose you were teaching an emergency programme to train diesel engine repair-men. What would you teach and how would you teach it? . . . Suppose instead you were coaching a group of pupils for success in physics examinations that asked for definitions in proper wording and calculations with carefully memorized formulae. What would you do? . . . And now suppose that you and I are all of us to teach young people science in a way which gives them a clear understanding that will be of lasting value to all educated citizens. Many of our young people, though not scientists themselves, will later on have to work with scientists; and all will live in an intellectual environment where science plays a very important philosophical part. What should we teach them, and how should we teach? . . . That is my question for this discussion.

I am thinking of our young people when they are grown up, not when they are learning science at school, but a dozen years later when they are out in the world: a young man in a bank presently to be a manager, an important person in business or industry, a history teacher in school or university; or, above all, the parent of young children giving the next generation a first view of science. Again I ask my question: what are our aims in science-teaching for these people, and how should we teach for these aims?

A dozen years after school education adults will not remember the facts clearly, or even the general principles unless they understand the science we teach them. If they understand, they may retain some sympathetic understanding all their lives.

We all say we want to teach for understanding, but what does that mean for the general pupil? Much of the welfare of civilization, and perhaps even its fate, depends on science. Does our school science teaching help educated people to understand this dependence? Scientists have a characteristic way of thinking and planning and working, which we call the scientific attitude or scientific method or science itself, that offers intellectual resources and guidance to all. Do we send our pupils out delighted with that understanding of science, and ready to turn it in new directions? Do the next generation of scientists and engineers make the most possible progress? Can governors and administrators who learnt science at school confer intelligently with scientists on the vital problems of our age? In general, does our science teaching make its proper contribution to education?

> *Nuffield Physics, Teachers Guide,*
> pp. 64–5, Longmans/Penguin Books, 1966

For discussion
How would you differentiate between an 'aim' as normally defined in educational theory and an 'objective' as normally defined in Programmed Learning?

5

We said, 'Right. What the student can do at the end of the course is important, but what we are mainly concerned with is what he will be able to do at some time in the future.' This conclusion was reached after careful inspection of educational objectives prepared by nationally recognized educators. No matter how many we looked at we found they all had one thing in common: they all intend for the student to be able to do something at some point in time *after* the instruction has ended, at some point after the influence of the instructor is terminated.

'Well,' we said, 'suppose we really wanted to take these objectives seriously. Suppose we really wanted to do everything we can to reach these objectives. What could we do?'

This question led us to a rather startling conclusion. That conclusion was that no matter what the nature of the instruction, no matter what the subject matter, no matter what the age level of the student, there is a universal objective appropriate to all instruction; that *at the very least* it should be the intent of the instructor to send the student away from the instruction with an attitude toward the subject matter at *least* as favourable as that with which he arrived.

Why? Because if we are to maximize the probability that a student will use in the future what he has learned, we must at least see that he is *willing* to use his knowledge, we must see to it he does not run in the opposite direction whenever he is faced with the subject we have taught him; in other words, we must act to see we don't teach the student to hate the very subject we are teaching him about. If education is for the future, we teachers must not be the agents through which the student becomes less inclined to come into contact with the very subject we have worked so hard to teach him. Indeed, we must send him away anxious not only to use what he has learned, but anxious to learn more about it as time goes on.

'But, really,' we were told, '*every* teacher wants to send his students away more favorably disposed toward his subject than when the student arrived.' And this was the most astonishing point of all. For if this is true, then for the most part it is a hollow wish, it is talk not followed by action, it is little more than another example of good intention. Because, you see, to act to achieve this goal requires that the objective be specified in a way that would allow one to recognize success. Some sort of measuring instrument would have to be prepared and administered to ascertain whether attitudes have been improved or degraded by the teacher, course procedures would have to be analyzed for techniques that tend to adversely influence attitude (approach tendency), and the course would have to be constantly monitored for its affective effect on the student. How many are demonstrating that much interest in reaching this objective?

'There can't be many,' we were told by one ex-student. 'After all,' he said, 'not all of us millions dropped out of school because we were pregnant.'

R. F. MAGER, Transcript of lecture given at
L.C.C. teachers' course on programme writing,
28 January 1964

For discussion

1 What can a teacher do to bridge the gap between the short-term and the long-term effects of his professed aims?

2 Do you agree that, for the most part, teachers do not greatly concern themselves with whether their pupils leave with favourable or unfavourable attitudes towards the subjects they teach?

6 Must an educator have an aim?

Given that 'education' implies, first, some commendable state of mind and, secondly, some experience that is thought to lead up to or to contribute to it, and given also that people are usually deliberately put in the way of such experiences, it is only too easy to think of the whole business in terms of models like that of building a bridge or going on a journey. The commendable state of mind is thought of as an end to be aimed at, and the experiences which lead up to it are regarded as means to its attainment. For this model of adopting means to premeditated ends is one that haunts all our thinking about the promotion of what is valuable. In the educational sphere we therefore tend to look round for the equivalent of bridges to be built or ports to be steered to. Hence the complaints of lack of direction when obvious candidates do not appear to fill the bill.

It is my conviction that this model misleads us in the sphere of education. We have got the wrong picture of the way in which values must enter into education; and this is what occasions the disillusioned muttering about the absence of agreed aims. But to bring out how we are misled we must look at the contexts where the means-end model is appropriate. There is, first of all, that of plans and purposes where we do things in order to put ourselves in the way of other things. We get on a bus in order to get to work; we fill up a form in order to get some spectacles. Our life is not just doing one thing after another; we impose plans and schedules on what we do by treating some as instrumental to others. Some of these we regard as more commendable than others, and what we call our scale of values bears witness to such choices. The second means-end context is that of making or producing things. We mix the flour in order to make a cake or weld steel in order to make a bridge. We speak of the end-product in a factory and of the means of production in an economic system.

In both these contexts we might well ask a person what he was aiming at, what his objective was. But in both cases the answer would usually be in terms of something pretty concrete. He might say something like 'getting a better job' or 'marrying the girl' in the first context; or something like 'producing a soundless aeroplane' in the second. Similarly if a teacher was asked what he was aiming at, he might state a limited objective like 'getting at least six children through the eleven-plus'. But he might, as it were, lift his eyes a bit from the scene of battle and commit himself to one of the more general aims of education – elusive things like 'the self-realization of the individual', 'character', 'wisdom', or 'citizenship'. But here the trouble starts; for going to school is not a means to these in the way in which getting on a bus is a means to getting to work; and they are not made or produced out of the material of the mind in the way in which a penny is produced out of copper. These very general aims are neither goals nor are they end-products. Like 'happiness' they are high-sounding ways of talking about doing some things rather than others and doing them in a certain manner.

It might be objected that education is an art like medicine and that in medicine there is a commonly accepted end-product – physical health. Why should there not be a similar one for education – mental health, for instance? The answer is fairly obvious. Doctors deal mainly with the body and if they agree about what constitutes physical health it is because it can be defined in terms of physical criteria like temperature level and metabolism rate. Also there is little objection to manipulating and tinkering with the body in order to bring about the required result.

In the case of education, however, there are no agreed criteria for defining mental health; for either it designates something purely negative like the absence of unconscious conflicts, or, in so far as it is a positive concept, it has highly disputable personal and social preferences written into it. Also education is not, like medicine or psychiatry, a remedial business. When we are concerned with the minds of men there are objections to bringing about positive results in certain sorts of ways. People make moral objection to pre-frontal leucotomy even as a remedial measure. How much more objectionable would it be to promote some more positive state of mind, like a love of peace, in all men by giving them drugs or operating on everyone at birth? Indeed, in my view, disputes between educationists, which take the form of disputes about aims, have largely been disputes about the desirability of a variety of principles involved in such procedures. Values are involved in education not so much as goals or end-products, but as principles implicit in different manners of proceeding or producing.

R. S. PETERS, *Authority, Responsibility and Education*,
Allen & Unwin, 1960

For discussion
'Must an educator have an aim?' asks Professor Peters. Do you accept his argument that, 'Values are involved in education not so much as goals or end-products, but as principles implicit in different manners of proceeding'?

7

After addressing a conference of teachers of mathematics on the subject of programmed learning and outlining what was being done in introducing students to programme writing, I was asked: 'Do you really teach this stuff to your students? I ask because I am appalled at the waste of time when you should be teaching them to keep discipline and how to write on the blackboard.' The answer to this kind of objection had already been provided by one of the students studying programming. An able third year student, he had attended the first few lectures on programming techniques. The main emphasis had been on the need for the careful definition of the task, of the main concepts involved, and the need for the careful structuring of the learning situation. During one of the very informal sessions he suddenly exclaimed: 'Now I see why you put "Aim" at the beginning of lesson notes'. This student had taken nearly three years to see the value of defining objectives; many students probably never reach this stage. Working on programming had in this case accomplished a very useful task.

> E. STONES, 'The Teaching of Programming Techniques
> in Teacher Education', *Education for Teaching*,
> Journal of the Association of Teachers in
> Colleges and Departments of Education, No. 69,
> February 1966

For discussion
It seems that there is something to be said for defining objectives. Agreed?

8

Finally, by way of putting the cat among the pigeons, we offer a viewpoint which is nothing if not provocative. Attempt a critical analysis of the argument, paying particular attention to (*a*) its underlying assumptions, (*b*) its consistency, and (*c*) the choice of language used in its statement of the school's primary purpose.

Signposts for the Future. It is the duty of the State, which means the duty of politicians and bureaucrats, to exercise prudent and farsighted management in the control of State schools.

They must first be clear in their minds as to what the schools are *for*. Their primary purpose is to instruct boys and girls in the skills which are necessary for personal and national wellbeing. That is not to say that this is the only or even the most important part of a child's upbringing, but it is the part which a school can do better than almost all parents, and a part which a great majority of parents cannot do at all. Religion is more important than Arithmetic, but a school can do little to kindle religious zeal in the hearts of children who come from a totally irreligious home.

As an agency for setting standards of character and conduct, the school is a much weaker influence than the home or the neighbourhood. Inside the school, the pupils have a greater influence on one another than the teachers.

We must not pitch our hopes too high or ask more of a school than a school can readily do. After all, a day pupil is in school for only one sixth of the year.

We must not consider any purposes which are damaging to the primary purpose. There are advocates of the Comprehensive school who argue that the acceptable social mixture cannot be achieved in a neighbourhood school which will be virtually one-class, at least in a city. They propose that a proletarian school should be diluted (or enriched) by middle class pupils.

Whatever social value this bright idea may have, it should be rejected out of hand. Clever children do not learn most readily when they have to travel across a town to a school in a district in which they have no roots, to be taught in company with classmates who are strangers in every respect. Schools are not social laboratories.

Everything about a school should be geared to the purpose of learning. Some palatial Secondary Modern schools were built just after the Second World War. They were far too expensive and they roused a good deal of local indignation, but the real objection to them was educational. It is unwise to teach children in material conditions which are intimidatingly superior to the conditions of their own home; the effect is depressing.

COLM BROGAN, *The Nature of Education*,
pp. 111–12, Oldbourne, 1962

For discussion
In view of the fact that he has to carry out policies laid down for him by the State, by the local education authority and by his own headmaster, is it any part of the assistant teacher's job to formulate *general* aims? Write down SIX statements of aim which seem to you to be essentially worthwhile to you personally. Ask other members of the group to do the same. Find out through discussion whether your set of statements meets with unanimous approval. (You can count yourself lucky if they do!)

4

General and Special Education

The problem of striking a balance between the claims of so-called 'liberal–cultural' education and the counter-claims of so-called 'vocational–technical' training is, of course, an extension of the one we have just been discussing. Any conflict between them arises from different emphases in aim.

In the past, 'liberal education' was restricted (*a*) to a leisured minority and (*b*) to a curriculum based mainly, if not exclusively, on literary studies. Neither of these restrictions is permissible in the contemporary situation. The first is ruled out by the provision of free secondary education for all, and the second has been rendered obsolete by the explosion of knowledge in every field, especially in the natural and applied sciences. It is no longer possible for anyone to be at home in the whole field of knowledge as it was, say, in Renaissance times, when the ideal of 'the well-rounded man' was identified, more or less, with a reading of the Classics. A hundred years ago the confrontation between Matthew Arnold (champion of 'the best that has been thought and said in the world') and Thomas Huxley (advocate of the claims of science) foreshadowed the controversy which has been waged over the Two Cultures in our own day. At the moment, the heat engendered by the Snow–Leavis fracas appears to have died down – but the issue remains controversial and has still to be resolved. On the one hand, it is clearly impossible for anyone to learn everything, so that specialization in one form or other is inevitable. On the other, the dangers inherent in the fragmentation of modern knowledge are no less obvious.

1 A nineteenth-century view

I do not think it is any part of the duty of Government to prescribe what people should learn, except in the case of the poor, where time is so limited that we must fix upon a few elementary subjects to get anything done at all. . . . The lower classes ought to be educated to discharge the duties cast upon them. They should also be educated that they may appreciate and defer to a higher cultivation when they meet it, and the higher classes ought to be educated in a very different manner, in order that they may exhibit to the lower classes that higher education to which, if it were shown to them, they would bow down and defer.

ROBERT LOWE,
Primary and Classical Education, 1867

For discussion
The viewpoint expressed here now strikes us as being unspeakably arrogant, yet it was sincerely held in its day and was, in fact, the basis for official policy. What has happened in the hundred years which have elapsed since these words were written, and why is it that our viewpoint is so different?

2 A modern viewpoint

What is the true education, who can say? For the best men the classical education may still, perhaps, be best. Gladstone thought it the true education, though he realized that this could be the case only for the few. 'It can only apply in full,' he said, 'to that small proportion of the youth of any country, who are to become in the fullest sense educated men.' Gladstone, H. G. Wells did not consider a really educated man. 'He was educated,' wrote Wells in the *Outline of History*, 'at Eton College, and at Christ Church, Oxford, and his mind never recovered from the process.' But Wells's editorial advisers did not agree, and there is a battle in the footnotes between Wells himself, Professor Ernest Barker, and the Professor Gilbert Murray. Gladstone, like Peel, gained the 'double first' in classics and mathematics. 'Men with such a training,' said Barker, 'were genuinely and nobly trained for statesmanship.' But, objected Wells – 'With no knowledge of ethnology, no vision of history as a whole, misconceiving the record of geology, ignorant of the elementary ideas of biological science, of modern political social and economic science, and modern thought and literature!' Gilbert Murray pointed out, however, how much the good man read *outside* the old classical curriculum – 'A good man was rather laughed at if he did not know Shakespeare and Milton.' Fisher's education was the classical education at its best; Wells's education though haphazard was sufficient to show him some of the deficiencies of the old and the need for an inclusion of modern science. But we are discovering to-day that it is impossible to teach everything; the school curriculum has been vastly overloaded. The best education, perhaps, is that which stretches a man's abilities to the full and gives him the feeling of rising superior to his environment. And that either classics or science may do.

T. L. JARMAN,
Landmarks in the History of Education,
p. 288, John Murray, 2nd edition 1963

For discussion

1 In terms of Victorian society Gladstone had certainly received a liberal education. Why, then, did H. G. Wells consider that he 'never recovered from the process'?

2 Is it always the case today that a good man is laughed at if he does not know Shakespeare and Milton?

3 Would you say that your own education has given you the feeling of rising superior to your environment?

3 The concept of general education

General education, as the name implies, prepares the educand for life in general, without consideration of any clearly marked-out kind or part of life. But we found as we went on an increasing difficulty in keeping the specific and the general apart from each other. At the earliest stages the general was practically included in the specific. Education was not analysed: its theory had not yet been evolved. When it came to be needful to consider the case of such persons as the ruler, the priest, the orator, theory of necessity made its appearance. But in the case of such vocations life was so full that the general swamped the particular, or, if it is preferred, the particular swamped the general. If a man were well educated as prophet, priest or king all his nature was concerned, and there was no room for an antagonism between the different elements. General and specific education coalesced. To be a good orator or poet takes as much out of a man as he is able to give, so long as he has free play for his energies in poetry or in oratory.

But with the growing complexity of human life there arose greater and greater need for specialisation, and much of the work that was thus set apart for certain groups of workers was in itself distasteful, and did not satisfy the demands of the whole nature of the persons who had to do it. The educand had to get a preparation for his vocational work, but also for the rest of his time. Both specific and general education were necessary, and were found as a rule in the education of mere living. No doubt there were certain favoured classes that had the benefit of an education deliberately given to meet purely general needs; but the common people had to make shift with what education they could find for themselves.

It was, however, in historical times and within the ranks of the educators themselves that a curious change took place in the meaning of what we have called general education. Instead of being applied to a preparation for life in general as opposed to a preparation for some particular walk in life, it began to be regarded as a preparation not for actual life at all, but as the preparation for a sort of potential life. Man was to be so trained that he became fitted not for this or that sphere in life, however wide or satisfying, but for any possible sphere that might claim him.

SIR JOHN ADAMS, *The Evolution of Educational Theory*
pp. 182–3, Macmillan

D

For discussion

1 Originally, *all* education had some kind of vocational aim: 'general and specific education coalesced', says Adams. Apparently this is by no means always the case nowadays. Why not?

2 The suggestion is that general education has come to be regarded as 'a preparation for a sort of potential life', and that, as such, it is pretty useless. Is this another way of saying that general aims are fated to be abortive unless special aims are constantly and firmly kept in view?

4 The case for and against a many-sided approach

A] HERBART

Many-sidedness of Interest – Strength of Moral Character How can the teacher assume responsibility for those aims of the pupil which we designated as *merely possible?*

As these aims will be chosen by the pupil after he has grown up and become independent their factual content is beyond the competence of the teacher, who can seek only to form will and tendencies, and also the demands which the future man will make upon himself. The power, the initiative, and the activity wherewith the future man may meet these demands can be prepared and cultivated by the teacher according to the ideas he has about a mature person. Thus it is not a certain number of separate aims that we, as teachers, ought to have in mind (for how can we foresee them) but the potential activity of the growing man, the quantum of his personal vitality and the spontaneity. The greater and more harmonious this quantum, the greater will be the man's maturity and perfection, and the greater the effect of the teacher's care.

Only the flower must not burst its calyx – abundance must not become weakness through losing direction because of too many distractions. Human society has long found division of labour necessary, that every one may perfect what he attempts. But the more sub-divided, the greater is that which each later receives from all the rest. Now, since intellectual receptivity rests on affinity of mind, and this on similar activities of mind, it follows that in the higher realm of human achievement labour ought not to be divided to the point where each man is ignorant of his neighbour's work. Every man must love all activities and be a virtuoso in one. The particular virtuosity is a matter of choice; but manifold receptivity is a matter of education for it grows out of manifold beginnings of a pupil's own efforts. Therefore we call the first part of the educational aim – *many-sidedness of interest*, which must be distinguished from its exaggeration – dabbling in many things. And since no one object of will, nor its direction, interests us more than any other, we must assure a *well-balanced* many-sidedness. We shall thus get at the meaning of the common expression 'harmonious cultivation of all powers'. But we must define what we mean when we speak of a 'multiplicity and harmony of mental powers'.

> HERBART, 'The Science of Education',
> *Allgemeine Pädogogik aus dem Zweck der*
> *Erziehung abgeleitet*, 1806, translated and revised
> from the 1902 Heath edition by Dr R. Ulich
> in *Three Thousand Years of Educational Wisdom*
> published by Harvard University Press

B] KERSCHENSTEINER

Kerschensteiner's principle was to base the whole of the teaching of the vocational schools on the students' trade, and, from that basis, so to broaden the scope of the teaching that the students eventually gained an insight and understanding into the changing yet changeless pattern of the world, where every force and every person interacted, the one on the other, in the formation of that unified harmony which is life. The students were to realize that all the citizens in the State were inter-dependent, that without the farmer they could not eat, that without the builder they would be homeless, that without steady production, increased trade, and a balanced economy the State could not prosper. They were to be made conscious of the fact that they all shared the responsibility for the continuous advancement and welfare of the state.

> DIANE SIMONS, *Georg Kerschensteiner*,
> pp. 94–5, Methuen, 1966

The first aim of education for those leaving the elementary school is training for trade efficiency and love of work. With these is connected the training of those elementary virtues which efficiency and love of work have in their train – conscientiousness, industry, perseverance, responsibility, self-restraint, and devotion to an active life.

Following close on that, the second aim must be pursued, which is to gain an insight into the relation of individuals to one another and to the State and to understand the laws of health. This knowledge and insight must then be used actively in the exercise of self-control, justice, devotion to duty, and in leading a sensible life characterised by a strong feeling of personal responsibility.

One can call the first aim that of technical education, the second, that of intellectual and moral education. But one must be conscious of the fact that the first aim also has high moments of intellectual and moral education, and that the second aim can only be attained through the first and as a continuation of it.

> *Staatsbürgerliche Erziehung der deutschen Jugend*, 1910

Vocational training leads to character training.

> *Berufs- oder Allgemeinbildung?* 1904

How then shall we tackle the question of educating the young citizen to develop an altruism which is born of insight? There only seems one answer possible to this question – at his work. . . . The vast majority of young people are engaged in some kind of employment and want to advance by means of their work. Their interests are centred on their job and nearly all the youngsters are to be won over through this sphere of interest. If we win the boy over in this way, we also gain his confidence and with that we can guide him both intellectually and morally.

Die drei Grundlagen für die Organisation des
Fortbildungs-Schulwesens, 1906

For discussion

1 Broadly speaking, the secondary school curriculum represents an attempt 'to assure a well-balanced many-sidedness', at any rate before the time comes when specialization is deemed necessary. Can anything be said in favour of Kerschensteiner's argument that we should begin the other way round, and that 'vocational training leads to character training?'

2 'Labour ought not to be divided to the point where each man is ignorant of his neighbour's work,' says Herbart. In advanced industrial societies, however, this is precisely what happens, with the result that 'at the top of the Establishment' (as Lord Snow called it in his famous Rede Lecture) there is the danger of a total breakdown of communication between literary intellectuals and scientific technologists.

Any comments?

5 The American view of the problem

Three extracts reprinted by permission of the publishers from General Education in a Free Society *(pp. 71–2, 54–5, and 93). Report of the Harvard Committee, Harvard University Press.*
Copyright © 1945 by the President and Fellows of Harvard College.

A]

The aim of general education, according to the Harvard Committee, is to produce the responsible human being and the citizen. By contrast, special education aims at giving competence in some occupation. General education is characterised by (*i*) effective thinking – the ability to draw sound conclusions from premises, (*ii*) communication – the ability to express oneself so as to be understood by others, (*iii*) making relevant judgments – the ability to bring to bear the whole range of ideas upon the area of experience, (*iv*) discrimination among values. Concerning the last of these the report has this to say:

The ability to discriminate in choosing covers not only awareness of different kinds of value but of their relations, including a sense of relative importance and of the mutual dependence of means and ends. It covers also much that is analogous to method in thinking; for example, the power to distinguish values truly known from values received only from opinion and therefore not in the same way part of the fabric of experience. Values are of many kinds. There are the obvious values of character, like fair play, courage, self-control, the impulse to beneficence and humanity; there are the intellectual values, like the love of truth and the respect for the intellectual enterprise in all its forms; and there are the aesthetic values, like good taste and the appreciation of beauty. As for the last, people are apt to locate beauty in picture galleries and leave it there; it is equally, if not more, important to seek beauty in ordinary things, so that it may surround one's life like an atmosphere.

Add to all this that the objective of education is not just knowledge of values, but commitment to them, the embodiment of the ideal in one's actions, feelings and thoughts, no less than an intellectual grasp of the ideal. The reader may object that we are proposing a confusion, that we are suggesting the turning of school or college into a moral reformatory or a church. For is not the purpose of educational institutions to train the mind and the mind only? Yet it is not easy, indeed it is impossible, to separate effective thinking from character. An essential factor in the advancement of knowledge is intellectual integrity, the suppression of all wishful thinking and the strictest regard for the claims of evidence. The universal community of educated men is a fellowship of ideals as well as of beliefs. To isolate the activity of thinking from the morals of thinking is to make sophists of the young and to encourage them to argue for the sake of personal victory rather than of the truth.

B]

In this epoch in which almost all of us must be experts in some field in order to make a living, general education therefore assumes a peculiar importance. Since no one can become an expert in all fields, everyone is compelled to trust the judgment of other people pretty thoroughly in most areas of activity. I must trust the advice of my doctor, my plumber, my lawyer, my radio repairman, and so on. Therefore I am in peculiar need of a kind of sagacity by which to distinguish the expert from the quack, and the better from the worse expert. From this point of view, the aim of general education may be defined as that of providing the broad critical sense by which to recognise competence in any field.

William James said that an educated person knows a good man when he sees one. There are standards and a style for every type of activity – manual, athletic, intellectual or artistic; and the educated man should be one who can tell sound from shoddy work in a field outside his own. General education is especially required in a democracy where the public elects its leaders and officials; the ordinary citizen must be discerning enough so that he will not be deceived by appearances and will elect the candidate who is wise in his field. . . .

Two complementary forces are at the root of our culture; on the one hand, an ideal man and society distilled from the past but at the same time transcending the past as a standard of judgment valid in itself and, on the other hand, the belief that no existent expressions of this ideal are final but that all alike call for perpetual scrutiny and change in the light of new knowledge. Specialism is usually the vehicle of this second force. It fosters the open-mindedness and love of investigation which are the wellspring of change, and it devotes itself to the means by which change is brought about. The fact may not always be obvious. There is a sterile specialism which hugs accepted knowledge and ends in the bleakest conservatism. Modern life also calls for many skills which, though specialized, are repetitive and certainly do not conduce to inquiry. These minister to change but unconsciously. Nevertheless, the previous statement is true in the sense that specialism is concerned primarily with knowledge in action, as it advances into new fields and into further applications.

Special education comprises a wider field than vocationalism; and correspondingly, general education extends beyond the limits of merely literary preoccupation.

c]

In view of these wide and deep differences, is a truly general education possible? We shall conclude by stating two broad propositions and then by sketching what seems to us the role of general education as conditioned by difference.

The first proposition is at once a confession and a question – a confession of ignorance and a question calling for answer. The line of reasoning in this report has been briefly this. First, our national life and, more broadly, our culture do in fact predicate certain traits of mind and ways of looking at man and the world. Second, these traits and outlooks embrace heritage and change, which in turn correspond, though not exactly and certainly in no wooden, perfunctory way, to general and special education, the one concerned with the more slowly changing relationships within knowledge as a whole, the other with its more quickly changing parts. Third, a successful democracy (successful, that is, not merely as a system of government but, as democracy must be, in part as a spiritual ideal) demands that these traits and outlooks be shared so far as possible among all the people, not merely among a privileged few. But, fourth, there exist in fact great differences among people, not only of opportunity, which have been and can be improved, but of gifts and interests, which either cannot be improved so quickly or, in the case of interests, are and should ideally be varied.

Our ignorance, which seems to us a widespread ignorance, and our question, which the question of the nation and age, follow these four steps as a fifth. It is, *how can general education be so adapted to different ages and, above all, different abilities and outlooks, that it can appeal deeply to each, yet remain in goal and essential teaching the same for all?*

The answer to this question, it seems not too much to say, is the key to anything like a complete democracy.

For discussion

1 'The educated man should be one who can tell sound from shoddy work in a field outside his own': he must have the ability to recognize competence in any sphere. To this end, the Harvard Committee recommended a broad-based curriculum with the Social Studies serving as a link between the Arts and the Sciences. Is this a viable solution?

2 If you think it is, perhaps you will explain just how an Arts man can tell sound from shoddy work in, say, the field of nuclear physics – and just how the scientist can be given the 'recognition of competence' in, say, the sphere of literary criticism.

3 'In view of these wide and deep differences is a truly general education possible?' That is the question. While the Harvard Committee's report may seem to end on an inconclusive note, at least it forces us to ask what is to happen if the answer to that question is 'No'. Consider the implications of such a denial.

6 Specialism defended

The habit of apprehending a technology in its completeness: this is the essence of technological humanism, and this is what we should expect education in higher technology to achieve. I believe it could be achieved by making specialist studies (whatever they are: metallurgy or dentistry or Norse philology) the core around which are grouped liberal studies which are relevant to these specialist studies. But they must be relevant; the path to culture should be through a man's specialism, not by by-passing it. Suppose a student decides to take up the study of brewing; his way to acquire general culture is not by diluting his brewing courses with popular lectures on architecture, social history, and ethics, but by making brewing the core of his studies. The *sine qua non* for a man who desires to be cultured is a deep and enduring enthusiasm to do one thing excellently. So there must first of all be an assurance that the student genuinely wants to make beer. From this it is a natural step to the study of biology, microbiology, and chemistry: all subjects which can be studied not as techniques to be practised but as ideas to be understood. As his studies gain momentum the student could, by skilful teaching, be made interested in the economics of marketing beer, in public-houses, in their design, in architecture; or in the history of beer-drinking from the time of the early Egyptian inscriptions, and so on in social history; or, in the unhappy moral effects of drinking too much beer, and so in religion and ethics. A student who can weave his technology into the fabric of society can claim to have a liberal education; a student who cannot weave his technology into the fabric of society cannot claim even to be a good technologist.

SIR ERIC ASHBY, *Technology and the Academics*, Macmillan, 1958

For discussion

1 'The path to culture is through a man's specialism, not by by-passing it.' This is reminiscent of Kerschensteiner's argument that vocational training leads to moral training. In a word, it insists that as much can be taught and learned *through* one field of study as *in* many. How valid do you think this argument is?

2 Supposing that the prospective brewer happens to come from one of the 'non-professional homes' mentioned in the previous extract, what then?

7 A Scottish plea for work-based courses

In the U.S.S.R. and the Communist-bloc countries the 'Life and Work' philosophy has led to some drastic changes in the school curriculum, the belief being that something needs to be done to lighten the burden of purely theoretical studies and to give all pupils actual on-the-job experience. Thus, the 1961 Education Act of the Hungarian People's Republic provides for 'a closer tie with life, with experience and production at all stages of education and training'. It seems that much the same philosophy pervades the Brunton Report.

THE BRUNTON REPORT (*From School to Further Education*), 1963

55 ... *We believe, and we are supported in this by very many of those whom we have consulted, that the case is unanswerable for the use in schools of the vocational impulse as the core round which the curriculum should be organised.* This is not to say that the vocational motive can or should be allowed to dictate the whole curriculum. All subjects of the curriculum should be seen as serving the end of developing all aspects of the personality of boys and girls; but they should also be seen as serving the additional end of widening the range of their experience and of preparing them for life after school. While there is general agreement that the introduction of vocational elements into secondary education is desirable, both for educational reasons and for the purpose of co-ordinating secondary education with further education, there are, however, wide divergencies of opinion on the way in which this should be done. Three main views emerge.

56 On the one hand, some people suggest that any vocational elements that are introduced should be of the most general nature only and should not relate exclusively, or even very closely, to any particular occupation or industry. Any bias should be given more through the approach of the teacher to existing courses of general education and through changes in methods of teaching and of learning than through alteration of the form and content of the courses. The work done in the various subjects of the curriculum should arise out of and be illuminated by frequent references to, and practical illustrations from, the various major industrial and commercial activities of the district as part of the local environment. On occasion, a substantial proportion of the work in the various subjects should be directed towards some activity such as steel making

or farming, or towards a group of related activities such as those connected with shipbuilding and commerce in a large river basin like the Clyde, which influences strongly the lives of the people in the community.

57 By contrast, some people believe that the courses provided in the secondary school should be largely of a vocational nature and should prepare pupils for entry into particular trades and occupations. These courses should include a substantial element of general education but should provide also specific preliminary training in the practical skills appropriate to the occupations, and in the related technology.

58 In between are those who advocate the introduction of courses which provide a broad general preparation for a group of occupations associated with a particular industry or service. By far the greater part of these courses would be concerned with general education and the all-round development of the pupils, but they should include elements of a definite vocational nature and should provide some experience of the practical skills appropriate to the various occupations in the industry. The vocational elements should be regarded primarily as providing a central interest which motivates the work of the whole course.

59 Though these three views represent different approaches, we regard them not as mutually conflicting but rather as appropriate to successive stages in the development of the vocational interests of young people. The very general approach described in paragraph 56 emphasises one aspect of the environmental considerations which should influence secondary education from its very start and should play a growing part in the instruction throughout. The type of course discussed in paragraph 58, offering a broad approach to a particular industry or service, has its place in the third year of the secondary course. The narrower vocational course referred to in paragraph 57 is appropriate at the state when the person's vocational ambitions tend to be clearly crystallised, i.e. after the age of fifteen; this type of course, therefore, should be provided either in a fourth year at a secondary school or in the first year of a college of further education.

60 At present the large majority of schools are undertaking no more than the very general approach and in many of them the references made to local industry are so casual and infrequent as to have little effect on the work and the attitude of the pupils. A major reason for this often lies in the inexperience and relative unfamiliarity of subject teachers with the principles and practices of local industry. There is an urgent need for the schools to improve this situation by enlisting the co-operation and seeking the advice of people in local industry and of teachers in further education. Even, however, when this general approach is well developed it fails to be wholly effective, especially with the older pupils. Their natural interest in the adult world which they look forward to entering soon demands from the school a curriculum which is in their eyes more manifestly and more directly connected with the daily work of that world. As we have already remarked, the efforts of the few schools which have so far developed in

their third year courses providing a broad approach to particular industries have proved remarkably successful in catching and holding the interest of the pupils not only in the more directly vocational parts of the course but also in the more general subjects. The whole attitude of the pupils towards school has sometimes been transformed. *We recommend that as many schools as possible should proceed to introduce courses of this type* (pp. 23–5).

For discussion

1 The Brunton Report was concerned only with pupils attending Junior Secondary schools (which broadly correspond with England's Secondary Modern schools). In urging that 'the vocational impulse' should be made the core round which the curriculum should be organized, the Report undoubtedly had in mind the fact that many of these pupils found the existing curriculum aimless and lacking in incentives. We are assured that courses more directly connected with daily work will lead to a transformation of attitudes. But how can we be sure that this is not simply a twentieth-century version of Robert Lowe's belief that 'the poor ought to be educated to discharge the duties cast upon them'?

2 No mention is made of the academic pupils attending Senior Secondary (i.e. Grammar school type) schools in Scotland. In their case, presumably, the 'vocational impulse' is satisfied by the traditional curriculum. Can you suggest reasons for this?

8 Two cultures?

It is the most pathetic of all educational fallacies to suppose that everything can be learned. At the same time, the Comenian ideal of teaching all things to all men persists to the extent that schools and colleges are committed to the task of providing a curriculum which will 'appeal deeply to each, yet remain in goal and essential teaching the same for all'. The dilemma posed by the demands of general education (already onerous enough to swell an overcrowded time-table), and the no less rigorous demands of special education (which necessitate the dropping of certain courses at an early age), is acute in secondary schools the world over; and although it has not yet given rise to anything like the same disquiet in the universities its effects are undoubtedly serious. No one can honestly deny that Sir Walter Moberley is right in asserting that a great many students graduate without ever being faced with 'the issues which are momentous' – another way of saying that they are *ipso facto* uncultured.

Nor can the issue be evaded, as has sometimes been suggested, by claiming that general education is not to be defined by its subject-matter. Granted, the only essential difference between general and special education is a difference of outlook and aim. The one has as its long-range target the production of 'the responsible human being and the citizen': the other has for its more immediate purpose the acquisition of competence in some occupation. The two are as indissociably linked as hydrogen and oxygen atoms in a molecule of water, and only the artifice of language enables us to think of them as existing apart. Any antithesis between 'liberal–general' and 'vocational–technical–special' aims is unreal. In Whitehead's well-worn phrase, education must turn out people who know something well and can do something well. Until comparatively recent times the problem of finding a common core of studies capable of fitting a man for any walk in life presented no great difficulty: the 'something' with which every responsible human being was supposed to be familiar consisted of the Seven Liberal Arts. Unfortunately the vast increase in the scope, variety and sheer amount of modern knowledge, and the tendency for its branches to become more and more disparate, has rendered any theory based upon a common core virtually impracticable. Compared with that of previous ages, the curriculum of the academic secondary school has more than doubled in scope and size. The change in the learning situation can best be expressed by comparing the pool of available knowledge in 1962 and in 1762 with a big-city reservoir and a village well. In some ways the situation is easier in that the supply is on tap and can be turned on at will, provided one knows how. In others, it is more difficult, for the pressure on the individual to step up his consumption is increasing all the time. The ever-growing burden the modern child has to carry is one of the penalties of being born in the twentieth century. That 'recognition of competence in any field', which the Harvard Committee rightly saw as the indispensable attribute of the free mind, can only be gained by hard-won mastery of the facts. There is no short cut to an understanding of the principles involved in any field of arts or science. The ability to recognize competence in literary criticism, say, or in nuclear physics, calls for a very considerable expenditure of time and effort even for those of more than average intelligence. Against this, it is certain that the complexities of a thousand and one different callings will see to it that more and more time has to be spent in mastering some specialism or other. Nowadays everyone needs to be an expert in something.

What happens in practice can perhaps best be illustrated diagrammatically. Suppose for the sake of argument that the various branches of knowledge can be represented as the segments of a circle. Let the circumference stand for the 'frontier' of knowledge. The further along each radius, the more advanced the study becomes. (In academic parlance this is the presumed dimension of 'depth'.) Looked at this way, general education may be seen as the attempt to provide an all-round introduction to as many branches as possible. Where this attempt is successful, the result, at sixth-form level, presents the kind of compact culture-profile shown in Fig. 1. Here is a sixteen-year-old boy who has just taken GCE with passes in eight subjects. One can see where the gaps in his formal education have been – he has done little or nothing as regards the fine arts, and biology, for example – but on the whole the areas he has covered, if that is the word, are evenly balanced. This balance begins to take on a decidedly one-sided look in Fig. 2, an undergraduate at the end of his Honours degree course in Physics. This student reads an occasional novel in his spare time and has a liking for long-playing records. Thanks to a subsidiary course on the History and Philosophy of Science, he has maintained a desultory interest in History, but says that he has forgotten nearly everything he learned at school in

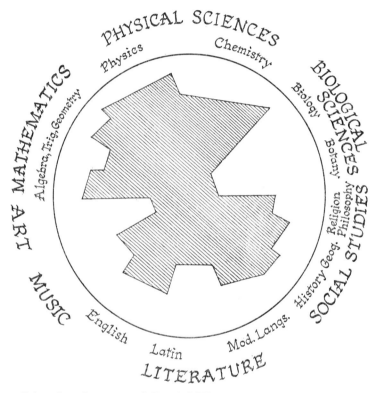

FIG. I Cultural attainments at O Level GCE stage

the way of Languages and the like. In the case of the two research-workers shown in Fig. 3, this lopsidedness has become even more pronounced. If the Snow Hypothesis is valid, A and B cannot communicate because they are at opposite poles. Like boll weevils, each has burrowed into his own narrow tunnel and cannot see what is going on to left and right, let alone at the other end of the diameter. Only by retracing his steps to the centre (the area of general education) can he hope to make any sort of contact; and when he does this it turns out that what remains of his pre-specialized knowledge has atrophied. Any Mathematics and Science which B may have known ten years previously has vanished into thin air; and except for Music, the one art which is common ground to all, A must now count himself an ignoramus in Literature, Painting, Architecture, History, Philosophy and everything that does not concern him in

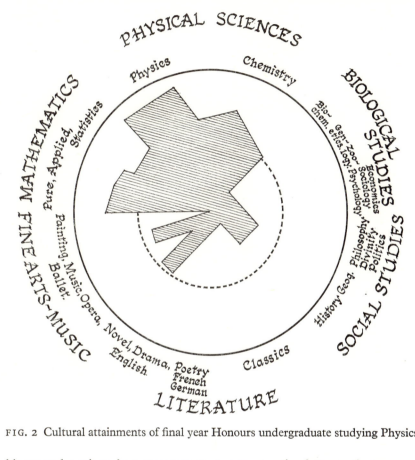

FIG. 2 Cultural attainments of final year Honours undergraduate studying Physics

his research project. As a consequence, any conversation between the two men will be limited to trivialities – the weather, or some such topic.

W. KENNETH RICHMOND,
Culture and General Education,
pp. 13–17, Methuen, 1965

For discussion

1 'The only essential difference between general and special education is a difference of outlook and aim.' Does this imply that we can ignore the intrinsic worth of the subject matter?

2 A difference of outlook, yes, but is it very helpful to say this if one outlook leads to the scholar-gentleman and another to the manual labourer?

3 How wide is the 'Great Divide' between Arts and Science? Need we take the blind-spots revealed in the two Ph.D. candidates very seriously?

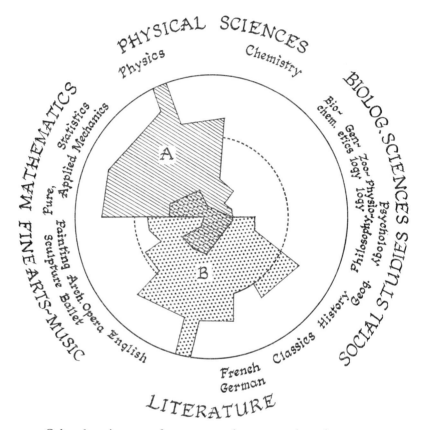

FIG. 3 Cultural attainments of two post-graduate research students

9 Towards a reconciliation

The antithesis between a technical and a liberal education is fallacious. There can be no adequate technical education which is not liberal, and no liberal education which is not technical: that is, no education which does not impart both technique and intellectual vision. In simpler language, education should turn out the pupil with something he knows well and something he can do well. This intimate union of practice and theory aids both. The intellect does not work best in a vacuum. The stimulation of creative impulse requires, especially in the case of the child, the quick transition to practice. Geometry and mechanics, followed by workshop practice, gain that reality without which mathematics is verbiage.

There are three main methods which are required in a national system of education, namely, the literary curriculum, the scientific curriculum, the technical curriculum. But each of these curricula should include the other two. What I mean is, that every form of education should give the pupil a technique, a science, an assortment of general ideas, and aesthetic appreciation, and that each of these sides of his training should be illuminated by the others. Lack of time, even for the most favoured pupil, makes it impossible to develop fully each curriculum. Always there must be a dominant emphasis. The most direct aesthetic training naturally falls in the technical curriculum in those cases when the training is that requisite for some art or artistic craft. But it is of high importance in both a literary and a scientific education.

A. N. WHITEHEAD, *The Aims of Education*,
pp. 74–5, Benn, paperback edition 1962

For discussion

1 Liberal and technical go hand in hand, says Whitehead, and so do theory ('knowing something well') and practice ('doing something well'). Why, then, the prejudice against technical education? Any why the heavy premium placed on the so-called 'Liberal Arts'?

2 'There are three main methods which are required in a national system of education, namely, the literary curriculum, the scientific curriculum, the technical curriculum. . . . Always there must be a dominant emphasis.'

How do you imagine Whitehead would have regarded the decision to abolish a tripartite system of secondary schools and adopt instead the comprehensive principle?

10 Concluding statement

The incompleteness of our philosophy is revealed clearly enough in current life, and especially in the prevailing doubts about the meaning of the vocational and the cultural. Thus, 'vocational' is still frequently used to apply only to the activities of manual workers, on a lower grade in status and salary than 'professional' workers, while 'cultural' still applies very often to certain selected activities – in art and literature, for example – rather than to a style and colour exhibited by life-activities generally. In other words, current use of the terms is still strongly reminiscent of a social order where it was regarded as a providential disposition that many should labour for a living, while the few, being already provided for, could devote themselves to the fine and good. . . .

Where all is so inchoate and undetermined it is not possible, certainly not for me, to attempt any complete or definitive integration of the two ideas. But a few suggestions, chiefly of a negative kind, may be hazarded.

1 The distinction between vocational and cultural does not work out as a distinction between two quite separate groups of 'subjects' or activities.

2 The distinction, similarly, does not appear to correspond to separate classes within the community.

3 Nor does the distinction correspond to any sharp separation of teaching methods or of underlying psychologies.

4 Finally, and this may appear a little startling, the distinction does not correspond to any difference of utility or disutility in the respective activities. The contrast is merely a survival of an older social order where it was forgotten that the traditional classical curriculum was, in origin, vocational in aim through and through. . . .

We have rejected the idea of any sharp distinction between vocational and cultural as representing separate groups of activities which have to be acquired separately and then brought together somehow in a unified life. We are left, then, with a new interpretation of Culture itself as the remaining alternative for a solution. That would seem to be the path we have to follow, feeling our way by the aid of all the light that present social facts can give. We shall proceed to clear our minds of a good deal of prejudice, for, as we approach the task, one thing we shall discover is the extent to which the septic debris of past social history corrupts our notions of culture. We shall discover, too, how fruitful in culture the ostensibly vocational can be, and how valuable for vocation may be those activities which are taught with purely cultural ends in view.

SIR FRED CLARKE, ' "Vocational" and "Cultural" ',
Forum of Education, VI, No. 3, November 1928.
Quoted in F. W. MITCHELL, *Sir Fred Clarke:
Master Teacher*, pp. 47–8, Longmans, 1967

For discussion

1 How far are our ideas about 'liberal–cultural' and 'vocational–technical' clouded by 'the septic debris of past social history'?

2 Granted that the distinction between cultural and vocational has become blurred, can we say that the distinction between the aims of general and special education are equally blurred?

5

The Concept of Educability

One of the stalest clichés in the business assures us that education is the art of the possible. Now, suddenly, that tedious truism is undergoing a sharp revision. Feats of learning and teaching which, only a decade ago, were thought to be beyond the reach of the average child and the average practitioner are now seen to be perfectly possible. The buoyant mood of educational theory in the second half of the twentieth century might well be summed up as an expression of the faith that the impossible takes a little longer.

Yet age-old modes of thinking are not sloughed off overnight. Ever since Plato's day, the belief that human beings can be classified into intellectual types, with an able minority constituting an élite, has remained more or less unshaken. This belief, and the idea of a limited Pool of Ability which went with it, is still held by a great many people, some of whom regard it as being self-evidently true. Recently its validity has been challenged so effectively that the whole tenor of educational policy making in Britain has been altered. The change is well brought out by contrasting the views of the Norwood Report (1943) with those of the Newsom Report (1963). The former sticks firmly to the Platonic doctrine, affirming the need for differential treatment of pupils in a tripartite system of secondary schools; whereas the Newsom proposals are based on a 'strong' definition of equality of opportunity which assumes that intelligence, far from being a fixed quantum, is largely an acquired characteristic.

This confrontation between two seemingly irreconcilable theories about the nature of human abilities and the 'art of the possible' is the contemporary version of a controversy which has been waged in seesaw fashion over the centuries. It is, of course, the controversy concerning the relationship between 'Nature' and 'Nurture' (i.e. heredity and environmental influences). The issue is clearly posed in the following passages. Ancient and/or Modern – Plato's Myth of the Metals or Bruner's hypothesis – which has the better of the argument?

Before going on . . .! (*Without comment*)
E

SOCRATES: Did you say that you believe in the separation of Church and State?

BRYAN: I did. It is a fundamental principle.

SOCRATES: Is the right of the majority to rule a fundamental principle also?

BRYAN: It is.

SOCRATES: Is freedom of thought a fundamental principle, Mr Jefferson?

JEFFERSON: It is.

SOCRATES: Then how would you gentlemen compose your fundamental principles if a majority, exercising its right to rule, ordained that only Buddhism should be taught in our public schools?

BRYAN: I'd move to a Christian country.

JEFFERSON: I'd claim the sacred right of revolution.

BOTH: What would you do, Socrates?

SOCRATES: I'd re-examine my fundamental principles.

WALTER LIPPMAN, *Imaginary Conversations*

I

A] 'THE REPUBLIC'

The Myth of the Four Metals 'And now we will have to devise one of those useful lies of which we spoke, and if possible get the rulers themselves to believe it, and in any case have it accepted by the rest of the citizens.' 'What kind of story would that be?' asked Glaucon. 'Oh, nothing very new,' I said: 'just a Phoenician story told by the poets, and located in many places. It has not happened in our time, and I am not sure that it could. It will certainly take a considerable amount of persuasion to put it over.' 'You seem reluctant to tell your story,' said Glaucon. 'Can you not just go ahead with it?' 'Very well, then,' I said. 'Here goes!

'I will inform the rulers and their assistants, and then the rest of the citizens, that the training and instruction they had seemed to get had all been a dream: that in reality they had been fashioned and nurtured in the depths of the earth, and on being completed had been sent up to the light of day by their Earth Mother. For that reason they must protect the land which had been nurse and mother to them from its enemies, and regard the other citizens as earth brothers. "All of you who dwell in the city," we will tell them, "are brothers, but the god who made you mixed gold in the composition of those among you who are fit to rule. Silver entered into the composition of their assistants, and brass and iron went to the making of the farmers and other craftsmen. Your children will usually be like yourselves, but since you are all akin it is possible that a silver child may sometimes be born to a gold parent, and the other way about. Similarly with the rest of you. The first and most imperative charge laid by God on the city's rulers is that they keep close watch on the children born among you and discern the metals that have gone to their making. If one of their own progeny has iron or brass in its composition they must have no scruple about putting the child among the farmers and workers whose nature it shares. If on the other hand, a child born in the lower class proves to have gold or silver in him, he must be made a warden or an assistant, as the case may be."

'Can you suggest any way of getting this story accepted?' I asked. 'No,' said Glaucon. 'I do not think there is any chance of the citizens to whom it is first told believing it, but possibly their children and the generations that follow may come to do so.' 'I daresay you are right,' I said. 'Even that would be quite a good thing to happen, would it not?'

PLATO, The Republic, III, 414-15

B] LOCKE, PLACE, OWEN, BRUNER

Of all the Men we meet with, nine Parts of ten are what they are, good or evil useful or not, by their Education. 'Tis that which makes the great difference in Mankind.

JOHN LOCKE, Some Thoughts concerning Education, 1690

The generality of children are organised so nearly alike that they may by proper management be made pretty nearly equally wise and virtuous.

FRANCIS PLACE, Letter to James Mill, 1816

Any general character, from the best to the worst, from the most ignorant to the most enlightened, may be given to any community, even to the world at large, by the application of proper means; which means are to a great extent at the command and under the control of those who have influence in the affairs of men. . . . Children are, without exception, passive and wonderfully contrived compounds; which may be formed collectively to have any human character. . . . Human nature is without exception universally plastic, and by judicious training the infants of any one class in the world may be readily formed into men of any other class.

ROBERT OWEN, A New View of Society, 1813

We begin with the hypothesis that any subject can be taught effectively in some intellectually honest form to any child at any stage of development. It is a bold hypothesis and an essential one in thinking about the curriculum. No evidence exists to contradict it; considerable evidence is being amassed that supports it.

JEROME BRUNER, The Process of Education, 1960

For discussion

Before going on, supposing you *had* to choose between Plato's Myth of the Metals and Bruner's hypothesis which would you prefer on rational grounds?

Points for further discussion

A] 'THE REPUBLIC'

1 In *The Open Society and Its Enemies* (vol. 1) Karl Popper maintains that Plato is a cheat and that Plato's entire argument centres upon a concept of justice which is essentially fraudulent. How do you react to this suggestion?
2 Plato professes to think that the myth stands little chance of gaining widespread acceptance. Why, then, has its apparent truth come to be taken for granted? Is it simply a case of a 'useful lie' being repeated so often that eventually it becomes credible – as in Nazi-type propaganda?
3 In the light of present psychological and sociological knowledge how far is it correct to say that 'your children will usually be like yourselves'?

B] LOCKE, PLACE, OWEN, BRUNER

1 Locke assigns 'nine parts of ten' in the adult's make-up to Education. How to reconcile this with his saying (also from *Some Thoughts*) that, 'We must not hope wholly to change their original Tempers, nor make the gay, pensive and grave; not the melancholy sportive, without spoiling them. God has stamped certain Characters upon Men's Minds, which like their Shapes, may perhaps be a little mended, but can hardly be totally alter'd and transform'd into the contrary'?
2 Place refers to 'proper management' and Owen to 'judicious training' as the means by which 'l'education peut tout'. Is this an over-optimistic position? Is it *conceivably* tenable?
3 Are there any reasons for thinking that Bruner's hypothesis is less unrealistic than the similar views put forward by earlier thinkers? What kinds of evidence can now be adduced in support of the hypothesis?

2 The Newcastle Commission Report 1861

Evidence of Rev. James Fraser, an assistant commissioner who later became Bishop of Manchester

It is quoted in the Report ('We agree with the following observations . . .')
. . . Even if it were possible, I doubt whether it would be desirable, with a view to the real interests of the peasant boy, to keep him at school till he was 14 or 15 years of age. But it is not possible. We must make up our minds to see the last of him, as far as the day school is concerned, at 10 or 11. We must frame our system of education upon this hypothesis; and I venture to maintain that it is quite possible to teach a child soundly and thoroughly, in a way that he shall not forget it, all that is necessary for him to possess in the shape of intellectual attainment, by the time that he is 10 years old. If he has been properly looked after in the lower classes, he shall read a common narrative – the paragraph in

the newspaper that he cares to read – with sufficient ease to be a pleasure to himself and to convey information to listeners; if gone to live at a distance from home, he shall write his mother a letter that shall be both legible and intelligible; he knows enough of ciphering to make out, or test the correctness of, a common shop bill; if he hears talk of foreign countries he has some notions as to the part of the habitable globe in which they lie; and underlying all, and not without its influence, I trust, upon his life and conversation, he has acquaintance enough with the Holy Scriptures to follow the allusions and the arguments of a plain Saxon sermon, and a sufficient recollection of the truths taught him in his catechism, to know what are the duties required of him towards his Maker and his fellow man. I have no brighter view of the future of the possibilities of an English elementary education, floating before my eyes than this.

For discussion
The witness found it inconceivable that the school-leaving age could be raised to 14 or 15. Why? Evidently his concept of the art of the possible was a very limited one. Why? Is it likely that your own ideas about the 'art of the possible' will be seen to be decidedly limited a hundred years hence?

3 The juvenile delinquents, the wild and the lost

Let me remind you of my suggested four groups of boys (a) the decent boys; (b) the average, good and bad, boys; (c) the evil boys; and (d) the low intelligence or E boys. The first group rarely cause any trouble. The second group cause some trouble, now and then, according to the circumstances. The third group are very few indeed. (I have had 5 in my ten years. I should, perhaps, include in this group the mentally unstable boys, exhibitionists all of them and unpredictable. I can remember three.) The fourth group is a different group from the other three. It is a certain block of boys cut out from the Roll of the School because of their low grading in intelligence. They can, and they do, contain the first three groups. But all of them, even the decent ones, are just that little bit more stupid so that they believe the wildest stories and cause trouble, and they are easily led into bad acts of mischief. They are a special group because of their inability to reason.

Out of my Roll of 700, about 140 are E boys. In the last ten years the average number of my boys appearing in the Juvenile Court is 36. Out of this 36, one half are E boys. When I consider my Incidents Book, in which I record the behaviour of bad boys in the School, I again find the E boys responsible for half of them. Quite often they are the same boys. Thus, taking it at its worst, out of 700 boys I have about 36 boys who are markedly bad or Juvenile Delinquents, i.e. five per cent, and out of this five per cent one half are E boys. Here are parts of a speech given recently by the Principal Psychologist of Wormwood Scrubs

Prison: 'Teachers are forward observation posts for the early detection of delinquency. The backward child, estimated at fifteen per cent of the child population, is anxious and full of frustration. The list given for the probable causes of Juvenile Delinquency is almost identical with the one we would give for the causes of Backwardness.' When asked for these the speaker said: 'Over-crowding, family conflict, neglect, lack of affection, lack of parental interest.'

He should simply have said: 'Low intelligence.'

NORMAN D. F. TOSH,
Being a Headmaster, pp. 74–5, Maclellan, 1964

For discussion
'He should simply have said: "Low intelligence".' Should he?

4

Hard wittes be hard to receiue, but sure to keepe: painefull without werinesse, hedefull without wauering, constant without newfanglenes: bearing heauie things, thoughe not lightlie, yet willinglie; entring hard things, though not easelie, yet deplie; and so cum to that perfitnes of learning in the ende, that quicke wittes, seeme in hope, but do not in deede, or else verie seldome euer attaine vnto.

ROGER ASCHAM, *The Scholemaster*

For discussion
If, by 'quicke wittes', Ascham means what we mean by 'bright pupils', – the ones with high I.Q.s – why was it that in Elizabethan times 'hard wittes' were often preferred?

5a The Norwood Report 1943

Tripartite Organization Even if it were shown that the differences between individuals are so marked as to call for as many curricula as there are individuals, it would be impossible to carry such a principle into practice; and school organization and class instruction must assume that individuals have enough in common as regards capacities and interests to justify certain rough groupings. Such at any rate has been the point of view which has gradually taken shape from the experience accumulated during the development of secondary education in this country and in France and Germany and indeed in most European countries. The evolution of education has in fact thrown up certain groups, each of which can and must be treated in a way appropriate to itself. Whether such groupings are distinct on strictly psychological grounds, whether they represent types of mind, whether the differences are differences in kind or in degrees, these are questions which it is not necessary to pursue. Our point is that rough groupings, whatever may be their ground, have in fact established themselves in general educational experience, and the recognition of such groupings in educational practice has been justified both during the period of education and in the after-careers of the pupils.

For example, English education has in practice recognized the pupil who is interested in learning for its own sake, who can grasp an argument or follow a piece of connected reasoning, who is interested in causes, whether on the level of human volition or in the material world, who cares to know how things came to be as well as how they are, who is sensitive to language as expression of thought, to a proof as a precise demonstration, to a series of experiments justifying a principle: he is interested in the relatedness of related things, in development, in structure, in a coherent body of knowledge. He can take a long view and hold his mind in suspense; this may be revealed in his work or in his attitude to his career. He will have some capacity to enjoy, from an aesthetic point of view, the aptness of a phrase or the neatness of a proof. He may be good with his hands or he may not; he may or may not be a good 'mixer' or a leader or a prominent figure in activities, athletic or other.

Such pupils, educated by the curriculum commonly associated with the Grammar School, have entered the learned professions or have taken up higher administrative or business posts. . . .

Again, the history of technical education has demonstrated the importance of recognizing the needs of the pupil whose interests and abilities lie markedly in the field of applied science or applied art. . . .

The various kinds of technical school were not instituted to satisfy the intellectual needs of an arbitrarily assumed group of children, but to prepare boys and girls for taking up certain crafts – engineering, agriculture and the like. Nevertheless it is usual to think of the engineer or other craftsman as possessing a particular set of interests or aptitudes by virtue of which he becomes a successful engineer or whatever he may become.

Again, there has of late years been recognition, expressed in the framing of curricula and otherwise, of still another grouping of pupils, and another grouping of occupations. The pupil in this group deals more easily with concrete things than with ideas. He may have much ability, but it will be in the realm of facts. He is interested in things as they are; he finds little attraction in the past or in the slow disentanglement of causes or movements. His mind must turn its knowledge of its curiosity to immediate test; and his test is essentially practical. He may see clearly along one line of study or interest and outstrip his generally abler fellows in that line; but he often fails to relate his knowledge or skill to other branches of activity. Because he is interested only in the moment he may be incapable of a long series of connected steps; relevance to present concerns is the only way of awakening interest, abstractions mean little to him. Thus it follows that he must have immediate returns for his effort, and for the same reason his career is often in his mind. His horizon is near and within a limited area his movement is generally slow, though it may be surprisingly rapid in seizing a particular point, or in taking up a special line. Again, he may or may not be good with his hands or sensitive to music or art.

5b 'Half Our Future'

The Newsom Report 1963 I Other advanced industrialized countries are also having to look critically at their educational systems, and attempts are being made to measure the national reserve of ability.

2 Can our pupils be regarded as one such reserve of ability? Will a substantial investment in their education produce people capable of fulfilling the industrial roles indicated above? If we look at what has happened when popular education has been extended in the past, the answer is an optimistic 'Yes'. New provision has always elicited new responses. Intellectual talent is not a fixed quantity with which we have to work but a variable that can be modified by social policy and educational approaches. The crude and simple answer was given by Macaulay 139 years ago: – 'Genius is subject to the same laws which regulate the production of cotton and molasses. The supply adjusts itself to the demand. The quantity may be diminished by restrictions and multiplied by bounties.'

3 A more subtle investigation into what constitutes the 'restrictions' and the 'bounties' in our society is of far more recent growth. The results of such investigation increasingly indicate that the kind of intelligence which is measured by the tests so far applied is largely an acquired characteristic. This is not to deny the existence of a basic genetic endowment; but whereas that endowment, so far, has proved impossible to isolate, other factors can be identified. Particularly significant among them are the influences of social and physical environment; and, since these are susceptible to modification, they may well prove educationally more important.

4 The problem is not solely a matter of social conditions. There are still large differences in the progress and attainments of children who appear to start with equal advantages, and even brothers and sisters in the same family differ from each other in talents. Factors of health and growth, character and temperament come into it, as well as native wit, which must be reckoned with, even if it cannot as yet be precisely measured. But when we refer to pupils in this report as 'more able' or 'less able' we are conscious that the terms are descriptive rather than diagnostic; they indicate the facts about the pupil's relative performance in school, but not whether that performance could be modified given different educational approaches.

For discussion

1 The Norwood Report accepted a threefold typology of pupils, adding that, 'Whether such groupings are distinct on strictly psychological grounds, or whether they represent types of mind, whether the differences are differences in kind or in degree, these are questions which it is not necessary to pursue.'

How far can the adoption of a tripartite system of secondary schools in England and Wales after 1944 be attributed to this refusal to ask such questions?

2 Do you agree that the language used to describe Grammar, Technical and Modern schoolchildren is highly generalized? Would you say that a phrase-by-phrase analysis of the passage reveals it as a tissue of falsehoods?

3 What kinds of evidence led the Newsom Committee to state categorically that 'intelligence . . . is largely an acquired characteristic'?

6

Marxist scholars have all along held that intelligence is entirely acquired, but Western scholars argue against this theory from their research on the similar achievements of identical twins separated at birth, and the different achievements of non-identical twins brought up together. Similar cases have suggested that there must be an inherent quality in intelligence, even if the acquired element is a large part of the whole. Nevertheless, those systems of education which, like the Russian, are based upon the assumption that all children are born equal, are probably more satisfactory in practice than those which, like our own (up to recently in the greater part of the country), have been based on the assumption that children are born – intellectually – sheep or goats.

A great deal of the debate about equality has now become out of date, since it is based upon three assumptions, none of which is any longer thought to be wholly correct. The first is that educational resources will always be scarce, so that a choice must be made between the children of any age group who should be adequately educated, and those who should receive second best. This is partly true at present. As we shall show below, the shortage of teachers is likely to last for some time. But compared with the past we are very much better off than we were, and projections of the future economic condition of Britain make it probable that the economic problem in its present form will be solved sooner or later, as Lord Keynes said it would be.

In any case, the most pressing problems of scarcity are not ours any longer; and we are no longer faced with choosing between a good education for the few and an indifferent education for the many. Our choices are more complex and less constrained by poverty than they were.

Secondly, it has always been assumed that society depended upon the identification of some exceptional people who would later become the leaders, while the great mass would be doing routine and humdrum jobs well within the capabilities of anybody with a minimum of intelligence and training.

This is now emphatically not the case. In a modern economy, jobs present a wide range of demands on talent and ability, and a highly productive society makes enormous demands upon people of all abilities, both on their general level of competence in such matters as reading, writing, calculating, driving, or managing technical equipment, and on their ability to meet the requirements of an increasingly complex social organization, while at the same time it requires a high level of emotional adjustment to situations of rapid change. Learning these techniques, abilities, and basic emotional adjustments depends to an increasing extent upon the educational system. It is becoming as important to educate the people of average and less than average ability as it is to educate the highly able. In any case, study after study has shown that unless a very wide range of ability is educated, some very able people are inevitably going to fall through the net. Even in a society such as ours, which has been organized for nearly fifty years on a basis of some equality of opportunity, two-fifths of the top ten per cent of the ability distribution still left school at fifteen in the mid-1950s.

The third assumption which is no longer thought to be true is that ability is a fixed quantum which can be identified and which to all intents and purposes remains constant throughout life. It has now been shown that the average level of ability has risen rather than fallen, if measured in terms of what the average person can do. It has been shown that children brought up in homes with satisfactory emotional adjustment, went to good schools, staying on at school until the latest possible date, and then taking up interesting work, become more intelligent in every sense than those to whom this does not happen. In so far as there is a rise in the standard of living of the average home, an improvement in the average school, and a lengthening of school life, the number of able people will therefore multiply.

This new knowledge makes it necessary to re-examine the whole concept of 'equality of opportunity'. Mr Anthony Crosland drew a vital distinction between the 'weak' and the 'strong' definition of equality of opportunity (a distinction that Sir Edward Boyle borrowed for his introduction to the Newsom Report). The weak definition (which had been generally accepted as the only definition up till that time) is that all children of equal (measured) ability should have roughly the same start in life. The strong definition takes account of recent psychological knowledge which points out that ability is largely acquired, and that a child can become more or less intelligent according to the kind of family he has and the social and educational experience he receives. It asserts that subject to differences in heredity and infantile experience, every child should have the same opportunity for *acquiring* measured intelligence, in so far as this can be controlled by social action. This is clearly a revolutionary principle.

JOHN VAIZEY, *Education for Tomorrow*,
Penguin Books, 1966

For discussion

1 Vaizey maintains that there is greater scope for the 'art of the possible' in an affluent society. Examine this view.

2 To what extent does a policy of Comprehensive secondary schooling depend upon the acceptance of a 'strong' definition of equality of opportunity?

3 'The generality of children are organised so nearly alike that they may by proper management be made pretty nearly equally wise and virtuous,' said Francis Place. Are we any nearer to finding the 'proper management' than teachers were at the beginning of the nineteenth century? How far will the establishment of 'educational priority areas' (recommended by the Plowden Report) help to equalize the general level of educability?

7 The nature of intelligence

All I can hope to do is point to certain developments that have been apparent over the past thirty years or so, and then restate what seems to me the position of the majority of middle-of-the-road psychologists.

1 There has been an increasing disinclination to accept the notion of intelligence as an inherited and measureable quality of the individual which simply matures as he grows older, regardless of upbringing and education.

2 The earlier belief in an antithesis between innate intelligence and acquired attainments has largely broken down; in particular the notion of the Achievement Quotient has been discredited. We realize that all types of ability develop through interaction between the maturing organism and a stimulating environment, and are intimately bound up with dynamic personality trends, motivations and social processes. This implies a greater disbelief in the long-term predictive value of the IQ.

3 There has been increasing interest in the psychological processes underlying intellectual performance, the nature of the child's percepts and concepts at different ages which Piaget has stressed, and the study of brain-functioning in the light of information theory and computer models.

4 There has been an increasing tendency to break down a single global intelligence or *g* into a large number of partly distinct ability factors, but attempts to develop differential tests for abilities along different lines, have not in fact met with much success.

5 There is increasing dissatisfaction with the types of multiple-choice items that make up the conventional group intelligence test, and greater realization that performance at these is considerably affected by previous practice and coaching. The increasing use of machine-scored tests, to facilitate the testing of large numbers, has not helped matters. At the same time there has been little progress in developing less restricted item forms, though the current concern with so-called divergent thinking and creative abilities is of interest.

6 There have, then, been many and varied critical attacks on the earlier, rather naïve, view of intelligence-testing commonly held in the 1920s – a view which is still all too widespread among teachers and educated laymen generally.

PHILIP E. VERNON, 'Development of Current
Ideas about Intelligence Tests' from
Genetic and Environmental Factors in Human Ability,
(eds.) J. E. MEADE and A. S. PARKES,
Oliver & Boyd, 1966

For discussion
An earlier generation of psychologists asserted that intelligence was innate and that the I.Q. was virtually unalterable. The present generation is much less inclined to be dogmatic. Why the change?

8

This belief in the overwhelming force of circumstances in the development of the individual plays an important part in the educational thinking of our times. It is a major factor in Soviet educational policy; and, though it has not been pressed to such extremes in this country, most left-wing thinkers look to deleterious social conditions as the chief inhibiting agent in educational advancement. A belief in the equalizing force of similar social conditions lies behind the 'comprehensive' philosophy; and it has been shown that even the I.Q., once thought to represent the native intelligence of the individual uncontaminated by family or environmental factors, is, in fact, to some degree affected by socio-cultural influences. Current concern for 'wastage' among working-class pupils is also influenced by the belief that the inhibiting influences are environmental.

There are, however, two important reservations to be made. Hereditary factors place considerable limitations on human adaptability. More important, the very power assigned to the environment should inhibit us from thinking that school education can bring about rapid reorientation. It is commonly admitted that the early years of childhood exercise a vital formative influence on later development; every child, by the time he gets to school, has already imbibed, consciously and unconsciously from his family background and neighbourhood, speech characteristics, emotional attributes, etc., which the relatively more superficial school environment, with its predominantly cognitive emphasis, can do little about except where unusual intellectual powers are in question. What can be changed most easily are the cognitive resources of the individual; what remain more impervious to alteration are the profounder emotional and unconscious aspects of the personality based on early experience. Human nature, because it always grows out of an historical context, is less plastic than our current environmentalists would like to think. Recent remarks on the failure of the comprehensive school to socialize its more difficult children will come as no surprise to those who bear this truth in mind.

G. H. BANTOCK,
Education and Values, pp. 133-4, Faber, 1965

For discussion
The writer is extremely critical of the trend towards the belief in intelligence as an acquired characteristic. Do you share his scepticism?

6

The Nature and Nurture
of Human Abilities

Is intelligence innate, or is it partly, largely (or even entirely) acquired through the process of learning? Is it true that some pupils are born clever, or do they become clever as a result of their upbringing?

In the final analysis, educational theory as a whole centres upon these crucial questions; and policy and practice cannot fail to be affected by the answers we give. The trouble is that, as often as not, these answers tend to be equivocal or self-contradictory. Indeed, the relationship between genetic factors ('Nature') and environmental influences ('Nurture') poses the knottiest and subtlest of all the problems the educationist has to face. So long as the arguments are bandied from one side to the other – and this is what educational theorists have been doing for centuries – the effect, inevitably, is to convert the problem into a pseudo-problem. If the problem is not to degenerate into a conundrum it is vital to realize that it is never a question of trying to assign this or that much importance to one side or the other – as if 'Nature' and 'Nurture' were somehow separate entities. Nature-Nurture (preferably without the hyphen!) provides the dimensions for the educationalist just as Space-Time does for the physicist.

The following discussion of the relationship is written in the form of a teaching programme, with both linear and branching sequences. In linear sequences the answer to a frame will be found in *italic* at the beginning of the next frame. In branching sequences the answers are scrambled, and you may find that you are referred either backward or forward.

After working through the programme you should be able to:

1 summarize the relevant facts concerning the nature and nurture of human abilities,
2 evaluate some of the statistical evidence adduced by psychologists and sociologists, and
3 see the point we were trying to make in the last sentence (i.e. that the relationship has to be thought of as one of mutual interaction).

Mendelian laws of inheritance, fundamental in the modern study of genetics, are based on chromosome theory. This theory postulates that the set of characteristics which produces the adult organism (phenotype) is, so to speak, blueprinted in the parental genes. In the fertilized germ cell these genes are present in pairs (zygotes, or singly gametes). Each chromosome – there are 46 in the body cell of a normal human being – has its own specific effects on the development of the organism, and retains its individuality throughout successive cell divisions. The mechanisms by which physical features, sex, etc., are determined are well established.

Are we correct in assuming that you are familiar with Mendel's early experiments in the cross-breeding of garden peas?

If so, *see* 2
If not, *see* 1

[1]

The typical, oft-quoted experiment was as follows: Tall-growing pea plants were crossed with short plants (P1, the first parental generation); their offspring (F1, the first filial generation) were all tall, and when self-fertilized, gave a second generation of hybrids (F2) consisting of tall and short plants in the ratio of three to one. The short plants from the F2 bred true for shortness when selfed, and a third of the talls bred true for tallness, while the other two-thirds of the talls again gave talls and shorts in the three to one ratio which had been found in the F2. Mendel's hypothesis was this: tallness and shortness are dependent on a pair of alternative factors, which we call T tall and t short. Each fertilized zygote, and each cell of the organism into which it develops, contains two of these factors, and may thus be TT, or Tt or tt; but the gametes each contain only one factor selected out of the two which are contained in the germ-mother cell out of which the gamete is formed. The first cross was between TT and tt, and gave a F1 of Tt; the fact that this F1 shows as tall plants must mean that during development the T factor 'dominates' over the t, which is said to be 'recessive'. When the F1 is selfed, each Tt plant forms equal numbers of gametes with T and with t, and if these unite at random they will give TT, Tt and tt plants in the ratio 1:2:1. Thus there will be three talls (of which one will be pure breeding TT and two Tt like the F1) to one pure breeding tt short.

Mendel's experiments succeeded in demonstrating that certain physical characteristics of garden pea plants are inherited.

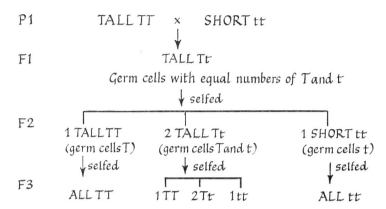

Do you agree? *See* **2**

If you do not agree there is no point in your continuing,– your best course is to learn the basic facts concerning heredity. Why not try C. H. Waddington's *Introduction to Modern Genetics* or, better still, one of the popular paperbacks on the subject?

----

[2]

Mongoloid babies are due to abnormalities in the chromosome structure of the fertilized egg-cell. Similarly, certain forms of colour blindness are known to be inherited as sex-linked characteristics. In human beings only males are affected, yet the condition is, in fact, transmitted by females.

Here is a family pedigree for red–green colour blindness. (Affected individuals marked black, squares denote males, circles, females.)

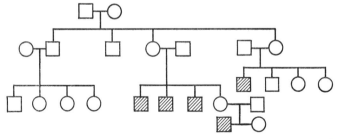

C. H. WADDINGTON, *Introduction to Modern Genetics*, Allen & Unwin

This shows that red–green colour blindness is in . . . . and that only
. . . . are affected. Even in this case, however, it has to be noted
that . . . . all individual males are affected.   *See* 3

---

[3]

inherited; males; not all

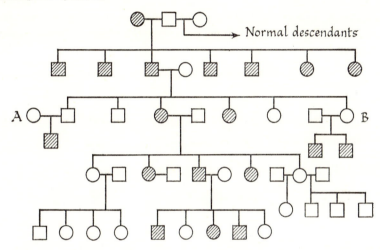

A Pedigree of Glaucoma – The character behaves as a dominant; it is usually
handed on only by individuals who themselves show it. But at A and B it is
transmitted by non-affected individuals, so that its penetrance is not complete.
Males squares, females circles, affected individuals black.
On this evidence would you say:

A Glaucoma is inherited.   *See* 4
B Glaucoma is transmitted through parents who are themselves affected by the
disease.   *See* 5
C Glaucoma appears to be normally transmitted by parents who are themselves
carriers of the disease.   *See* 6

F

[4]

You said that glaucoma is inherited. Invariably? In fact, the condition can arise quite apart from any genetic factor. You are drawing conclusions which are not warranted by the evidence as presented in the diagram.   *See* **6**

----

[5]

You said that glaucoma is transmitted through parents who are themselves affected by the disease. No doubt it would be easy to find pedigrees in which the transmission is 100% – but this is not one of them. Look at the F2 generation in the diagram.   *See* **6**

----

[6]

You said that glaucoma appears to be normally transmitted by parents who are themselves carriers of the disease.
Agreed.
This family tree looks very like the pedigree of glaucoma.

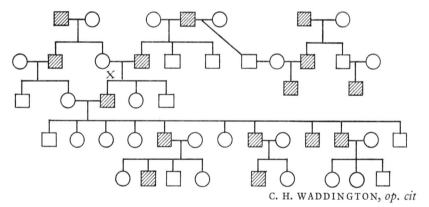

C. H. WADDINGTON, *op. cit*

A Pedigree of the Darwin Family as an example of how intelligence 'runs in families'. – Males squares, females circles. The males marked in black attained intellectual eminence, most of them having been Fellows of the Royal Society; no attempt has been made to assess the intellectual achievements of the women. Charles Darwin is marked with an X; note that he married his cousin, and that the inbred family was extremely successful.

This shows that high intelligence is determined by the parental genes in the same way as a disease like glaucoma is handed on from one generation to another.

If you agree, *see* **13**
If you disagree, *see* **12**

[7]

Spectacular advances have been made in the field of molecular biology in recent years, not least in the elucidation of the structure of the nucleic acids, e.g. D.N.A., which control the sequence and the rates of synthesis of proteins in the living cell. The work of deciphering the genetic 'code' proceeds apace, giving rise to the hope that eventually the mechanisms of hereditary transmission will be more fully understood than they are at present.

Before going on, two points are worth noting. First, even at the level of protein-synthesis, geneticists agree that *external* stimuli play an important part in the development of an organism. Second, the theory of genetic transmission adumbrated by Mendel and refined by his successors remains essentially unchanged. The theory may be summarized thus: The GENOTYPE sets the pattern of growth for individual members of the species, but this pattern is subject to variations in the course of the individual's development – the PHENOTYPE. In other words, genetic factors determine the chemical machinery of the organism and provide the *potential* for its future growth. The *actual* growth will, however, depend to some extent on the conditions to which the organism is subjected.

Genotype is to Phenotype as (potential/actual) growth is to (potential/actual) growth.   *See* 8

---

[8]

potential; actual
These two terms should be clearly understood:
    1 GENOTYPE – the genetic make-up of the individual
    2 PHENOTYPE – the end-product of the genotype, resulting from its interaction with its environment.
To repeat, genotype is to phenotype as .... is to ....   *See* 9

---

[9]

potential; actual
This distinction between potential and actual is worth bearing in mind. It should be remembered, too, that growth is not *simply* a biological concept. To say that the chemical machinery of the human organism controls its brain structure and rates of maturation is one thing. To say that 'mind' and 'character formation' are similarly pre-determined is quite another.

One psychologist, Hebb, classifies intelligence under two headings, Intelligence 'A' (innate intelligence) and Intelligence 'B' (measured intelligence as demonstrated in learned behaviour). Here again, a distinction has to be drawn between .... and ....   *See* 10

---

[10]

potential; actual

1 INTELLIGENCE A – 'innate intelligence'
2 INTELLIGENCE B – ('measured intelligence' as demonstrated in learned behaviour)

Which of the above corresponds to: Genotype; Phenotype?   *See* 11

---

[11]

Genotype – Intelligence A
Phenotype – Intelligence B

Now select the correct statement:

A The phenotype of an individual is limited by his genotype.
B The genotype of an individual pre-determines his phenotype.
C The genotype of an individual is limited by his phenotype.   *See* 14

---

[12]

You disagreed with the statement, and rightly.

The fact that Darwin's father and father-in-law, were both F.R.S.s and that four of his sons achieved the distinction is not, in itself, proof that 'intelligence runs in families'. It may be that social conditions (akin to those which effectively prevented any of the womenfolk from becoming F.R.S.s) were in one way or other at least partly responsible. No one denies that it is an advantage to have brilliant parents, but this is not the same as to say that intellectual ability is transmitted by the parental genes exclusively. In any case, intellectual ability, unlike shortness, tallness, colour of eyes, or even sex, is not a single, clear-cut characteristic which can readily be attributed to a combination of genetic factors. True, the latter determine the physical constitution of the newly-born child, including the central nervous system and the brain, and so must be thought of as providing him with the mental apparatus with which he enters the world. A great deal depends, however, on the *use* he makes of that apparatus, and this in turn depends upon the circumstances of the child's growth.   *See* 7

---

[13]

You agreed with the statement. Watch it! Superficially, the Darwin family-tree may resemble the Glaucoma pedigree, but aren't you missing one obvious and important difference? None of the female members gained the F.R.S. distinction. Was this because (*a*) they were less intelligent than the men, or (*b*) they were prevented from doing so for reasons which had nothing to do with inherited intelligence?

If you think (*a*) there is really no point in your continuing.
If you think (*b*) continue.   *See* 7

[14]

A

Psychologists who argue in favour of the concept of innate intelligence often appeal to the evidence concerning identical twins. Statistically, the evidence is certainly impressive. A positive correlation of 0·925 for the intelligence test scores of twins born from the same mother germ cell means that so far as their mental capacity is concerned they are virtually indistinguishable.

Study the figures in the table, then select the statement which fits best with the evidence.

TWINS — CORRELATIONS BETWEEN INTELLIGENCE TEST SCORES
(From Burt 1955, Table 1)

| | Burt and Conway | | | Freeman, Holzinger and Newman | |
| | | | | *r* Group test | *r* Individual test |
	N	*r*	*N*		
Identical twins reared together	83	0·925	50	0·922	0·910
Identical twins reared apart	21	0·876	19	0·727	0·670
Non-identical twins reared together	172	0·551	50	0·621	0·640
Siblings reared together	853	0·538	—	—	—
Siblings reared apart	131	0·517	—	—	—
Unrelated children reared together	287	0·269	—	—	—

S. WISEMAN, *Education and Environment*
Manchester University Press

This is conclusive proof that intelligence is inherited. *See* **15**
It looks very much as though intelligence is largely inherited. *See* **16**
The evidence is inconclusive because the figures cannot be trusted. *See* **17**

[15]

Conclusive proof? Are you so sure?

Study the figures in the table below, noting especially the correlations for general educational attainment and for reading and spelling for identical twins reared apart compared with those for siblings reared together. Evidently environmental influences *do* make a difference.

TWINS – CORRELATIONS OF EDUCATIONAL ATTAINMENT
(From Burt 1955, Table I)

	Freeman et al.	*Burt and Conway*		
	General Attainment	*General Attainment*	*Reading and Spelling*	*Arithmetic*
Identical twins reared together	0·955	0·898	0·944	0·862
Identical twins reared apart	0·507	0·681	0·647	0·723
Non-identical twins reared together	0·883	0·831	0·915	0·748
Siblings reared together	—	0·814	0·853	0·769
Siblings reared apart	—	0·526	0·490	0·563
Unrelated children reared together	—	0·535	0·548	0·476

S. WISEMAN, *op cit.*

Go back to 14

[16]

Yes. It certainly looks as though this is a valid inference. Still, a difference between 0·922 (the correlation between the I.Q.s of identical twins reared together) and 0·727 (the correlation for identical twins reared apart) is significant – and as you will see from the table in frame 15 this difference is magnified when it comes to correlations between the educational attainment of identical twins reared apart. Evidently the use made of the child's inborn mental apparatus, as we have called it, varies according to the circumstances of his upbringing. Suppose, for the sake of argument that one identical twin were to be removed at birth to Outer Mongolia and the other brought up in an English home and eventually sent to Eton College, is it not a fair presumption that in twenty years' time the two would exhibit massive differences in intellectual ability? Culture patterns help to decide the learner's level of educability quite as much as any genetic factor.

In any case, where do we draw the line between genetic factors and environmental influences? It is arguable that from the moment the germ cell divides it is already in an environment, i.e. the mother's body. *See* 18

[17]

This evidence may be inconclusive but the figures are trustworthy. *Back to* **14**

---

[18]

Talking of Eton College, you may like to consider the achievements of school-leavers who failed the 11-plus examination. Those pupils referred to in the table below (column 2) attended English Public Schools or direct grant Grammar schools. Those referred to in column 4 attended Secondary Modern schools. Note the respective numbers of boys attending the two types of school.

ACHIEVEMENTS OF LEAVERS KNOWN TO HAVE 'PASSED'
OR 'FAILED' THE 11 + EXAMINATION

Examination achievements	Survey schools		% Maintained schools (boys only)	
	'Passed' 11 +	'Failed' 11 +	Grammar	Sec. Mod.
O-level passes				
None*	2	8	11	92
Four or more	92	72	67	3
Eight or more	47	20	20	*
A-level passes				
One or more	74	35	38	*
Two or more	67	27	33	*
Awarded a university place	50	15	17	*
Number of boys	4,923	913	58,290	218,890

* Including none attempted.   G. KALTON, *The Public Schools*, Longmans

Given the same measured intelligence at 11-plus, or at any other age for that matter, it appears that the level of educability reached by pupils depends to a great extent upon the kind of schooling they receive.   If you agree, *see* **23**
If you disagree, *see* **22**

---

[19]

Correct. But is this the only inference to be drawn from the figures?
Have another look at the table.   *Then see* **21**

---

[20]

Correct. But is this the only inference to be drawn from the figures?
Have another look at the table.   *Then see* **21**

[21]

Yes – two factors *among others*. Of the various environmental influences which go into the making of a national culture and its sub-cultures social class is perhaps the one which has received the greatest attention from English sociologists in recent years. Some typical findings are summarised in the table below from the Robbins Report.

PERCENTAGE OF CHILDREN AT MAINTAINED GRAMMAR SCHOOLS
ACHIEVING FIVE OR MORE 'O' LEVELS
England and Wales

		Percentage	
		Entrants in 1946 (leaving in 1949/50– 53/54)	*Leavers in 1960–1*
		(1)	*(2)*
11 + grading	*Father's occupation*		
Upper third	Professional and managerial	80	91
	Clerical	65	79
	Skilled manual	60	77
	Semi- and un-skilled	42	49
	All children	61	78
Middle third	Professional and managerial	62	68
	Clerical	53	60
	Skilled manual	43	55
	Semi- and un-skilled	27	46
	All children	43	56
Lower third	Professional and managerial	48	53
	Clerical	36	47
	Skilled manual	33	32
	Semi- and un-skilled	20	22
	All children	31	36
Transfer from secondary modern school		46	45

In the light of this evidence which of the following statements seems most appropriate?

A This shows that the proportion of working-class children gaining 5 or more O-level passes is smaller than the proportion of middle class children. *See* **25**

B This shows that fewer working class children gain 5 or more O-level passes than children of the same measured ability from other classes. *See* **24**

[22]

You disagreed with the statement. Fair enough. Maybe you are hard to convince, or possibly the argument as presented so far is less than convincing. Let us pursue it further and hope that a scrutiny of the evidence underlying the importance of environmental influences (of which schooling is only one) will help to make you change your mind. *See* **23**

[23]

Schooling makes a difference, yes. So does the host of pre-school experiences, e.g. the language used in the home, the mother–child relationship in earliest infancy, the mores of the peer group, the sub-culture, etc., which influence the learner's attitudes and attainments which he acquires before setting foot inside the school.

We have already agreed that the mental capacities of identical twins are strikingly similar. If this similarity were attributable solely to the parental genes there would presumably be a family likeness between the mental capacities of siblings born of the same parents.

Examine the O-level, A-level and degree-level performances of children from small and large families in the table, then select the statement which strikes you as being most appropriate:

HIGHEST COURSE OF EDUCATION: BY PARENTS' SCHOOLING AND BY FAMILY SIZE   Great Britain: Children born in 1940–1

		Percentage				
		Higher education				Other post-school course or 'O' level
		Full time			'A' Level or S.L.C.	
Parents' schooling	Number of children in the family	Degree-level	Other	Part-time		
One or both parents at a selective school	One only	13·0	5·1	7·6	12·4	45·6
	Two	11·4	9·7	7·2	7·7	41·0
	Three	9·0	4·3	6·6	5·1	45·4
	Four	8·0	1·1	3·4	6·2	39·5
	Five or more	3·2	1·9	4·0	6·1	31·6
	All children	9·4	5·4	6·1	7·4	41·1
Neither parent at a selective school	One only	3·3	2·1	4·3	3·2	56·1
	Two	2·8	2·1	4·4	2·1	44·0
	Three	1·2	2·5	2·0	1·8	43·4
	Four	1·0	1·0	1·4	1·1	33·4
	Five or more	0·2	0·9	0·6	0·2	23·7
	All children	1·6	1·9	2·4	1·6	38·8

Source: Survey of 21-year-olds.

A The child's educational attainment depends to some extent upon the kind of education his parents received.   See 19

B So far as his educational attainment is concerned, the only child has an advantage over children from large families.   See 20

C Two factors which affect the child's educational attainment are the size of the family and the kind of education his parents received.   See 21

[24]

The same point is underlined in the next table, also from the Robbins Report. This gives the percentages of successful candidates of equal measured intelligence, but from different social–economic backgrounds, at O-level, A-level and degree-level examinations.

ACADEMIC ACHIEVEMENT OF CHILDREN AT MAINTAINED GRAMMAR SCHOOLS: BY I.Q. AT 11 AND FATHER'S OCCUPATION
England and Wales: Children Born in 1940–1

		Percentage				
I.Q.	Father's occupation	Degree level course (1)	At least 2 'A' levels (2)	At least 5 'O' levels (3)	Weighted sample numbers (= 100%)	Un-weighted sample numbers
130 and over	A. Non-manual	37	43	73	67	50
	B. Manual	18	30	75	60	63
	A divided by B	2·06	1·43	0·97		
115–129	A. Non-manual	17	23	56	201	151
	B. Manual	8	14	45	403	237
	A divided by B	2·12	1·64	1·24		
100–114	A. Non-manual	6	9	37	138	80
	B. Manual	2	6	22	236	124
	A divided by B	3·00	1·50	1·68		

Source: Survey of 21-year-olds.

This shows that:

A Manual workers' children are less academically inclined because they are not so clever, on the whole, as non-manual workers' children. *See* **29**
B The proportion of manual workers' children who drop out before reaching the university is roughly twice as great as the proportion of non-manual workers' children with the same measured intelligence. *See* **30**

---

[25]

Correct. But the main point is that working class children fare considerably worse than children of equal ability in other classes. *See* **24**

---

[26]

Bright pupils tend to deteriorate between the ages of 8 and 11. Correct. But aren't you missing the point? *Back to* **30**

---

[27]

Low scorers in verbal reasoning tests tend to improve slightly between the ages of 8 and 11. Quite so. But aren't you missing the point?   *Back to* **30**

---

[28]

On the whole, the performance of lower manual workers' children in verbal reasoning tests tend to deteriorate between the ages of 8 and 11.

Correct. And this state of affairs becomes progressively worse for many children with the result that, according to the Robbins Report, a boy or girl whose father's occupation is unskilled or semi-skilled stands only one chance in twenty of gaining a university place compared with a boy or girl whose father's occupation is professional or managerial. The extent of the discrepancy, which cannot be accounted for in terms of difference in measured intelligence at 11-plus, may be gauged from the next table.

PERCENTAGE OF CHILDREN BORN IN 1940–1 REACHING FULL-TIME HIGHER EDUCATION: by Father's Occupation, Great Britain

		Percentages				
		Full-time higher education		No full-time higher	All	Numbers
	Father's occupation	Degree-level	Other	education	children	(= 100%)
BOYS AND GIRLS	Non-manual					
	Higher professional	33	12	55	100	15,000
	Managerial and other professional	11	8	81	100	87,000
	Clerical	6	4	90	100	38,000
	Manual					
	Skilled	2	2	96	100	248,000
	Semi- and unskilled	1	1	98	100	137,000
BOYS	Non-manual	15	4	81	100	70,000
	Manual	3	2	95	100	189,000
GIRLS	Non-manual	9	10	81	100	70,000
	Manual	1	2	91	100	196,000

This shows that the percentage of children reaching full-time higher education varies enormously according to their fathers' occupation.

(*a*) For children whose father is in the higher professional bracket the percentage is ………

(*b*) For those whose father's occupation is unskilled or semi-skilled the percentage is ………   *See* **31**

[29]

Oh, come on – if you believe that you'll believe anything. You may be right in thinking that working class children are on the whole 'less academically inclined' (whatever that means), but even if this is the case it must be for reasons which are unconnected with any inherent 'cleverness'. If the figures in column I mean anything at all, the point is that the children in all three groups are roughly equal in ability *regardless of social class.*

On this understanding, have another look at the table and see whether or not you wish to change your opinion.   *Then go to* **30**

[30]

You said that the proportion of manual workers' children who drop out before reaching the university is roughly twice as great as it is for non-manual workers' children. Correct. Moreover, the disadvantages suffered by these underprivileged children increases and becomes cumulative in the course of time. In the table we have just been considering all the pupils in the three groups had the same measured intelligence at 11-plus. But some of them have had to overcome the disadvantages of inferior social-economic backgrounds before reaching the age of 11, as the next table shows. The rot may have set in as early as age 8, or even before!

CHANGES IN AVERAGE MEASURED ABILITY BETWEEN 8 AND 11:
BY SOCIAL CLASS AND ABILITY AT 8
England and Wales: Children born in 1946

	Test score at the age of 8					
Social class	60 or more	56–60	51–55	46–50	41–45	Under 41
Non-manual:						
Upper	−2·3	+1·5	+1·8	+3·4	*	*
Lower	−1·9	+0·6	+1·7	2·4	+1·8	+2·5
Manual:						
Upper	−3·2	−0·8	+0·2	+0·6	+0·9	+0·5
Lower	−4·6	−2·3	−0·8	No change	−0·2	+0·7

Select the statement which seems most appropriate:

A Pupils with high measured ability tend to deteriorate between the ages of 8 and 11 regardless of their home background.   *See* **26**
B Pupils with low measured ability tend to improve slightly between the ages of 8 and 11 regardless of their home background.   *See* **27**
C On the whole, the measured ability of lower manual workers' children tends to deteriorate between the ages of 8 and 11.   *See* **28**

[31]

(a) 45%; (b) 2%

The point to bear in mind being an enormous difference between the total numbers of the groups involved, 15,000 against 137,000.

In view of the facts which have already emerged, in particular those concerning the unequal attainments of pupils of the same measured intelligence, the only possible deduction seems to be:

A Equality of opportunity is impossible so long as a policy of differential treatment – Grammar schools for the few, Secondary Modern schools for the many – is pursued.   *See* **34**

B There must be vast reserves of concealed ability which remain untapped.
                                                                             See **35**

C The statistics misrepresent the actual state of affairs in our schools.   *See* **36**

----

[32]

The tendency to drop out is most marked in the middle and lower third of the ability range, granted. But this is not the main significance of the figures.
                                                                             See **33**

----

[33]

Yes, the figures are significant because they indicate that the tendency to drop out is in some way connected with the father's occupation.

Before we start blaming it all on poor old Dad, however, let's have a look at the Brown boys and the Robinson boys whose collective case histories are so revealingly documented in 'Half Our Future' (see table overleaf). They are all attending Secondary Modern schools and are at the point when they are about to enter the world of work. The Brown boys represent the top 25% of all the so-called non-academic pupils in the country as regards general educational attainment. The Robinson boys represent the bottom 25%. But this is not the most interesting difference which emerges from the comparison.

Compare then for height and weight for a start. Physical characteristics of this sort, we know, can be hereditary, but taking into consideration all the other factors which are operating – the size of family, type of neighbourhood, economic circumstances, etc. – it seems unlikely that a purely genetic explanation will suffice.

The profiles indicate that:

A As a class, boys whose fathers are in unskilled occupations tend to be undersized and underweight at school-leaving age.   *See* **37**

B Compared with boys whose fathers are in non-manual occupations the proportion of manual workers' children who are undersized and underweight is significantly greater.   *See* **38**

PROFILE OF THE BROWN BOYS

Average Age 14 years 8 months

Height			
Under 5′ 0″	5%	5′ 4″–5′ 7″	59%
5′ 0″–5′ 3″	23%	5′ 8″ or more	23%

Weight			
90 lbs. or less	6%	131 lbs.–150 lbs.	21%
91 lbs.–110 lbs.	26%	151 lbs. or more	8%
111 lbs.–130 lbs.	39%		

Father's Occupation			
Non-Manual Worker:		Manual Worker:	
Professional or Managerial	7%	Skilled	59%
Clerical, etc.	11%	Semi-skilled	14%
		Unskilled	9%

Size of Family, Only Child 17%			
Number of Brothers or Sisters:		Three	13%
One	30%	Four	7%
Two	23%	Five or more	10%

Free Meals			
Receive free school dinners	3·5%	Do not receive free school dinners	96·5%

PROFILE OF THE ROBINSON BOYS

Average Age 14 years 8 months

Height			
Under 5′ 0″	14%	5′4″–5′ 7″	37%
5′ 0″–5′ 3″	35%	5′ 8″ or more	14%

Weight			
90 lbs. or less	16%	131 lbs.–150 lbs.	14%
19 lbs.–110 lbs.	32%	151 lbs. or more	4%
111 lbs.–130 lbs.	34%		

Father's Occupation			
Non-Manual Worker:		Manual Worker:	
Professional or Managerial	2%	Skilled	53%
Clerical, etc.	7%	Semi-skilled	18%
		Unskilled	20%

Size of Family, Only Child 7%			
Number of Brothers or Sisters:		Three	17%
One	17%	Four	14%
Two	20%	Five or more	25%

Free Meals			
Receive free school dinners	8·2%	Do not receive free school dinners	91·8%

[34]

You said that equality of opportunity is impossible so long as a policy of differential treatment is retained. You are probably correct in thinking so, but this is not the only possible deduction which can be made. It is arguable, for example, that the situation could be improved very considerably without 'going Comprehensive'. Let us see what conclusion was drawn by the Robbins Report.   *See* **35**

----

[35]

Correct. Levels of educability are influenced by levels of aspiration and expectation – and these vary in different walks of life. In professional class families, for instance, it is the done thing to stay on at school until 17 or 18, but this is by no means always the case in lower working-class families. Look at the table.

PERCENTAGE OF LEAVERS FROM MAINTAINED GRAMMAR SCHOOLS
HAVING 2 OR MORE PASSES AT ADVANCED LEVEL: by grading 11+ and
father's occupation   England and Wales, 1960–1

Grading in 11+	Father's Occupation	*Percentage of leavers of all ages who have 2 or more 'A' levels* (1)	*Percentage of leavers of all ages who leave aged 18 and over* (2)	*Percentage of leavers aged 18 and over who have 2 or more 'A' levels* (3)
Upper third	Professional and managerial	57	55	79
	Clerical	44	39	74
	Skilled manual	38	40	77
	Semi- and un-skilled	21	23	81
Middle third	Professional and managerial	33	42	63
	Clerical	18	29	56
	Skilled manual	18	27	59
	Semi- and un-skilled	10	15	58
Lower third	Professional and managerial	14	32	43
	Clerical	16	22	58
	Skilled manual	10	18	51
	Semi- and un-skilled	4	7	53
Transfer from secondary modern school		15	29	49
All groups at 11	Professional and managerial	37	46	67
	Clerical	26	32	64
	Skilled manual	22	29	65
	Semi- and un-skilled	11	17	56
All children		24	31	65

These percentages are significant because they indicate that:

A The tendency to drop out is more marked in the middle and lower third of the ability range. *See* **32**

B The tendency to drop out is in some way connected with the father's occupation. *See* **33**

---

[36]

You said that the statistics misrepresent the actual state of affairs. In that case it is up to you to explain just how they do this. We can sympathize with you as regards your reluctance to draw conclusions from a set of statistical tables, and we agree that it is essential to get behind the bare figures wherever and whenever this is possible – e.g. by reading such intensely human documents as Marsden and Jackson's *Education and the Working Class* – but aren't you being over-cautious?

See **35** for the conclusion drawn by the Robbins Report.

---

[37]

Not at all! You are reading more into the evidence than it is safe to do. *As a class*, the Robinson boys exhibit only negligible differences as regards height and weight. Only a minority are at a disadvantage compared with the Browns. No doubt we misled you by inserting the phrase 'tend to be'. Sorry! *See* **38**

---

[38]

The proportion of manual workers' children who are undersized and underweight is significantly greater than it is in the case of non-manual workers' children. At the same time, it has to be recognised that any disadvantage – and if the physical shortcomings of the Robinsons are slight we can be sure that their mental handicaps are a good deal more serious – arises from a whole complex of social-economic *and* cultural factors.

It is a fact of common observation that 'tough' schools are, for the most part, situated in 'problem areas'. 'Where they live', indeed, is as important a factor as any. Judging by the next table, England seems to be full of 'problem areas'.

PERCENTAGE OF 17-YEAR-OLDS AT SCHOOL: BY L.E.A. AREA
England and Wales; January 1960

Counties	Per-centage	County boroughs	Per-centage
Highest		Highest	
Cardiganshire	27·9	Merthyr Tydfil	15·2
Caernarvonshire	24·8	Bath	14·8
Merionethshire	21·0	Swansea	13·9
Carmarthenshire	19·5	Blackpool	13·9
Pembrokeshire	18·6	Lincoln	13·6
Lowest		Lowest	
Staffordshire	6·8	Nottingham	4·7
Nottinghamshire	6·7	Salford	4·7
Durham	6·5	Dudley	4·4
Ely	6·3	West Ham	2·9
Lincolnshire (Holland)	5·5	Bury	2·5

Notes

1 The figures relate to 17-year-olds at school in January 1960 as a percentage of 13-year-olds at school in January 1956.

2 The highest English Counties were Westmorland (14·5%), Surrey (13·9%), Hertfordshire (13·8%) and Cheshire (12·9%).

Entry to full-time higher education

The range of variation for entry to full-time higher education is equally striking. Again the highest proportion was in Cardiganshire (24·9%); the lowest was in West Ham (1·7%). These variations are best explained by saying that:

A Cardiganshire children are more intelligent than those in West Ham. *See* **40**
B Rural areas are more enthusiastic about education than industrial areas.

See **39**

C Opportunities of enjoying an extended school-life seem to be a matter of geographical luck. *See* **41**

G

[39]

Your view was that rural areas are more enthusiastic about education than industrial areas. There is probably something in this idea. But what about Merthyr Tydfil – and what about Lincolnshire (Holland)? Evidently there is something in the Welsh culture pattern, for in this league table it tops the list in industrial as well as in rural areas. In the case of the five Welsh counties, the obvious explanation for the 'enthusiasm' is the lack of job prospects in the area: for the able and ambitious 'getting on' means 'getting out' – and education (i.e. some kind of paper qualification) is seen as the only road to a worthwhile career. The same is true of the Highlands and Islands of Scotland which have been exporting trained manpower for many a long year. In these areas there is no doubt that parents are prepared to make sacrifices for the children and that, in general, education is held in high esteem. There is no doubt, too, that 'enthusiasm' for education is shared by some cultures, (e.g. the Jewish) and not by others. However, this is not the point we wish to make. *See* **41**

[40]

Your view was that Cardiganshire children are more intelligent than those in West Ham? You must be joking! *See* **41**

[41]

Your view was that opportunities to enjoy an extended school-life seem to be a matter of geographical luck. A sweeping conclusion, but one which is apparently justified.

The English system of education is often satirized as being a patchwork quilt, a crazy pavement which rationalizes its irregularities by calling them diversity. Even within the boundaries of a single county it appears that there are wide variations in educational opportunity.

ACADEMIC PERFORMANCE OF SECONDARY SCHOOL CHILDREN
IN DIFFERENT AREAS OF THE WEST RIDING OF YORKSHIRE

Area	Percentage of all children allocated to grammar schools	Percentage of those allocated to grammar schools who went to university
Coalfield	17·8	9·7
North	30·4	14·0
West	34·9	10·8

Source: Evidence of the West Riding of Yorkshire Education Committee.
Note: The table relates to those entering grammar schools in 1949–53 (inclusive) and to those taking up County awards to the university in 1956–60 (inclusive).

In the coalfield area of the West Riding ——% of all children were allocated to Grammar schools, while in the western division the percentage was ——%. Moreover, of the children allocated to Grammar schools, ——% went to the university from the northern division and only ——% from the coalfield division. This, despite the fact that the coalfield took a much (higher/lower) percentage than either of the other two areas.

See **42**

------

[42]

17·8; 34·9; 14·0; 9·7; Lower
To recapitulate:
'This raises the fundamental issue of whether the pool of ability, as it is usually called, can be measured and, if so, how is it possible to tell what proportion of the population are so constituted at birth that, growing up under the most favourable circumstances, they could reach a level of attainment suitable for entry to higher education?

'The answer is "no": that is to say, one cannot specify an upper limit.

'There is, however, a great deal of evidence which suggests that the reserve of untapped ability in this country is still very considerable and that on present trends it is most unlikely to be fully mobilised within the next twenty years.'

(Robbins Report)

A somewhat gloomy prediction, but so much remains to be done before all children can be said to enjoy opportunities for 'growing up under the most favourable circumstances', that there is nothing for it but to agree that the prediction is realistic. The numbers staying on to A-levels are steadily rising, but not fast enough to meet the requirements of an advanced industrial society which calls for increasingly high standards in occupational skills as well as in general education. If the Robbins projections are accurate, as you can see from the table overleaf, even in 1985 the percentage of the age-group (boys and girls) who complete the equivalent of a sixth-form course will still amount to only ——%.

Read table then see **43**

QUALIFIED SCHOOL LEAVERS: ENGLAND AND WALES
PERCENTAGE OF EACH AGE GROUP AT SCHOOL IN JANUARY
England and Wales

Boys and girls	19 and over	18	17	16	15
			Percentage		
			Age in January		
1950	0·3	2·1	6·6	14·1	29·8
1954	0·3	2·5	7·9	15·8	31·6
1955	0·3	2·7	8·1	16·6	32·4
1956	0·4	2·8	8·7	17·7	33·9
1957	0·4	3·2	9·2	18·7	35·1
1958	0·4	3·4	10·0	19·2	36·6
1959	0·4	3·7	10·4	20·7	38·4
1960	0·4	3·7	11·1	21·5	39·8
1961	0·4	3·9	11·7	22·0	40·0
1962	0·4	4·1	12·0	22·4	42·2
1965	0·5	4·8	13·7	25·3	63·6
1970	0·6	5·8	16·3	29·3	67·6
1973	0·7	6·4	18·0	31·8	69·9
1975	0·7	6·8	19·0	33·4	71·6
1980	0·8	7·8	21·7	37·5	75·6
1985	0·9	8·8	24·4	41·6	79·6

Based on *Statistics of Education 1962*, H.M.S.O.

Notes

1 Figures for 1965 and after are estimated.

2 Figures for 1950–7 include estimates for independent schools not recognised as efficient.

3 In the first column, those at school aged 19 and over have been added to those at school aged 19 and expressed as a percentage of all those aged 19.

[43]

9·7 (i.e. 8·8% + 0·9%)

In talking about the pool of ability three terms are often used:

(*a*) Innate potential, biologically inherited;

(*b*) Measured ability, as estimated by the use of intelligence tests; and

(*c*) Attainment in a specific branch or branches of knowledge.

It is important to be as clear as possible about the nature of measured ability, and its relationship to innate potential, on the one hand, and attainment on the other.

Views of what is measured by intelligence tests have changed since they were first invented. Then, it was thought that measured intelligence depended mainly on heredity, and that in most western countries the influence of the environment on test scores was small. More recently, comparative studies in widely different social and cultural groups have modified this view. Genetic factors are undoubtedly important, but the influence of the environment is great, and its extent cannot easily be determined. For our present purposes it is enough to say that measured ability is a function of two variables, innate and environmental, and that the contribution of the latter increases with age.

Is this a fair summary of the argument as presented so far?

Yes.   *See* **45**

No.   *See* **46**

---

[44]

1 Sex. 2 Where they live. 3 National culture. 4 Secondary Schooling. 5 The language used in the home. 6 Father's occupation. 7 Family size, etc., etc.

Any suggestion that 'More means worse' must therefore be rebutted. The idea that there are only a few clever people in the world and that the supply of high intelligence is somehow limited is almost certainly false. The supply is growing all the time! By now the idea that we learn to become intelligent should not seem so strange as it may have seemed at first.

As yet there is relatively little evidence to prove that 'More means better', but what there is supports the contention. In the U.S.A., where the proportion of the school-leaving age-group going on to college and university is much higher (and increasing faster than it is in Britain) standards of scholastic aptitude appear to be rising.

AVERAGE SCORES ON VERBAL SCHOLASTIC APTITUDE TESTS OF ENTRANTS TO CERTAIN AMERICAN INSTITUTIONS: BY YEAR OF ENTRY

Institution	1947	1953	1960
A	490	—	550
B	430	460	500
C	—	570	650
D	—	590	640
E	—	420	500
F	510	520	620
G	—	440	570
H	590	580	640
I	530	520	640
J	530	510	610
K	600	620	630
L	640	640	680
M	—	450	580

Source: Orlans, H., *The Effects of Federal Programs on Higher Education*, Brookings Institution, 1962.

* 36 institutions were approached, but only 13 had reasonably comprehensive records of scores since the war.

Work out the average increment in test scores for the eight institutions which kept records between 1947 and 1960.   *See* **47**

[45]

Yes. Now let's take the argument a step further.

'There has been another change in general ideas about ability (both actual and potential). What was at one time assumed by scientists, as it still is by some laymen, to be a single trait has been gradually broken down, with the help of experimental evidence, into a number of distinguishable components, each requiring measurement of its own. Some of these components are not even cognitive: and what is generally called 'intelligence' is partly dependent upon personality and motive. Thus, while the distinction between measured ability and innate potential has been increasingly emphasised, the distinction between measured ability and attainment has tended to become less clear. Recent work has called in question the view that intelligence in some way comes prior to attainment and partly determines it. Nevertheless it is still true, that, because of early leaving or failure to enter higher education, there are many young adults of high measured ability whose educational attainments are modest.'

We have already considered some of the social, economic and cultural influences which combine to keep the level of attainment of the majority of children well below their level of educability. One of the most obvious is the influence of social class. Can you suggest others?

1 ...... 2 ...... 3 ...... 4 ...... 5 ...... etc. *See* **44**

----

[46]

No.

In that case either there is something wrong with the programme or you have not been studying the evidence as carefully as you were asked to do. *See* **45**

----

[47]

68·7

So far as British universities are concerned what little evidence there is is encouraging.

AVERAGE SCORES OF UNIVERSITY STUDENTS IN A VERBAL
INTELLIGENCE TEST: PRE-WAR AND POST-WAR PERFORMANCE

	Average score	*Numbers tested*
Undergraduates at Edinburgh		
1935–37	155·6	380
1945–48	157·0	619
1957–60	156·5	844
Cert. Ed. students at Liverpool		
1932–42	151·3	621
1943–50	156·3	262

Source: Edinburgh: Data supplied by Professor J. Drever. Liverpool: Tozer, A. H. D., and Larwood, H. J. C., *Brit. Jnl. Psych.* **XLIV**, 347–58, 1953.
Note: Data for Edinburgh relate to a representative sample of undergraduates in arts and science.

This shows that although the number of university students has increased quite considerably since the 1930s:

A The average I.Q. has risen significantly.   *See* **49**
B The average I.Q. has risen slightly.   *See* **50**
C The average I.Q. has certainly not fallen.   *See* **51**

----

[48]

from Weekend Telegraph, 18th November, 1966.   OPINION by Colin Wilson

ONE RAT IN TWENTY IS A LEADER

One of the most closely guarded secrets of the Korean war was why there were no escapes of American prisoners. The Chinese wanted to economise on manpower. So, instead of keeping all the prisoners under heavy guard, they watched them for a day or two, and picked out all the 'leader' figures: anyone who seemed to have imagination or enterprise. These were guarded heavily. The rest were left with almost no guard at all. And without the leaders no one tried to escape.

The 'dominant' types, the Chinese found, were always precisely five per cent of the total number of soldiers. The same figure also applies to animals. In experiments concerned with the effect of overcrowding among rats, Dr John B. Calhoun of the U.S. National Institute of Mental Health discovered that the 'dominant' rats numbered five per cent of the total.

The rats were put into four cages, all interconnected. There was enough room for all the rats to be fairly comfortable. But what happened was that two of the rats were very dominant indeed – 'king rats'. Each of these two took a cage for himself, and established himself in it with his harem. The rest had to crowd into the remaining two cages, creating a kind of slum.

And now the really interesting thing happened. The remainder of the dominant five per cent did not actively challenge the authority of the 'king rats'. Instead, they formed themselves into 'criminal' gangs, and went around attacking the other rats, stealing food, and generally creating a nuisance. Rats normally have an extremely elaborate courting ritual, which is never violated under normal conditions. The criminal gangs abandoned it and went in for rape. A percentage of them became homosexuals.

The point I am making should be ominously clear. Any society needs to provide an outlet for its dominant five per cent. A hundred years ago a boy of this sort might run away to look for gold in Alaska. There were many outlets for the urge to adventure.

G. K. Chesterton once remarked that an adventure is only an inconvenience rightly considered, and an inconvenience is an adventure wrongly considered. And it was A. N. Whitehead who pointed out that civilisation cannot survive without adventure. Civilisation may be defined as an attempt to do away with the inconvenience of living: so in a sense, civilisation aims at the destruction of adventure. If Professor Whitehead is right, then civilisation is aiming at its own destruction.

What is your reaction to this?

A Plato was right after all; leaders are born not made. *See* 52
B The first concern of any wise educational policy should be to find and train a natural élite. *See* 53
C In any society there are bound to be dominant types and 'king rats' so let's preserve our Grammar schools at all costs. *See* 54
D It's a matter of opinion whether the views expressed in the article should be taken seriously, or whether they should be regarded as cheap journalism. *See* 55

----

[49]

Let's hope you are right! We would remind you, however, that the sample was a rather small one and that for this reason alone it would be wrong to place too much confidence in the figures. *See* 51

----

[50]

That's what the figures suggest. At the same time, the sample was a relatively small one so that it would be unsafe to conclude that the slight increase in test scores applies to the student body as a whole. *See* 51

----

[51]

Agreed. The belief that 'More means better' would still be tenable even if it could be shown that existing standards will *not* rise in the future. The 'strong' definition of equality of opportunity insists that many more children are capable of reaching these standards than has been thought possible hitherto. It is now generally conceded that a system of secondary schooling based on differentia treatment, i.e. segregating 'academic' and 'non-academic', can result only in a split-level of educability which does less than justice to the great majority. Well meaning as it is, the philosophy of 'separate but equal' has proved to be delusive.

'We may reasonably conclude, then, that in the local secondary schools of England and Wales as a whole, a system based mainly on separate grammar and "modern" schools, about ten per cent of each age-group proceed to take a "good" GCE around the age of sixteen.

'Only two areas in Britain are completely comprehensive; the Isle of Man and Anglesey. Culturally they have no special advantages. Nevertheless, in the Isle of Man on average sixteen and a half per cent of the relevant age group gained a "good" GCE during the four years 1959–62. In Anglesey the average for 1959–61 was over fourteen per cent. In those Welsh counties other than Anglesey where a large number of the schools are comprehensive, the proportion gaining "good" GCEs is impressive; during 1958–61 the average for Cardiganshire was twenty-one per cent.'

R. PEDLEY, The Comprehensive School, Penguin

It seems, then, that in the long run there is no quarrel between those who appeal to 'excellence' and those who uphold 'equality'. The cause of social justice will best be served, not as Plato advocated by singling out the Children of Gold, but by broadening the educational base for all. Agreed? *See* **48**

----

[52]

Conceivably, Plato may have been right, but you are certainly wrong in concluding that leaders are born, not made, at any rate on the basis of the evidence presented in the article. This tells you nothing about the previous history of the alleged dominant types and the 'king rats'. You can do better than this!

See **55**

----

[53]

One of the concerns of any wise educational policy should be to see that the ablest receive the kind of education which enables them to realise their potentialities to the full. But should it be the *first* concern? In a democracy, surely, the mass of average children have equal claims to consideration. *See* **55**

----

[54]

Alright, let's suppose that in any society there are bound to be dominant types, but isn't it a *non sequitur* to go on to say that the best way of catering for them is by keeping a highly selective system of secondary schools? If they're cut out to be leaders anyway, wouldn't they be better off in a mixed-ability school where they can exercise their talents for leadership? *See* 55

[55]

It's perhaps as well that the article appeared under the heading of OPINION. When it comes to topics of this kind – and educational theory is full of them – value judging is inescapable. The question is whether the opinion expressed (which entails a value judgment) is sufficiently well-informed.

In working through this programme you have been doing two things:

1 looking at some of the evidence (information) concerning the relationship between 'Nature' and 'Nurture', and
2 evaluating this evidence so as to decide just what can safely be deduced from it. The rest is up to your own judgment.

Two last words before we leave it at that. *See* 56

[56]

We take it for granted that education is a Good Thing. How, then, do you interpret the findings of a 19th century French sociologist outlined in the graph below

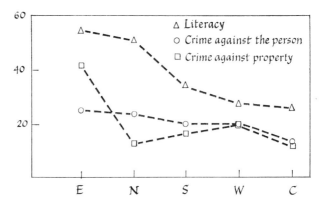

FIG. 9 Guerry's results. Rates of literacy and crime for the five French regions. Units: literacy – percentages; crime – rates (whole of France = 100)

A This shows that high standards of literacy are accompanied by a high incidence of crime.   *See* 57
B This merely goes to show that one needs to treat statistics with a certain amount of caution.   *See* 58

---

[57]

You chose answer A. On the face of it, this may seem to be what the graph shows. Unfortunately, the graph leaves out a great many things which need to be known before we can say that literacy is in some way linked with crime.

See 58

---

[58]

You chose answer B. Certainly this is the construction we should prefer you to make. One of the objectives of this programme (which you may well think is replete with facts and figures) has been to provide exercises in the critical reading of evidence. Much of this evidence is statistical and full of pitfalls for the unwary.

Figures can be misleading – and so can words, as a careful reading of the following passage reminds us.

We are tempted to say that an organism responds to environmental stimuli, only to meet the objection that environmental events would have no stimulus value but for the needs of the organism to which they relate; and though we may take refuge from the difficulty by emphasizing that the organism and the environment together constitute a field of forces we are not thereby provided with words and grammar that allow us to describe particular features of the interaction without starting from one side or the other. The individual's relation to his social environment provides one form of this general difficulty, and until we have mastered a new grammar for discussing interaction we must verbally misrepresent the process by making subject and object out of equal interacting forces.

D. W. HARDING, *Social Psychology and
Individual Values*

In working through this programme you have almost certainly felt that the argument was shifting its ground, first dwelling on the importance of genetic factors, then veering towards explanations which emphasized the part played by environmental influences. This is because of the inherent difficulty in language usage: the moment we write or speak of 'Nature', 'heredity', 'innate' ability, or whatever else we choose to call it, it becomes a noun in a sentence. Grammatically, it is permissible to say, 'Nature is just as important, less important, or more important (as) (than) Nurture' – where one is the subject and the other the object in the sentence. Strictly speaking, however, whenever we do this we are guilty of murdering to dissect.

Perhaps now you are ready to agree with the point which was made at the outset: in dealing with the interaction between potential and actual human ability it is essential to think in terms of Nature Nurture without a hyphen. If not, words fail us!

7

Punishment

If this happens to be one of the bulkiest sections in the book the reason is simple; this is one topic on which everyone feels strongly and has plenty to say! Can it be that as teachers (and parents) we are preoccupied, even obsessed, with the need for punishment? If so, how far does the preoccupation stem from religious convictions, in particular the doctrine of original sin, and how far from unconscious (possibly sadistic) motives? If not, how does it come about that we have so little to say about the positive and more agreeable aspects of the teacher–pupil relationship and the learning process? To what extent are sociological factors responsible?

How do we define punishment, anyway? What forms does it assume in the classroom, and for what offences is it admissible? – at what ages? How effective is it, and how do we justify its use? Looking back over the history of education it is arguable that too often, for too many, the learner has, through no fault of his own, been placed in a persecutory situation; and that the constant fear of 'correction' has been symptomatic of a deep-seated malaise in educational theory and practice alike. Despite Quintilian's indictment, corporal punishment persists, nowhere more obviously than in the home. True, it has been made illegal in most European school systems, and in England (though less so in Scotland) its use has steadily dwindled. If and when the recommendation of the Plowden Report is implemented it will be forbidden in England's primary schools. But the resort to physical violence, now generally condemned, may all too easily be replaced by violence of the tongue or by a lack of sympathy which can in the long run be just as callous and as damaging – as a reading of the following extracts serves to remind us.

NOTE

This is one topic on which it is fatally easy to be swayed by personal prejudices. For this reason, you are asked to *read the extracts in the order in which they are presented*. In each case, before considering any of the questions for discussion, indicate your reaction to the general viewpoint expressed in the passage by under-lining one of the choices at the bottom of the page:

STRONGLY AGREE | AGREE | NOT SURE | DISAGREE | STRONGLY DISAGREE
    (score 4)   (score 3)   (score 2)   (score 1)   (score 0)

Keep a record of your choices in order (*a*) to check your responses for consistency, (*b*) to detect any changes in attitude resulting from second thoughts. Remember St Augustine's caveat: 'It often happens that a man, when asked a question, gives a negative answer, but by further questioning can be brought to answer in the affirmative.' In any case, we have one or two surprises in store for you!

I

I disapprove of flogging, although it is the regular custom and meets with the acquiescence of Chrysippus, because in the first place it is a disgraceful form of punishment and fit only for slaves, and is in any case an insult, as you will realise if you imagine its infliction at a later age. Secondly, if a boy is so insensible to instruction that reproof is useless, he will, like the worst type of slave, merely become hardened to blows. Finally there will be absolutely no need of such punishment if the master is a thorough disciplinarian. As it is, we try to make amends for the negligence of the boy's *paedagogus,* not by forcing him to do what is right, but by punishing him for not doing what is right. And though you may compel a child with blows, what are you to do with him when he is a young man no longer amenable to such threats and confronted with tasks of far greater difficulty? Moreover when children are beaten, pain or fear frequently have results of which it is not pleasant to speak and which are likely subsequently to be a source of shame, a shame which unnerves and depresses the mind and leads the child to shun and loathe the light. Further if inadequate care is taken in the choices of respectable governors and instructors, I blush to mention the shameful abuse which scoundrels sometimes make of their right to administer corporal punishment or the opportunity not infrequently offered to others by the fear thus caused in the victims. I will not linger on this subject; it is more than enough if I have made my meaning clear. I will content myself with saying that children are helpless and easily victimised, and that therefore no one should be given un-limited power over them.

QUINTILIAN, *Institutes of Oratory,* translated in R. ULICH, *Three Thousand Years of Educational Wisdom,* Harvard University Press

VERDICT: Children are helpless and easily victimized.

STRONGLY AGREE | AGREE | NOT SURE | DISAGREE | STRONGLY DISAGREE

For discussion
How far can the teacher's readiness to use punishment in one form or another be explained by the fact that 'children are helpless and easily victimized'?

2

My Teachers and I use a simple maxim, warn once, and then punish. And always give a reason for the punishment, because Discipline must be seen to be intelligent. I try to impress on my young Teachers never to punish a boy in half hearted fashion. This is not brutality, it is common sense. Better three good strokes with the strap and no more nonsense than a continual succession of weak punishment. Any Teacher who shows in the first week that he expects quietness and discipline and shows that he is prepared to use the strap to get it, can put the strap away for the rest of the session. There is some quality in a Teacher that we sum up as personality, some inner core of hardness and integrity which the pupils recognise and react to with quiet respect. If a Teacher hasn't even the beginning of this, he will never be much use. If Mr John Smith is the best Teacher in the world but no one in his class listens to him, then Mr John Smith would be of more use as a labourer. It is as simple as that.

> NORMAN TOSH, *Being a Headmaster*, p. 56,
> Maclellan, 1963

STRONGLY AGREE | AGREE | NOT SURE | DISAGREE | STRONGLY DISAGREE

For discussion
Is it really as simple as that? If there is 'some inner core of hardness and integrity which the pupils recognise and react to with quiet respect' why should the teacher 'show he is prepared to use the strap'? If he lacks this 'inner core' we are told that 'he will never be much use', which is fair enough – but isn't this precisely the kind of teacher who is most liable to become 'strap happy'?

3

Owen's son, Robert Dale Owen, tells of an incident that appears to have taken place in 1824. He and his father had visited Bell's central school:

A class was standing up for arithmetic. 'Seven times eight are fifty-six,' said one boy. 'IS, not Are,' sternly cried the teacher, dealing the offender such a buffet on the ear that he staggered and finally dropped to the ground; then adding, 'Get up! Now perhaps you'll remember that another time.' But whether it was the blow or the bit of doubtful grammar he was bidden to remember seemed not very clear.

'I still recollect how my nature revolted against this outrage – for such it appeared to me. 'Father,' I said, as we left the room, 'I'm very sorry you gave any money to this school.' He smiled, and apologized for the teacher, saying, 'The man had probably been treated in the same manner when he was a child, and so knew no better.'

VERDICT: The incident reflects gross professional misconduct on the part of the teacher concerned.

STRONGLY AGREE | AGREE | NOT SURE | DISAGREE | STRONGLY DISAGREE

Question for discussion

Does corporal punishment tend to perpetuate itself for the reason given by Robert Owen in condoning the teacher's brutal treatment of the boy in this monitorial school?

4

I had *one* just flogging. When I was about thirteen, I went to a shoemaker and begged him to take me as his apprentice. He, being an honest man, immediately brought me to Bowyer, who got into a great rage, knocked me down, and even pushed Crispin rudely out of the room. Bowyer asked me why I had made myself such a fool? to which I answered, that I had a great desire to be a shoemaker, and that I hated the thought of being a clergyman.

'Why so?' said he. 'Because, to tell you the truth, sir,' said I, 'I am an infidel!' For this, without more ado, Bowyer flogged me – wisely, as I think; soundly, as I know. Any whining or sermonizing would have gratified my vanity, and confirmed me in my absurdity; as it was, I was laughed at, and got heartily ashamed at my folly.

S. T. COLERIDGE, *Table Talk*

Poor J.B.! – may all his faults be forgiven; and may he be wafted to bliss by little cherub boys, all head and wings, with no bottoms to reproach his sublunary infirmities.

S. T. COLERIDGE

VERDICT: Coleridge was knocked down by Bowyer in a fit of rage just like the boy in the incident described in the previous extract, yet from what he says, it seems that he did not think the teacher guilty of gross professional misconduct.

STRONGLY AGREE | AGREE | NOT SURE | DISAGREE | STRONGLY DISAGREE

5

'Girl number twenty,' said Mr Gradgrind, squarely pointing with his square forefinger. 'I don't know that girl. Who is that girl?' 'Sissy Jupe, sir,' explained number twenty, blushing, standing up, and curtsying. 'Sissy is not a name,' said Mr Gradgrind. 'Don't call yourself Sissy. Call yourself Cecilia.' 'It's father as calls me Sissy, sir,' returned the young girl with a trembling voice, as with another curtsy. 'Then he has no business to do it,' said Mr Gradgrind. 'Tell him he musn't. Cecilia Jupe. Let me see. What is your father?' 'He belongs to the horse riding, if you please sir.' Mr Gradgrind frowned, and waved off the objectionable calling with his hand. 'We don't want to know anything about that here. You mustn't tell us about that here. Your father breaks horses, don't he?' 'If you please, sir, when they can get any to break, they do break horses in the ring, sir.' 'You mustn't tell us about the ring here. Very well, then. Describe your father as a horse-breaker. He doctors sick horses, I dare say?' 'Oh yes, sir!' 'Very well, then. He is a veterinary surgeon, a farrier, and horse-breaker. Give me your definition of a horse.' (Sissy Jupe thrown into the greatest alarm by this demand.) 'Girl number twenty unable to define a horse,' said Mr Gradgrind, for the general benefit of all the little pitchers. 'Girl number twenty possessed of no fact of reference to one of the commonest animals! Some boy's definition of a horse. Bitzer, yours.'

Bitzer: 'Quadruped. Graminivorous. Forty teeth, namely, twenty-four grinders, four eye-teeth, and twelve incisive. Sheds coat in spring; in marshy countries, sheds hoofs too. Hoofs hard, but requiring to be shod with iron. Age known by marks in mouth.'

CHARLES DICKENS, *Hard Times*

VERDICT: This exemplifies the truth of Quintilian's saying that 'children are helpless and easily victimized'.

STRONGLY AGREE | AGREE | NOT SURE | DISAGREE | STRONGLY DISAGREE

Question for discussion
According to Bernstein, because of the low-level language used in the home, the child of unskilled and semi-skilled parentage often finds himself in a persecutory situation in the classroom. To what extent is the story of Sissy Jupe still repeating itself in our schools? Are pupils punished for offences which are, in effect, created by the difference between the school's rules and values and those of the sub-culture?

6

The fact that we do need reminding of the nature of the thing that we are dealing with may perhaps be illustrated by the following story. A good many years ago I visited a school many hundred miles from here and picked up the composition book of a 9-year-old boy. In it I read a composition entitled 'My real father'. The

H

subject set to the class had been 'My father', and the author of this particular composition had asked whether he might be allowed to write on his *real* father. I mention this circumstance because it shows that the teacher did receive a warning that the subject had some special significance for the child. The composition was as follows:

'My father is on the broad side and tall side. My father was a hard working man and he had a lot of money. He was not fat or thin. . . . His age was about 30 years when he died, he had a good reputation, he is a married man. When he was in hospital I went to see him every Sunday afternoon. I asked him how he was going on, he told me he was getting a lot better. My father was very kind to me and gave me and my cousins cigarette cards. He likes doing woodwork, my father, for me, and he likes a little game of cards now and then; or a game of darts. He chops the wood and saws the planks and he is a handsome man but he is dead. He worked at the rubber works before he died.'

The comment that the teacher had thought fit to write at the foot of this intensely moving and, in its way, beautiful piece of writing, was: 'Tenses. You keep mixing past and present.'

JOHN BLACKIE, *Good Enough for the Children?*
p. 16, Faber, 1963

VERDICT: Lack of understanding can be just as callous and as damaging as the resort to physical violence.

STRONGLY AGREE | AGREE | NOT SURE | DISAGREE | STRONGLY DISAGREE

Question for discussion
Would it be fair to call the teacher's comment a *punishment*? If not, why not?

7

True, there is difficulty in deciding what is and what is not punishment. One day, a boy borrowed my best saw. The next day I found it lying in the rain. I told him that I should not lend him that saw again. That was not punishment, for punishment always involves the idea of morality. Leaving the saw out in the rain was bad for the saw, but the act was not an immoral one. It is important for a child to learn that one cannot borrow someone else's tools and spoil them, or damage someone else's property or someone else's person. For to let a child have his own way, or do what he wants to *at another's expense*, is bad for the child. It creates a spoiled child, and the spoiled child is a bad citizen.

Some time ago, a little boy came to us from a school where he had terrorized everyone by throwing things about and even threatening murder. He tried the same game with me. I soon concluded that he was using his temper for the purpose of alarming people and thus getting attention. One day, on entering the playroom I found the children all clustered together at one end of the room. At the other end stood the little terror with a hammer in his hand. He was threatening to hit anyone who approached him. 'Cut it out, my boy,' I said sharply. 'We aren't afraid of you.' He dropped the hammer and rushed at me. He bit and kicked me. 'Every time you hit or bite me,' I said quietly, 'I'll hit you back.' And I did. Very soon he gave up the contest and rushed from the room. This was not punishment. It was a necessary lesson: learning that one cannot go about hurting others for one's own gratification.

Punishment in most homes is punishment for disobedience. In schools, too, disobedience and insolence are looked upon as bad crimes. When I was a young teacher and in the habit of spanking children, as most teachers in Britain were allowed to do, I was always most angry at the boy who disobeyed me. My little dignity was wounded. I was the tin god of the classroom, just as Daddy is the tin god of the home. To punish for disobedience is to identify oneself with the omnipotent Almighty: Thou shalt have no other gods.

Later on, when I taught in Germany and Austria, I was always ashamed when teachers asked me if corporal punishment was used in Britain. In Germany, a teacher who strikes a pupil is tried for assault, and generally punished. The flogging and strapping in British schools is one of our greatest disgraces.

A. S. NEILL, *Summerhill*, pp. 166–8, Gollancz, 1962

As regards the last sentence, what is your own opinion?

STRONGLY AGREE | AGREE | NOT SURE | DISAGREE | STRONGLY DISAGREE

Questions for discussion

1 We are not told the age of the boy who borrowed the saw. Supposing he was fifteen years old – old enough to 'know better', why was his act *not* an immoral one?

2 As regards the little boy with the hammer, it's a nice story – but supposing he had been a VERY BIG BOY (and supposing he had not dropped his weapon), what then?

3 No doubt many teachers would resent the suggestion that they think of themselves as 'the tin god of the classroom', but is it not a human failing to administer punishment when one is angry?

8

A Swabian schoolmaster, Häuberle by name, with characteristic Teutonic attention to details, has left it on record that, in the course of his fifty-one years and seven months as a teacher, he had, by a moderate computation, given

911,527 blows with a cane, 124,010 blows with a rod, 20,989 blows and raps with a ruler, 136,715 blows with the hand, 10,235 blows over the mouth, 7,905 boxes on the ear, 1,115,800 raps on the head, and 22,763 'nota benes' with the Bible, Catechism, singing-book and grammar. He had 777 times made boys kneel on peas, 613 times on a triangular piece of wood, had made 3,001 wear the jackass, and 1,707 hold the rod up, not to mention various more unusual punishments he had contrived on the spur of the occasion. Of the blows with the cane, 800,000 were for Latin words; of the rod 760,000 were for texts from the Bible or verses from the singing book. He also had about 3,000 expressions to scold with, two-thirds of which were native to the German tongue and the remainder his invention.

> E. P. CUBBERLEY, *History of Education*, quoted in
> J. S. ROSS, *Groundwork of Educational Theory*,
> p. 159, Harrap, 1952

VERDICT: Even allowing for the *autre temps autre mœurs* argument, the verdict must be that Häuberle's approach to teaching was in some way psychopathic.

STRONGLY AGREE | AGREE | NOT SURE | DISAGREE | STRONGLY DISAGREE

Question for discussion

Is it possible to see a connexion between this grisly record of a German school-master and the horrors of the Nazi concentration camps?

And here is a 'nota bene' which the modern teacher does well to heed.

9

I must tell you a rather horrifying cautionary story of an incident which happened in the early career of a classical master I know very well. He was a young man, keen on his work and at that time taking the fifth form in a grammar school and most eager to get them good results in the G.C.E. – for their sakes and his own. One afternoon he found his teaching being hopelessly interfered with by a violent din in the room next door. Obviously a master had left his boys, who were getting more and more out of hand. So he left his class, opened the door on the adjoining riot and rampage, and saw in a moment where the trouble lay – in one loutish ring-leader, whom he knew and everyone knew as a thoroughly bad hat. He was in rather a fury and was about to go up to this youngster and give him a good bang on the head, which was his first thought. But his training and his own principles made him hesitate – he was not a man, this classical master, who believed in taking it out of boys physically, and he stopped short. He glared, gave the boy an hour's detention, restored order and withdrew to his classroom.

He did well to hesitate. An hour later that loutish boy lay dead in the school gym. Unknown to anyone he had got into some fracas on the way to school and taken a violent fall which had severely damaged his neck. He had not realized his own injury; a few exercises in the gym completed the fracture and he died on the spot. You will say that this is a case in a million. It is, in fact, a case in many millions; boys are made of tough timber. But my friend, as you can imagine, remembers with intense gratitude that hesitation, that instinct for keeping to the regular customs of the school about punishment. If he had let himself go, that boy's life would have seemed to lie at his feet, and, whatever medical examination might later have shown, there would have remained a doubt which would have pursued my friend through life.

WALTER JAMES, *The Teacher and His World*, pp. 102–3, Gollancz, 1962

VERDICT: The rule is that punishment should never be administered impulsively.

STRONGLY AGREE | AGREE | NOT SURE | DISAGREE | STRONGLY DISAGREE

Question for discussion

1 As rules go, this sounds fine. It is applied in Jesuit schools, where offenders receive a ticket and are subsequently dealt with by the Master of Discipline (see James Joyce's 'Portrait of the Artist as a Young Man' for an account of how it works). Nevertheless, the majority of offences need to be dealt with on the spot; and for this purpose, say the anti-abolitionists, corporal punishment has the advantage of being short, sharp, and effective. Better to get it over quickly than to leave the pupil in suspense.
Examine the pros and cons of the argument.
2 In this instance, the master gave the boy an hour's detention. There are many schools in which a detention system is virtually unworkable, however. What are the alternatives? And what is to happen when the teacher meets with open defiance – 'Make me!'?

10

A moral value has been attached to flogging. 'This has been called "licking the boys into shape",' wrote a distinguished Headmaster. 'Not unnaturally one result of this schooling has been to perpetuate in adult life the conviction, not merely that compulsion is necessary for police purposes, but that human beings can be improved by being made afraid.' The police methods of the Fascist state he characterized as 'simply another outbreak of the Public School Philosophy'. What is the lesson that this teaches? '– College taught me no learning, brought me no fame, but it taught me to smile while I was being thrashed,' comes the answer from a typical Public School product.

Is there nothing to be said in favour of this discipline? It is said that it 'develops' character. This is a myth – you cannot be said to 'develop' a jelly when you put it in a tin. The net result of this militaristic rule is a mere deadening of the individual spirit. Add to this the unnatural segregation of a single-sex boarding school, and the psychological damage wreaked as a result over the years on the English Upper classes has been incalculable. It is indeed a curious comment on the blessings of the family life that the well-to-do prefer to send their children away for nine months in the year from the ages of eight to eighteen. During this time their only possible sexual outlet is pretty small boys instead of the girls on whom they would naturally fix their romantic feelings. 'If the Public School training is effective,' writes Wellard, 'the Public School man can never achieve humanity – either with strangers or friends, or father, mother, or wife. He is condemned to forty years of gelidity, and for the rest to a model senescence, pitifully interspersed with ill-timed attempts at lechery.'

This might be funny if it were not so pathetic. And so serious. For this emotional freeze-up has long been the recognized and crippling characteristic of the Englishman. Connolly calls it the 'Theory of Permanent Adolescence'. Public School boys, declares another critic, 'conspicuously suffer from arrested development, conspicuously fail, disastrously, however charmingly, to grow up'. They pass from first to second childhood without ever touching maturity – except in body.

With these fifty-year-old teenagers at the helm, no wonder we are lagging behind other countries in many vital fields – behind Germany in economic performance, Scandinavia in social planning, America in technology and innovation.

A. CHEETHAM and E. PARFIT (eds), *Eton Microcosm*,
p. 189, Sidgwick and Jackson, 1965

VERDICT: Any policy of 'licking the boys into shape' is misguided.

STRONGLY AGREE | AGREE | NOT SURE | DISAGREE | STRONGLY DISAGREE

Question for discussion
1 Need a policy of 'licking the boys into shape' result in 'permanent adolescence'?
2 Is the 'emotional freeze-up' – tight upper lip. Britain can take it, etc. – which is said to be a national characteristic *caused* by the system of punishment adopted in schools, or is that system itself a product of the society in which we live?

II

A lot of nonsense has been written about Spartan discipline. A Spartan has been identified as one who never flinches from personal and physical pain. We have been taught that the Spartan boys endured agonies to inculcate self-discipline, and most children know the story of the Spartan boy who hid a stolen cub in his tunic, where it bit its way into his entrails. The boy faced his accusers, lied about having stolen the cub, and then died, showing no sign of the pain he experienced. (We wonder?)

Spartan discipline was imposed from without, prompted by the fear of, firstly, being dubbed a coward, and secondly, of being sent to live with the women. The second punishment is indicative of the times. Women were the weaklings of the civilisation. There are many who think so still. There is no conclusive evidence upon this point. We know that they do not surpass the men in foolishness now that they possess the vote, but in point of fact, the woman's life is a life of pain cheerfully borne for the sake of the next generation. If ever there were Spartans in our civilisations, then they are to be found among the women.

Spartan training sets up a wrong set of values. It is a relic of the barbarous beginnings of civilisation.

It controls by repression. The new discipline controls by the removal of repression by trusting the child, as Arnold trusted in his pupils.

There is a story which we believe will interest our readers. It concerns Peter the Great.

Peter the Great was witnessing the flogging of two men, one a Russian and the other a German. When the strokes fell on the back of the Russian he took his punishment without a murmur. When the German was being flogged he screamed and writhed until the whole count was done. A friend of the Emperor's standing by, turned to Peter: 'You see, sire,' he said, 'with what fortitude our splendid Russian took his flogging. The German is a coward.' 'Nonsense,' replied Peter. 'The German is the better man. His whole being cried out against the brutality of the sentence. It is the cry of humanity. While the Russians will suffer indignities as this Russian did, my nation is dead.' The historian among our readers may smile at this picture of Peter. We give it as a story that is told. Its wealth of meaning is apparent. Yet the Russian was the 'Spartan'.

A. B. ALLEN, The Psychology of Punishment,
pp. 103–4, Allman, 1936

VERDICT: Spartan discipline is a relic of barbarism.

STRONGLY AGREE | AGREE | NOT SURE | DISAGREE | STRONGLY DISAGREE

Question for discussion

Those who advocate the retention of corporal punishment are flogging a dead horse! All the evidence is against them. The practice has died out practically everywhere, and survives only as a barbarous relic. Yet among the ranks of practising teachers there is a strong body of opinion which declines to accept such conclusions. Why?

12

Study the map on the facing page. Each square denotes a Local Education Authority which had 6 or more clauses restricting the use of corporal punishment in its schools at the time of the National Educational Research Foundation's survey (1950–1). Each circle denotes an L.E.A. which imposed no restrictions on the teachers in its employment. You can ignore the triangles.

What do you deduce from this map as regards the 'ecology' of punishment in schools in England and Wales?

When you have done so, but not before, read the conclusions drawn in 'A Survey of Rewards and Punishments' overleaf.

The concentration of instances of high Index of Restriction in regions of dense population and industrialisation is shown visually in the accompanying map (facing page).

II CORPORAL PUNISHMENT REGULATIONS AND URBANISATION. POSSIBLE CONNECTIONS

It may be taken as proved that over England and Wales as a whole there is a definite relation between a high Index of Restriction and a high degree of urbanisation.

Some qualifications are necessary in the interpretation of this relation.

It must be noted clearly that the connection analysed above is not between corporal punishment as such or frequency of punishment and degree of urbanisation. Corporal punishment, as we have seen, has been a characteristic feature in all traditional schools. It was not only expected; in some cases it was prescribed. Head teachers who have had experience in both urban and rural conditions during the period of evacuation after 1939, with whom this point has been discussed, state that in their experience, there is not much difference between urban and rural schools at the present time. In any given case, much depends on the personality and skill of individual teachers, and upon the beliefs and influence of individual head teachers.

The real connection lies between conditions of urbanisation and the incidence of severe corporal punishment. A study of the regulations in detail has already shown that the object of the regulations has been, in the main, not the prohibition of corporal punishment as such, but its control within reasonable limits.

If this position is accepted, and it appears to be borne out of the evidence so far, then the most likely link between local teaching conditions and the infliction of excessive or severe corporal punishment must be sought in the degree of strain, mental and physical, which some urban conditions impose on some teachers.

In so far as this is a correct interpretation it appears to follow that the complete prohibition of corporal punishment would increase the strain. It would tend to

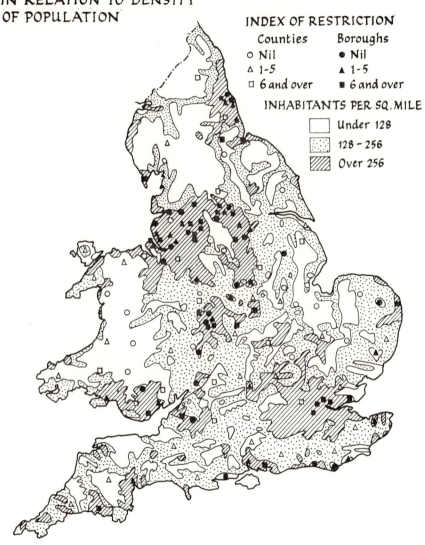

DISTRIBUTION OF INDEX OF RESTRICTION
IN RELATION TO DENSITY
OF POPULATION

INDEX OF RESTRICTION

Counties	Boroughs
o Nil	● Nil
△ 1-5	▲ 1-5
□ 6 and over	■ 6 and over

INHABITANTS PER SQ. MILE

Under 128
128 - 256
Over 256

From *A Survey of Rewards and Punishments in Schools*, A Report by the National
Foundation for Educational Research in England and Wales, Newnes, 1952

intensify feelings of insecurity and thereby increase anxiety in many teachers, particularly if the prohibition were by legal enactment. Moreover the arbitrary prohibition by decree of a central authority would ignore local conditions and impose a heavier strain on teachers in the less favourable conditions.

> From *A Survey of Rewards and Punishments in Schools.* A Report by the National Foundation for Educational Research in England and Wales based on researches carried out by M. E. Highfield and A. Pinsent.

13

A Survey of Rewards and Punishments in Schools gave the following reasons for thinking that the total abolition of corporal punishment was unwise.

TEACHERS' PERSONAL PROBLEMS

A further source of difficulty relevant to our topic is to be sought in the teachers themselves. The evidence touches upon this source only incidentally. Nevertheless in any consideration of the problem of corporal punishment the problem of professional teaching competence and of personality deficiencies in some teachers must be noted.

In this connection, the total prohibition of all corporal punishment might very well lead to deterioration rather than improvement in the mental health of both pupils and teachers. The psychiatrist quoted in a preceding section said that his greatest concern was the teacher who thwarts initiative, spontaneity and other evidences of healthy growth to the extent that pathological submission is the only acceptable behaviour reaction. He felt that the teacher who depends on ridicule, isolation and other ego-deflationary techniques to obtain submission is more dangerous to emotional development than the teacher who uses corporal punishment.

VERDICT: Until all teachers are professionally competent and free from personality deficiences there is no point in recommending the total prohibition of corporal punishment.

STRONGLY AGREE | AGREE | NOT SURE | DISAGREE | STRONGLY DISAGREE

For discussion

The inference must be that pupils are often punished for offences which are artificially created by school conditions – large classes, strain of teaching conditions, etc. Is this just another example of the don't-blame-the-criminal – blame-society argument so popular nowadays?

14 What teachers think about punishment

As part of the Plowden Committee's investigations, 2,239 teachers answered a questionnaire, section 21 of which asked:

Do you think the use of corporal punishment in primary schools should be

(a) a regular means of discipline?   1 ☐
(b) a last resort only?   2 ☐
(c) forbidden?   3 ☐
(d) Undecided?   4 ☐

How would you answer this question?

15 Appendix 1 'Children and Their Primary Schools', Table D 21

Should corporal punishment be used in primary schools?

Teachers in primary schools	Percentage of teachers			
	Regular means of discipline	Last resort only	Forbidden	Undecided
Infant	1·9	84·8	9·3	4·0
Infant/Junior	2·7	89·3	5·2	2·8
Junior	4·7	89·2	4·2	1·9
Men	5·1	90·2	3·1	1·5
Women	2·4	87·5	6·9	3·2
Head teachers	1·9	91·7	4·3	2·1
Assistant teachers	3·6	87·3	6·2	2·9
Teachers aged:				
20–29	3·7	84·6	6·4	5·3
30–49	2·9	88·6	5·8	2·7
50 and over	3·2	89·7	5·4	1·7
All teachers in primary schools	3·2	88·3	5·8	2·7

A statement from the Association of Head Teachers, commenting on the Plowden Committee's recommendation that corporal punishment should be forbidden, said: 'We believe that the recommendation has gone against the weight of the evidence.' Do you agree? What reasons may have prompted the Committee's decision?

16

The teacher should have knowledge of MacDougall's theory of 'the levels of moral control' ('Social Psychology'). These levels are four in number:

The prudential
The authoritative
The social
The personal

Translated into action the first postulates a control by fear, the second a control by the agency of rewards and punishments, the third control is effected by the bestowal of praise and blame, the fourth is inspired by a form of internal discipline.

These four levels of moral control suggest the four classes into which punishment may fall:

There is punishment that is imposed to protect society. This is the protective form and is the basis of our prison system to-day.

There is punishment inflicted to deter others from a repetition of the 'crime'. This is the preventative form, and is often used as the guiding principle in the Institutes for Young Delinquents.

There is the form of punishment inflicted in order to bring about a change in the nature of the 'criminal'. This is the reformatory form.

Finally, there is the retributive form, revenge taken by society against those who perpetrate anti-social acts.

It is one thing to place these groups into convenient and water-tight compartments. It is another thing to decide which of the groups to apply, and when the time is ripe for the application.

A. B. ALLEN, *The Psychology of Punishment*, pp. 65–7,
Allman, 1936

VERDICT: Retributive punishment represents the lowest level of moral control, as reformatory punishment represents the highest.

STRONGLY AGREE | AGREE | NOT SURE | DISAGREE | STRONGLY DISAGREE

17 The meaning of 'punishment'

In a school situation a proclivity to punish people is often confused with discipline; but this is to confuse one way of preserving discipline with discipline itself. 'Discipline', etymologically speaking, is rooted in a learning situation; it conveys the notion of submission to rules or some kind of order. The rules may be those of what is learnt, e.g. the rules of grammar or of morals; they may be those of the method of learning, e.g. rules of practice and training; or they may be more general rules necessary for something to be learnt, e.g. rules relating to silence, posture, and diet. Such rules may be externally imposed by someone in authority or imposed by the learner on himself. Whenever we think about rules or a system of order from the point of view of their impress on a mind or minds it is appropriate to talk of 'discipline'. 'Discipline' is thus a very general notion which is connected with conforming to rules.

'Punishment' on the other hand is a much more specific notion which is usually only appropriate when there has been a breach of rules. It involves the intentional infliction of pain or of something unpleasant on someone who has committed such a breach of rules. The pain always must be inflicted by someone who is in authority, who has a right to act in this way. Otherwise, it would be impossible to distinguish 'punishment' from 'revenge'. People in authority can, of course, inflict pain on people at whim. But this would be called 'spite' unless it were inflicted as a consequence of a breach of rules on the part of the sufferer. Similarly a person in authority might give a person £5 as a consequence of his breaking a rule. But unless this were regarded as painful or at least unpleasant for the recipient it could not be counted as a case of 'punishment'. In other words at least the three criteria of (*i*) intentional infliction of pain (*ii*) by someone in authority (*iii*) on a person as a consequence of a breach of rules on his part, must be satisfied if we are to call something a case of 'punishment'. There are, as is usual in such cases, examples that can be produced which do not satisfy all criteria. For instance there is a colloquialism which is used about boxers taking a lot of punishment from their opponents, in which only the first condition is present. But this is a metaphorical use which is peripheral to the central uses of the term.

In so far as the different 'theories' of punishment are answers to questions about the meaning of 'punishment', only the retributive theory is a possible one. There is no conceptual connection between 'punishment' and notions like those of 'deterrence', 'prevention' and 'reform'. For people can be punished without being prevented from repeating the offence, and without being made any better. It is also a further question whether they themselves or anyone else is deterred from committing the offence by punishment. But 'punishment' *must* involve 'retribution'; for 'retribution' implies doing something to someone in return for what he has done. It may involve something pleasant as in the case of gratitude or reward; or it may involve something unpleasant as in the case of punishment. Punishment in other words is one type of retributive transaction. Punishment, therefore, must be retributive – by definition.

R. S. PETERS, Ethics and Education, pp. 267–8,
Allen & Unwin, 1966

VERDICT: *All* punishment involves retribution.

STRONGLY AGREE | AGREE | NOT SURE | DISAGREE | STRONGLY DISAGREE

Questions for discussion

1 If you agreed with the previous statement (and it seems likely that many of you did) and *if* the argument advanced here is correct, the inference is that you have fallen into a logical trap. Can you argue yourself out of it?

2 According to Peters, *all* punishment is retributive. In this connexion you may like to consider the following anecdote.

Some years ago a questionnaire on school punishment was sent to head-masters of English Grammar and Public schools. When the return from the great Sanderson of Oundle was examined it was found that he had simply scribbled the words, 'Never punish except in anger', on the form. Disconcerted by this, the organizers of the survey sent Sanderson a letter saying, in effect, that the dictum must have been an inadvertent slip of the pen. Back came the uncompromising reply, 'OF COURSE I MEANT NEVER PUNISH EXCEPT IN ANGER'!

What do you think Sanderson meant?

18

Once we have arranged the particular type of consequence called a reinforcement, our techniques permit us to shape the behaviour of an organism almost at will. It has become a routine exercise to demonstrate this in classes in elementary psychology by conditioning such an organism as a pigeon. Simply by presenting food to a hungry pigeon at the right time, it is possible to shape up three or four well-defined responses in a single demonstration period – such responses as turning around, pacing the floor in the pattern of a figure-8, standing still in a corner of the demonstration apparatus, stretching the neck, or stamping the foot. Extremely complex performances may be reached through successive stages in the shaping process, the contingencies of reinforcement being changed progressively in the direction of the required behaviour. The results are often quite dramatic. In such a demonstration one can *see* learning take place. A significant change of behaviour is often obvious as the result of a single reinforcement.

From this exciting prospect of an advancing science of learning, it is a great shock to turn to that branch of technology which is most directly concerned with the learning process – education. Let us consider, for example, the teaching of arithmetic in the lower grades. The school is concerned with imparting to the child a large number of responses of a special sort. The responses are all verbal. They consist of speaking and writing certain words, figures, and signs which, to put it roughly, refer to numbers and to arithmetic operations. The first task is to shape up these responses – to get the child to pronounce and write responses correctly, but the principal task is to bring this behaviour under many sorts of stimulus control. This is what happens when the child learns to count, to recite tables, to count while ticking off the items in an assemblage of objects, to respond to spoken or written numbers by saying 'odd', 'even', 'prime', and so on. . . .

Now, how is this extremely complicated verbal repertoire set up? In the first place, what reinforcements are used? Fifty years ago the answer would have been clear. At that time educational control was still frankly aversive. The child read numbers, copied numbers, memorized tables, and performed operations upon numbers to escape the threat of the birch rod or cane. Some positive reinforcements were perhaps eventually derived from the increased efficiency of the child in the field of arithmetic, and in rare cases some automatic reinforcement may have resulted from the sheer manipulation of the medium – from the solution of problems or the discovery of the intricacies of the number system. But for the immediate purposes of education the child acted to avoid or escape punishment. It was part of the reform movement known as progressive education to make the positive consequences more immediately effective, but anyone who visits the lower grades of the average school today will observe that a change has been made, not from aversive to positive control, but from one form of aversive stimulation to another. The child at his desk, filling in his work-book, is behaving primarily to escape from the threat of a series of minor aversive events – the teacher's displeasure, the criticism or ridicule of his classmates, an ignominious showing in a competition, low marks, a trip to the office 'to be talked to' by the principal, or a word to the parent who may still resort to the birch rod. In this welter of aversive consequences, getting the right answer is in itself an insignificant event, any effect of which is lost amid the anxieties, the boredom, and the aggressions which are the inevitable by-products of aversive control.

B. F. SKINNER, 'The Science of Learning and the Art of Teaching', *Harvard Educational Review*, 24:2 (Spring 1954), pp. 86–97. Copyright © 1954 by President and Fellows of Harvard College

VERDICT: Methods of teaching which rely on punishment are essentially negative and need to be replaced by a more positive approach.

STRONGLY AGREE | AGREE | NOT SURE | DISAGREE | STRONGLY DISAGREE

Question for discussion

1 The gist of Skinner's argument is that nothing succeeds like success. His psychology of operant conditioning provides one of the bases for programmed learning, in which the pupil is constantly reinforced (i.e. derives immediate satisfaction from being told that most of his responses are correct). In this way, the fear of failure which attends trial-and-error learning, is largely avoided.

In short, methods of teaching which rely on punishment are negative and have been proved to be inefficient. A more positive approach is needed.

How does the group respond to this final talking point?

Now that you have worked through the sequence you may like to check your responses with the Editor's! His own naturally reflects his personal viewpoint, which you are not bound to accept, and is offered solely for the purpose of comparison.

EXTRACT NO	1	2	3	4	5	6	7	8	9	10	11	13	16	17	18
EDITOR'S RESPONSE	3	0	3	2	4	4	1	4	3	4	2	3	3	3	4

8

Discipline

Before launching upon any discussions about this topic we do well to follow Wittgenstein's advice and look at the various contexts in which the word 'discipline' is used. 'Spartan discipline', 'Military discipline', 'mental discipline', 'the discipline of mathematics', 'the discipline of being a disciple', 'discipline in the classroom' – each of these in some sense implies submission to rules and conforming to order. In each case, however, the implications are liable to lead to opposite conclusions. Military discipline, for instance, may mean 'theirs not to reason why' – the unquestioning heroism of the Charge of the Light Brigade – or it may mean 'the Nelson touch' which is tantamount to refusing to obey orders when it comes to the crunch of battle.

These contradictory interpretations arise from the tension between Freedom and Authority – two concepts which demand the closest scrutiny. Is it to be 'freedom from' – i.e. release from restrictions which are felt to be irksome – or 'freedom for' – i.e. the initial acceptance of restrictions, however irksome, in order to serve a higher cause later on? Does it simply mean doing as one pleases provided one does not interfere with others – or are we to take in it the biblical sense of 'knowledge of necessity', the freedom which comes of 'perfect service'? And what *is* necessity? Does authority stem from some absolute source, or are its rules and sanctions man-made, explainable in terms of social convention?

Easy enough to say that discipline begins by being externally imposed and ends by being internalized as voluntary self-control. Not so easy to decide how the formal process of education can best be geared to the stages of the child's development. Discipline, we have been told, is always rooted in a learning situation. That situation, needless to say, varies from activity to activity. The techniques involved in learning to play the piano, for example – or to drive a car – demand a rigorous willy-nilly observance of the 'rules' if any sort of progress is to be made. Whether he likes it or not, the pupil must submit to the master's 'authority' if he is eventually to be 'free' to interpret Beethoven's Emperor Concerto. In other activities – child-art offers as good an example as any – the

I

nature of the technique may provide greater latitude for self-expression at an early stage.

For the great majority of students and teachers, however, the question of discipline centres on the purely practical problem of handling thirty, forty (or fifty) children in the classroom. Let us begin at that point and see where it leads.

I

School teaching, however scholarly, keen, or enlightened, profits little in the absence of discipline. Now discipline has a mystique of its own which I have never fathomed. For over thirty years I interviewed applicants for staff vacancies, and at the end I was no more capable of judging from mere appearances and demeanour whether an applicant was likely to be able to keep order than when I started. A six-foot Oxford 'blue' would appear, seeming to have all the manly virtues and social graces, and the next day he would be found impotent in the classroom with a company of small boys dancing ring-a-ring-a-roses triumphantly round him. This actually occurred.

On the other hand, when the Second War started and male staff became nearly unobtainable, a slip of a young lady arrived, extremely quiet and almost timid in our interview, who had never taught before but said she would like to. I pointed out that discipline might be a problem, and mentioned that a forbidding middle-aged and highly experienced lady teacher had fled the day before in horror from the scene. The young lady said nevertheless that she would like to try: 'At any rate I have a degree in English,' she added shyly. Much good may that do you, I mused. So into the classroom she walked that afternoon; and for three years she took classes up and down the school, including some of the toughest, with complete and absolute success. Order was exemplary; it never seemed to occur to a boy to give any trouble or to do anything other than the young lady requested. I sometimes wondered what was her secret, and after she had eventually left I ventured to ask a small boy how it was done. 'She was very nice,' said the boy, and left it at that. And at that I will leave it too.

GUY BOAS, *A Teacher's Story*, pp. 123–4, Macmillan, 1963

For discussion

At the end of a long and distinguished career as a headmaster, the writer admits that the secret of maintaining good teacher–pupil relations escapes him. ' "She was very nice," said the boy, and left it at that.'

A nice point. Can you enlarge on it?

2

Many teachers have fears and misgivings about discipline, and sometimes these fears are justified and the teacher finds his control, and with it his confidence, slipping away. He tries one thing after another to restore order, but the more he tries the worse things become. When he appeals for help to someone more experienced or more successful the advice seems so reasonable and easy that he is all the more disappointed when he finds that he still fails. Then he is told that discipline is a matter of personality – which is not very helpful. There are many reasons for lack of discipline, not all of them due to the failure of the teacher concerned, but the situation is serious because it is a tragic waste of human energy to try to teach in face of disorder. It may be that a train of events has been started which cannot be halted, and that the only thing for the teacher to do is to move to a totally different situation where he can start again, possibly to teach a different age range or in a different kind of neighbourhood. But this seems too much like admitting defeat and most people would rather stick it out. But 'sticking it out' is likely to be very unsatisfactory unless some cause for the unfavourable situation can be found.

J. E. SADLER and A. N. GILLETT, *Training for Teaching*, p. 258, Allen & Unwin, 1962

For discussion

1 Confidence is not enough, evidently. Consider the circumstances in which indiscipline occurs through no fault of the teacher. (They are by no means confined to 'tough' schools in slum areas.) Do its causes lie (*a*) in a clash between different social–cultural levels, (*b*) in the curriculum and methods used in the school, (*c*) in the internal organization of the school?

2 It is arguable that a fully competent professional worker should be able to cope with any situation. Could more be done to train teachers as social workers?

3 The gist of the extract seems to be that there is nothing much to be done to help the beginner in the matter of 'keeping discipline'. Apparently, proficiency comes through personal, practical experience and has to be acquired through trial and error. Is this a satisfactory state of affairs?

3

Before World War II it was far easier to impose a barrier on a class of children, but certain conditions which have even affected industrial discipline and public attitudes have made the imposition of arbitrary punishments far more explosive. It is easier to inflict a mechanistic system of reward and punishment on a group of young folk than to use one's personality and tolerance, but in the long run the older method runs into difficulties. Firstly since 1944, the extra year at school has had far greater effects on discipline than has been realised. These fourth year boys, aged 15, are adolescents brought up under the protection of the Welfare State. They are not the ragged little urchins who left school at 14 to become errand boys and underdogs. Just as people would put up with more subjection years ago, so did the children; today it isn't so; these 15-year-olds, in spite of appalling ignorance in some fields, are rather more mature, in the slick sense of the word, than before. Consequently they want to know Why? How? What for? Who does he think he is? and so on. You cannot beat them down all the time within our present social framework and expect things to run smoothly, because they won't. Thus the barrier needs to be reassessed in the general light of tolerance which reflects itself at adult level in such items as joint consultation, arbitration, colonial freedom and so on; the classroom is the prototype of a changing world and it is changing very fast.

If one goes too far the other way, towards the viewpoint that no boy is ever wrong, then the whole situation will be chaotic, but one assumes that the average teacher appreciates this fact. Some adults will, of course, disagree with this more liberal approach to children and teenagers. They may not agree that it is a superior way of handling situations when compared with the old. This completely misses the point. It is not a question of which way works better, because both systems have a different time scale. One cannot put the clock back; children are what they are today because of certain social changes and so one has to face the problem as it is and make due allowance for those changes, whether one is in sympathy with them or not. The elemental groundwork of any action should be – What is best, practicable and effective for the young people of the present generation, giving due consideration to present-day tendencies.

RICHARD FARLEY, *Secondary Modern Discipline*, pp. 98–9, Black, 1960

For discussion
Keeping them down won't do! Both inside and outside the school the climate of opinion has changed very considerably since the turn of the century – and the change is continuing.

How would you trace the *directions* this social change has taken since World War II?

4 What the Newsom children think

187 The views on school discipline expressed by the recent leavers provide an interesting comparison.

'We were made to have a maroon uniform which I really detest.'

'Quite often before entering the buildings in the morning we would have to stand in lines, while the head marched up and down checking our uniform. You could say we were like guards being inspected by the major.'

'The rules were quite strict about silly little things, for instance, the size of the check on our summer dresses.'

'Girls of fifteen even seventeen not being allowed to eat a sweet or even be seen in a sweetshop in school uniform.'

'Our uniforms left much to be desired. Ugly, big-knotted ties and a shocking colour of bright red for jumpers. And those hats. I really felt ashamed to walk down my street with it on.'

188 'There were so many rules that no one could ever remember them, but no actual discipline as such. No two teachers were alike. This left us in a state of perpetual unbalance.'

'I think that what went wrong with us, our teachers were so young they could not control us.'

'I never liked the young teachers we had. Some of them were not much older than us and it seemed a bit silly. I much prefer the older teachers who know how to teach.'

'It was not so much a case of ignorance as that they could not put the subject over properly, or they did not explain.'

'There was always a change of teachers in my form. That's the reason most of us were uninterested and glad to leave.'

'Teachers came and went like water.'

189 'Our headmaster thought the school was marvellous and wouldn't face up to the facts.' Fifteen year-old school-leaver.

'A boy who had just left school was asked by his former headmaster what he thought of the new buildings. "It could all be marble, sir," he replied, "but it would still be a bloody school." '

Half our Future The Newsom Report, p. 2

For discussion

1 The evidence suggests that the 'Newsom children', at any rate, are less amenable to authoritarian discipline, and more articulate in their criticisms of it, than formerly. Is this because the school has failed to keep abreast of the social changes we have just been discussing?

2 Can problems of discipline ever be divorced from problems of curriculum and method?

3 There is a great deal of talk nowadays about the 'generation gap' between adults and adolescents. According to one witness, some teachers actually create conflict because of their 'lack of perception'. Does a young teacher stand a better chance of establishing rapport with 'swinging' youth, or do you agree with the Newsom Committee in thinking that the answer is to be sought in smaller classes and more experienced teachers?

5 Indiscipline

When the children came for the first time to play in the house they thought it 'smashing'. They raced up and down the stairs in a wild frenzy of curiosity, happiness and astonishment; and when the house was closed in the evening most of the toys had disappeared. Two days later the rest had gone, because somebody had broken into the house by smashing windows in the basement. . . . That the children got the house is due to the fact that they were so incredibly misbehaved. The workers of the voluntary organisation had first met the children in the surface shelter of Branch Street in the autumn of 1941. From the beginning the control had been rather disappointing. The children had scorned the workers who had come into the shelter to bring them nice materials for work and play. They had torn everything out of their hands and had been 'the most rude, unruly and difficult group we have met so far among our 40 play centres . . .'

On that first evening in October I saw and heard them streaming in, howling, shouting and pushing. I spread out my material under a chaotic tumult. After a while every child had what it wanted and there was a normal atmosphere of enjoyment of the work. . . . But only too soon the bigger ones started to use the painting material as projectiles with which to shoot at the rest of us and a battle of quite considerable dimensions started, accompanied by hooliganism and diabolic shouting. They tore pieces of canvas from the bunks, and the kapok out of the cushions. They produced pieces of wood and card-board and these and most of the material which I had brought into the shelter flew through the air. They upset all the water jars. They climbed to the top of the bunks and shot at us all sorts of things. There was no stopping them.

> MARIE PANETH, *Branch Street, A Sociological Study*,
> quoted in *Children and Their Primary Schools*,
> Plowden Report, 1967

For discussion

1 How does one account for this sort of behaviour?
2 How would you have attempted to cope with this situation? Could *anyone* have coped single-handed?

6

It is regrettable that the word 'discipline' is often used as if it were a synonym for 'order', and it will help to clarify our thinking if we use it in a more limited sense. Discipline, we suggest, is a term that should be reserved to describe a state of mind; order, on the other hand, is merely a state of affairs. Order is of two kinds, somewhat similar in outward appearance but radically different in origin. It may be a state of affairs imposed on unwilling pupils by external authority, or it may be a state of affairs resulting naturally from the fact that pupils have willingly submitted themselves to certain good influences. This willing submission to outside influence is the very essence of discipline. When a teacher is able to keep a class in order, we usually call him a good disciplinarian, but the term 'disciplinarian' ought to mean much more than that. A disciplinarian is a person who can help pupils to submit themselves willingly to disciplinary influences; he is a person who has the art of making disciples. Bertrand Russell's description of the modern parent expresses admirably the qualities of a real disciplinarian: 'He wants his children to be as unconstrained in his presence as in his absence; he wants them to feel pleasure when they see him coming; he does not want a fictitious Sabbath calm while he is watching, succeeded by pandemonium as soon as he turns his back.'

It is clear that discipline is a state of mind, the acquirement of which needs the active co-operation of the pupil himself. True discipline is always in the last resort self-discipline. It is equally important, however, to remember that there can be no discipline without disciplinary influences. When we talk of 'free discipline' we do not mean that children are left free to do what they like. As a matter of fact, this is impossible, for if all external constraint could be removed, children would still be at the mercy of their own conflicting impulses. Free discipline, as far as the term has any meaning, implies that the children submit themselves freely or willingly; it therefore means nothing more than the term 'discipline' as we have defined it. Schools that work on 'free-discipline lines' are schools in which little importance is attached to order imposed by any authority other than the child himself. They are aiming, as all good schools aim, at promoting real discipline, but they differ from ordinary schools in that they leave children at all times as much as possible to their own devices. Many modern psychologists believe there is a danger that such methods may put too great a strain on young children. On the other hand, it is probable that those advocates of 'free discipline' who make a success of it exercise far more control over their pupils than they are aware of.

A. G. HUGHES and E. H. HUGHES, Learning and Teaching,
pp. 189–90, Longmans, 1946

For discussion

1 'Discipline is a state of mind, the acquirement of which needs the active co-operation of the pupil himself.' 'True discipline is always in the last resort self-discipline.' But the findings of developmental psychology indicate that the young child's concepts of rule-formation are quite alien to those of adults. Does this mean that in the early stages the teacher has no option but to impose exterior controls – in which case what becomes of 'true discipline'?

2 Can the school begin to operate on 'free discipline lines' too early?

3 How do these 'lines' differ from those followed in 'ordinary' schools?

7

Conceding the point that it is usually desirable that things should be done decently and in order, that order makes for efficiency and economy of effort, one may still maintain that very good order may be bad discipline. On the other hand, it is generally true that really good discipline will always tend to bring order in its train. What is the real relation between the two?

. . . The distinction was quite clear in the writings of Herbart. His terms were *Zucht*, meaning 'discipline' or 'training', and *Regierung*, meaning 'government' or 'order'. *Regierung* refers to the behaviour of the pupils in school and in class, but *Zucht* bears a wider and higher meaning; it is 'character-training' and it refers to the whole influence of the school in this direction. 'The aim of government lies in the present, whereas training has in view the future adult.' 'To maintain quiet and order in the lessons, to banish every trace of disrespect to the teacher, is the business of government: direct action on the temperament of youth with a view to culture is training.' For Herbart the educational aim was morality, but believing, as he did, that 'the will takes its root in the circle of thought', he regarded instruction as the chief means of reaching his objective. Now instruction could not proceed without government, therefore good government had to be aimed at in order that the pupil might profit by instruction. Government or order, then, was a means by which discipline was achieved. Order and discipline, in fact, are related to each other as means to end. Discipline, is much the wider notion, and it ought always to refer to the effect of the school on the pupil's character. It is concerned not merely with outward behaviour, but with the inner motives of conduct.

J. S. ROSS, *Groundwork of Educational Theory*,
pp. 157–8, Harrap, 1952

For discussion

1 The distinction drawn by Herbart between Discipline (in the sense of moral training and character formation) and Order (i.e. government for the sake of getting things done) suggests that the two are related as ends and means. Is the distinction clear to us? Is it a valid distinction?

2 'The old order changeth, giving place to new.' If he were brought back from the grave, how do you imagine Herbart would have reacted to the conditions now prevailing in a school conducted on 'free discipline lines'?

8

The proper aim of education is positive, to encourage free activity, not negative, to confine or to repress it. What becomes, then, of the concept of *discipline* which is so essential in the traditional ideas about school training? To gain a clear answer to this question, we must first distinguish between discipline and school *order*, and see that though they overlap and indeed interpenetrate, they are derived from quite different psychological roots. School order consists in the maintenance of the conditions necessary if school life is to fulfil its purpose; and . . . is most effective when based on imitation and the routine tendency. Discipline, on the other hand, is not an external thing, like order, but something that touches the inmost springs of conduct. It consists in the submission of one's impulses and powers to a regulation which imposes form upon their chaos, and brings efficiency and economy where there would otherwise be ineffectiveness and waste. Though parts of our nature may resist this control, its acceptance must, on the whole, be willing acceptance – the spontaneous movement of a nature in which there is an inborn impulse towards greater perfection or 'expressiveness' . . . We may properly speak of the movement of an athlete as disciplined; for they have gained their perfect form and efficiency – in a word, their expressiveness – largely through conscious effort. Similarly, we may speak of a person as disciplined by circumstances when he has deliberately used the lessons of hard experience to give shape to his impulses and powers. But though a person may discipline himself, as those do who rise to greatness in spite of hostile circumstance, yet discipline is, in general, the influence of a wider or better organized mind upon one narrower or less developed. In all cases there is, in a disciplinary process, a definite psychological sequence. First there must be something that one genuinely desires to do, and one must be conscious either of one's inability or of someone else's superior ability to do it. Next, the perception of inferiority must awaken the negative self-feeling with its impulse to fix attention upon the points in which one's performance falls short or the model's excels. Lastly, comes the repetition of effort, controlled now by a better concept of the proper procedure, and accompanied, if successful, by an outflow of positive self-feeling which tends to make the improved scheme permanent.

SIR PERCY NUNN, Education: Its Data and First
Principles, pp. 229–30, Arnold, 1930

For discussion
As teachers and parents, can we be certain that there is 'an inborn impulse to greater perfection' in all children? If so, why not leave well alone? Why the need for 'a wider and better organized mind upon one narrower and less developed'?

9 The two moralities of the child

For ourselves, we regard as of the utmost importance the experiments that have been made to introduce democratic methods into schools. As Foerster[1] has so ably said, it is unbelievable that at a time when democratic ideas enter into every

[1] F. W. Foerster, *L'Ecole et le Caractère*. French translation by Bovet.

sphere of life, they should have been so little utilized as instruments of education. If one thinks of the systematic resistance offered by pupils to the authoritarian method, and the admirable ingenuity employed by children the world over to evade disciplinarian constraint, one cannot help regarding as defective a system which allows so much effort to be wasted instead of using it in co-operation.

One should study, for example, the evolution of a born educator like Sanderson to see how this headmaster, who was at first a partisan of strict authority and even of corporal punishment, ended by introducing democracy and the system of collaboration into his boarding-school. We therefore do not at all agree with Durkheim in thinking that it is the master's business to impose or even to 'reveal' rules to the child. A 'priest' is the last thing a schoolmaster should be: he should be an elder collaborator, and, if he has it in him, a simple comrade to the children. Then only will true discipline come into being – discipline that the children themselves have willed and consented to. Every educationalist who has really made the experiment has found that this is what actually happens. The sense of a common law which, as we have shown in connection with the rules of a game, is possessed by children of 9–12, shows clearly enough how capable is the child of discipline and democratic life, when he is not, as at school, condemned to wage war against authority.

It is true that the problem of discipline is bound up with that of functional education as a whole. Autonomous and inner discipline can exist in a class only to the extent that the work enlists the major part of the child's spontaneous initiative and activity. Interest being, according to Dewey, the participation of the 'Ego' in the work done, it is obvious that it is necessary to the elaboration of a discipline proper to a system of autonomy.

Only the Activity school, *i.e.* that in which the child is not made to work by means of external constraint, but where he works of his own free will (from the psychological point of view the work done in these two cases is completely different) – only the Activity school is able to realize co-operation and democracy in the class-room.

J. PIAGET, *The Moral Judgement of the Child*, pp. 366–7, Routledge & Kegan Paul, 1932

For discussion

The accent should be placed firmly on freedom, not on authority, says Piaget: only the Activity School can serve as the model for a democratic community of children. How do we respond to this argument? What evidence can be adduced in favour of it? (Cf. S. Wiseman, *Education and Environment*, for comparisons between the educational attainments of pupils attending 'activity-type' and 'conventional' schools. Also *Children and Their Primary Schools* (Plowden Report) and the Scottish Education Department's 1965 Memorandum, *The Primary School*.)

10

Though there have been changes in *the system of authority, power and privilege* in the public schools, that system still remains yet another of the distinctive attributes of these schools. Authority (which I define as power which is accepted as legitimate) is distributed at staff and pupil levels over an elaborate and carefully laid down hierarchy. The authority of staff and pupils which is derived from office or status is defined in a vertical sequence of divisions for each of the parallel subsystems of house, school teams, C.C.F. and so on. The distribution of authority among the boys is therefore complex: one boy exercising one level of authority in the house, but another level or perhaps being subordinate in school or corps or games. The exercise of such authority is legitimated by the values of the school as the exercise of responsibility for others, involving power over them, obligations towards them, control over self and loyalty to one's superior in the chain of command. There can be few boys who pass through a public boarding school who do not hold some post of authority in one of the school's many subsystems. By this means the school attains a more thorough administration (much of the administration of the boarding or social side is left to the pupils), trains the boys to its goals and standards (particularly in learning both to obey and exercise authority) and manipulates the pupils by sub-dividing them and identifying them more closely with the staff. In this whole matter, the state school, even the state boarding school, differs profoundly possessing less formal hierarchy, fewer boys exercising authority over others, and even that authority will be less great and diverse. In the state school, staff and pupils who exercise real power or influence may not have any formal authority, whereas in the public school, informal power and formal authority more often coincide: the school will more often try to manipulate its informal power figures by bestowing some kind of formal authority upon them. With the hierarchy of authority there goes a hierarchy of privilege by which authority is denoted and rewarded: privileges can be utilitarian (studies, domestic service, greater freedom) or purely symbolic, especially in dress. This carefully graded privilege system is another common feature of the schools, though one which is being gradually eroded: many of the more absurd symbolic privileges (hands in or out of pockets, buttons done up or not) are disappearing. Any closed society, of course, creates privileges by withholding freedoms taken for granted in the outside world and conferring them back as rewards or incentives for conduct which aids its purposes.

ROYSTON LAMBERT, pp. xxii–xxiii, in G. KALTON,
The Public Schools: A Factual Survey, Longmans, 1966

For discussion
The accent should be placed firmly on authority, not on freedom, says the writer: the best way to promote a sense of personal responsibility is to organize the school

so that every pupil has opportunities of exercising authority as well as subordinating himself to it. How do we respond to this argument?

II

Most of our national leaders agree that it is far more important to have strong moral character in our citizens than to have good rockets, yet as a nation we have done astonishingly little with character education. Research in this field has demonstrated fully that most traditional approaches to character education will not suffice. For example, great strength of character does not result from negative ethics – from telling people what not to do. Not very long ago, I was talking to a group of twelve- to fourteen-year-old boys and asked them first what it was wrong to do. Since they had been majoring in that for some time, they knew many answers. They told me it is wrong to steal, wrong to lie, wrong to hit young children and so on. Then I asked them what it is right to do, and they had no idea whatsoever. Finally, one of them did say, 'It's right not to steal and not to lie,' but when I rejected this answer and said, 'No, I want you to tell me not what it is right *not* to do but what it is *right* to do,' they did not have a single suggestion.

The key to strong character is to define to youth what it is right to do and to challenge them to build moral and spiritual strength with a positive approach. However, knowing what is right to do is no simple task. Ours is a very complex world. Once in a while a parent will say, 'My child knows the difference between right and wrong.' I am always envious, because every day I face a dozen problems in which I am not at all sure of the difference between right and wrong. Our world is so exceedingly complex that character education today consists, in part at least, in discovering what are the right and wrong things to do.

It takes skill as well as will to do right. Today's older generation may have meant well, but did not have the skill to carry out their good intentions. So character education must be concerned with teaching young people *how* to do the right thing, even after they know what it is. For example, I have not deliberately set out to make anybody angry in forty years, but I have done it many times, always unintentionally, because I have lacked skill in right human relations. Hence, we must try to give young people the skills as well as the will for moral conduct.

ERNEST M. LIGON, p. 57, in *Philosophies of Education*, (ed.) P. H. PHENIX, Wiley, 1961

For discussion
The writer is an American, but the criticism he is making applies equally to us. Is our approach to discipline (apart from the question of keeping children in order) essentially negative?

12 The moral effects of school studies

The advocates of each school subject are fond of asserting that it not only gives valuable knowledge and habits of thought but also strengthens the will and enlightens the conscience. If we are to believe them, arithmetic makes you truthful; science makes you patient; geography makes you love your neighbors in the Phillipines as yourself; history makes you humble and brave and honorable; literature stirs every noble emotion and gives birth to all the virtues.

There is no doubt that the primarily intellectual work of learning the school subjects does produce secondarily certain moral results. But there is also no doubt that such statements as those given are gross exaggerations. It is necessary in estimating the moral effect of any study to bear in mind: (1) That a certain habit formed in a connection with a school subject will rarely extend far beyond it. We must not base hopes of moral education upon the false dogma of formal discipline. (2) That there is a fundamental difference between getting ideas of what is good and wishing to be good. The first is a response of knowledge; the second of attitude. (3) That there is an equal difference between wishing to be good and being good. The latter is a response not of attitude, but of action. (4) That the aesthetic emotions do not necessarily or even often predispose to their real counterparts. A boy may read tales of courage with appreciation and still be timid; a girl may adore a virtue in the heroine and practice its opposite none the less the next day.

With these four warnings to preserve us from overestimating the moral effect of studies and from expecting it in the wrong places, a just idea may be obtained of what the school studies can do for moral education and of how they may be taught so as to fulfil that function.

E. L. THORNDIKE, *The Principles of Teaching Based on Psychology*, pp. 189–90, Seiler, 1906

For discussion

1 If Thorndike is right, the moral effect of most school studies is negligible. What, then, *can* the school hope to achieve in the way of moral training? How is it to be done?
2 In this connexion it seems that many of the duties formerly discharged by the family, the Church, and other institutions are now expected to be taken over by the school. Traditionally, the school's task has concentrated on the imparting of *knowledge* rather than on bringing about changes in *attitude* in its pupils. Is the school's function changing? Is it equipped to meet the demands being made upon it?

13 Formal discipline – myth or reality?

The powers of the mind are supposed to work irrespective of the data with which they work. The power of observation is supposed to be uninfluenced by the nature of the fact observed; the power to reason to be uninfluenced by the nature of the problem and data; the power of attention to be capable of direction to any kind of object. It is even said that improvement of any one will improve all the mental powers; e.g. that learning to attend to Latin forms will make one not only attend but remember, reason and observe better than he did before.

The observation of facts proves this answer to be false. . . .

Training the mind means the development of thousands of particular independent capabilities, the formation of countless particular habits, for the working of any mental capacity depends upon the concrete data with which it works. Improvement of any one mental function or activity will improve others only in so far as they possess elements common to it also. The amount of identical elements in different mental functions and the amount of general influence from special training are much less than common opinion supposes. The most common and surest source of general improvement of a capacity is to train it in many particular connections.

Do not rely on any general mental improvement as a result of your teaching unless you have actual evidence of it. Teach nothing merely because of its disciplinary value, but teach everything so as to get what disciplinary value it does have. Consider in the case of every subject what ideas and habits of attitude and method the subject should develop that will be of general influence. After securing these ideas and habits in the special subject, give abundant practice in applying them to other fields. The price of the acquisition of general power is eternal vigilance in the formation of particular habits. The special training that is of the greatest value in and for itself will commonly also possess sufficient disciplinary value.

> E. L. THORNDIKE, *The Principles of Teaching Based on Psychology*, pp. 237–49, Seiler, 1906.

For discussion

1 Reviewing your own education, would you say that Thorndike's advice, 'Teach nothing merely for its disciplinary value' is sound? In some subjects, no doubt, most of the information you acquired through school lessons has been forgotten. What remains?

2 Subsequent studies of transfer of training have modified Thorndike's views, but most psychologists and educationists would probably still agree with him in thinking that it is better not to rely on any *general* mental improvement taking place automatically. On the other hand, the belief that certain studies – mathematics, Latin, history, etc. (but not Education!) have their own inherent discipline persists strongly in academic circles. Is the belief well-founded?

14

But now for many years I cannot endure to read a line of poetry. My mind seems to have become a kind of machine for grinding general laws out of a large collection of facts, but why this should have caused the atrophy of that part of the brain on which the higher tastes depend, I cannot conceive. The loss of these tastes is a loss of happiness, and may possibly be injurious to the intellect and more probably to the moral character, by enfeebling the emotional part of our nature.

CHARLES DARWIN, *Autobiography*

For discussion

It seems that in the long run, formal discipline or no, the effects of purely intellectual studies are real and lasting – and affect the learner's moral outlook. Darwin regrets that a lifetime's scientific training has 'caused the atrophy of that part of the brain on which the higher tastes depend'. Is a well-disciplined mind any guarantee that its owner will be capable of leading the good life?

It seems, too, that we are in deep waters. Inevitably, the question of discipline leads on to the question of moral training, to which we turn next.

9

Moral Education

To the question, 'Can virtue be taught?', Socrates gave a cryptic answer – 'Virtue is knowledge.' If only in the sense that moral behaviour is *learned* behaviour we are forced to agree with him; but Socrates' assertion that no man knowingly does wrong runs counter to the Christian belief in the essentially sinful nature of mankind, a belief summarized in St Paul's confession, 'When I would do good evil is present with me.'

This conflict between a rational-humanistic and a religious approach to the problems of moral conduct is complicated in our own time by disagreements and uncertainties which are no less fundamental. Time was when teachers, parents and clergy shared a common orthodoxy, when the child was instructed on a kind of 'agreed syllabus' and received a built-in code of do's and don'ts which was intended to serve him for the rest of his life. Today, thinks Riesman, we are moving into an other-directed society in which 'sensitive attention to the expectation of contemporaries' is the only guidance which the individual can rely on. In this situation, inevitably, there is bound to be considerable confusion. The dilemma of the fourteen-year-old who complained that, 'It's hard to say who's right and wrong these days about anything,' is one which we all have to face. Too often the standards and values exhibited in school are flagrantly denied in the home and in society at large – nowhere more obviously perhaps than in the world of the mass media, television, films, the press, and advertising. We cannot shut our eyes to the nasty contradictions which beset us in an age of ethical pluralism, nor can we dismiss them by saying that they are symptomatic of rapid social change. If education is a setting in order of a ferment in the mind some way of producing order out of the existing chaos needs to be found, otherwise the moral upbringing of the young is likely to go by default. As things are, it seems that instead of pulling together, the formal and informal agencies of moral education in our society are working in different directions.

HOW MORAL ARE YOU, ANYWAY?

If only for the sake of putting your own self-discipline to the test – and of raising questions about the reliability and validity of the test itself – why not carry out the instructions on this page? The test is reproduced from *Creativity and Intelligence* by J. W. Getzels and P. W. Jackson.

You are allowed up to 15 minutes to make your 20 choices. Though we suspect that there is not much point in warning you against choosing adjectives which the test-makers want you to choose, try to be as sincere with yourself as you can. You will find this far from easy! After completing the list (BUT NOT BEFORE!) you can calculate your own score using the method described at the end of this section (p. 152). There are no prizes for high scorers – and if your score is a low one at least it will leave you plenty to argue about!

DESCRIPTIVE WORDS[1]

Below are listed a number of words in groups of three. These are words which describe qualities you might like to possess. In each group you are to decide which word describes you as you would *most* like to be, and which word describes you as you would *least* like to be. On your answer sheet place an 'M' beside the letter which corresponds to the adjective describing the quality you would *most* like to have. Place an 'L' beside the letter which corresponds to the adjective which describes the quality you would *least* like to have. For each group of three words you should have two letters on the answer sheet, one 'M' and one 'L'.

Example	*Answer Sheet*
45 *a* intelligent	45 *a* M
b witty	*b* L
c humorous	*c*

In the foregoing example the person answering would most like to be intelligent and would least like to be witty. In some cases you may find it difficult to make a decision, since you might like to possess the qualities described in all three words. Nevertheless, you are to choose the one word which appeals to you most and the one word which appeals to you least in each group. Obviously there are no 'right' or 'wrong' answers. DO NOT WRITE ON THE TEST BOOKLET

1 *a* honest		4 *a* brave/lovely
b strong/cute		*b* helpful
c popular		*c* kind
2 *a* handsome/pretty		5 *a* good
b likable		*b* clean
c loyal		*c* friendly
3 *a* truthful		6 *a* agreeable
b cooperative		*b* dutiful
c skilful/graceful		*c* active

[1] Separate forms were prepared for boys and girls. When two adjectives appear side by side below (e.g. 'strong/cute') the first appeared in the boys' form of the instrument and the second in the girls' form.

K

7 *a* cheerful
 b muscular/beautiful
 c modest
8 *a* sociable
 b well-dressed
 c courageous
9 *a* conscientious
 b courteous
 c alert
10 *a* athletic/poised
 b fair-minded
 c amusing
11 *a* neat
 b polite
 c just
12 *a* honorable
 b refined
 c personable
13 *a* tall/slender
 b jolly
 c moral

14 *a* agile/bubbling
 b responsible
 c well-mannered
15 *a* rugged/gorgeous
 b unselfish
 c interesting
16 *a* vigorous
 b impartial
 c exciting
17 *a* faithful
 b amiable
 c good-looking
18 *a* ethical
 b desirable
 c attractive
19 *a* congenial
 b lively
 c consistent
20 *a* understanding
 b generous
 c energetic

J. W. GETZELS and P. W. JACKSON,
Creativity and Intelligence, pp. 246–7, Wiley, 1962

I

Now if discourses on ethics were sufficient in themselves to make men virtuous, 'large fees and many' (as Theognis says) 'would they win', quite rightly, and to provide such discourses would be all that is wanted. But as it is, we see that although theories have power to stimulate and encourage generous youths, and, given an inborn nobility of character and a genuine love of what is noble, can make them susceptible to the influence of virtue, yet they are powerless to stimulate the mass of mankind to moral nobility. For it is the nature of the many to be amenable to fear but not to a sense of honour, and to abstain from evil not because of its baseness but because of the penalties it entails; since, living as they do by passion, they pursue the pleasures akin to their nature, and the things that will procure those pleasures, and avoid the opposite pains, but have not even a notion of what is noble and truly pleasant, having never tasted true pleasure. What theory then can reform the natures of men like these? To dislodge by arguments habits long firmly rooted in their characters is difficult if not impossible. We may doubtless think ourselves fortunate if we attain some measure of virtue when all the things believed to make men virtuous are ours.

ARISTOTLE, *Nicomachean Ethics*, Book x,
Loeb Classical Library

For discussion

At the outset we are warned that the problems of moral education are age-old and admit of no easy solutions. Do you agree with Aristotle in thinking (*a*) that the majority of people live 'by passion' and are incapable of rising to the intellectual level of 'what is noble and truly pleasant'? (*b*) that it is difficult if not impossible to change habits and moral attitudes by means of argument?

2

Virtue being, as we have seen, of two kinds, intellectual and moral, intellectual virtue is for the most part produced and increased by instruction, and therefore requires experience and time; whereas moral or ethical virtue is the product of habit (*ethos*), and indeed has derived its name, with a slight variation of form, from that word. And therefore it is clear that none of the moral virtues is engendered in us by nature, for no natural property can be altered by habit. . . .

Moreover, the faculties given us by nature are bestowed on us first in a potential form; we exhibit their actual exercise afterwards. This is clearly so with our senses: we do not acquire the faculty of sight or hearing by repeatedly seeing or repeatedly listening, but the other way about – because we had the senses we began to use them, we did not get them by using them.

The virtues on the other hand we acquire by first having actually practised them, just as we do the arts.

ARISTOTLE, *Nicomachean Ethics*, Book ii,
Loeb Classical Library

For discussion

1 Aristotle draws a distinction between intellectual and moral virtue. What is it? Do you accept it as a valid distinction?
2 Contrast the Ancient World's concepts of moral excellence with Christianity's 'supernatural virtues' – Faith, Hope and Charity.
3 Do you agree that moral training of any kind is ineffectual unless it provides opportunities for regular practice?

3

That which every gentleman (that takes any care of his education) desires for his son, besides the estate he leaves him, is contained, I suppose, in these four things, virtue, wisdom, breeding and learning. I will not trouble myself whether these names do not some of them sometimes stand for the same thing, or really include one another. It serves my turn here to follow the popular use of these words, which, I presume, is clear enough to make me understand, and I hope there will be no difficulty to comprehend my meaning.

I place virtue as the first and most necessary of those endowments that belong to a man or a gentleman, as absolutely requisite to make him valued and beloved by others, acceptable or tolerable to himself. Without that, I think, he will be happy neither in this nor the other world.

As the foundation of this there ought very early to be imprinted on his mind a true notion of God, as of the independent Supreme Being, Author and Maker of all things, from whom we receive all our good, who loves us and gives us all things. . . .

You will wonder, perhaps, that I put learning last, especially if I tell you I think it the least part. This may seem strange in the mouth of a bookish man; and this making usually the chief, if not only, bustle and stir about children, this being almost that alone which is thought on when people talk of education, makes it the greater paradox. When I consider what ado is made about a little Latin and Greek, how many years are spent on it and what a noise and business it makes to no purpose, I can hardly forbear thinking that the parents of children still live in fear of the schoolmaster's rod, which they look on as the only instrument of education, as a language or two to be its whole business.

JOHN LOCKE, *Some Thoughts Concerning Education,*
1693

For discussion

Throughout the ages, educational thinkers have agreed on one point: that the ultimate purpose of education is an ethical one, not simply intellectual. They have, of course, disagreed violently about the ways and means. Locke puts virtue first and learning last in his order of priorities. Is this order reflected in the everyday practice of our schools? If not, why not?

Is this the order you approve of yourself?

4

We may reduce almost all the lessons of morality that have, or can be, formed for the use of children, to the following formula.

MASTER: You must not do so.
CHILD: And why must I not do so?

MASTER: Because it is naughty.

CHILD: Naughty! what is that being naughty?

MASTER: Doing what you are forbid.

CHILD: And what harm is there in doing what one is forbid?

MASTER: The harm is, you will be whipped for disobedience.

CHILD: Then I will do it so that no body shall know anything of the matter.

MASTER: O, but you will be watched.

CHILD: Ah! but then I will hide myself.

MASTER: Then you will be examined.

CHILD: Then I will tell a fib.

MASTER: You must not tell fibs.

CHILD: Why must not I?

MASTER: Because it is naughty, etc.

Thus we go round the circle; and yet, if we go out of it, the child understands us no longer. Are not these very useful instructions, think you? I could be very curious to know what could be substituted in the place of this fine dialogue. Locke himself would certainly have been embarrassed had he been asked so puzzling a question. To distinguish between good and evil, to perceive the reasons on which our moral obligations are founded, is not the business, as it is not within the capacity, of a child.

Nature requires children to be children before they are men. By endeavouring to pervert this order, we produce forward fruits, that have neither maturity nor taste, and will not fail soon to wither or corrupt. Hence it is we have so many young professors and old children. Childhood hath its manner of seeing, perceiving, and thinking, peculiar to itself; nor is there any thing more absurd than our being anxious to substitute our own in its stead. I would as soon require an infant to be five feet high, as a boy to have judgment at ten years of age. In fact, of what use would reason be to him at that age? Reason is given us as a check upon our power; a child has no need of such restraint.

ROUSSEAU, *Émile*

For discussion

1 According to Locke, the first task of the educator is to 'settle' moral habits in the child. According to Rousseau, it is not the business of the young child to distinguish between good and evil. Is there a fundamental disagreement here?

2 Do you agree that moral training should follow a developmental approach. If you do agree, would you explain just what you mean by 'following a developmental approach'? Is there such a thing as 'Readiness for Religion'? Is childhood 'the sleep of reason', as Rousseau said it was, and if so, what rational methods can the teacher rightly use in moral training?

5

The problem of moral training in day schools is still further complicated by the fact that pupils are under the teacher's control for one-fourth of their waking hours, that there are thirty or forty different moral natures for one teacher to help, that the present demands of schools in the shape of intellectual education reduce moral training to an incident, a by-product, of school work. A teacher is also limited in the means at his disposal for moral training. The tone of the family, the treatment received from friends, public opinion and practice, and hopes and fears of supernatural intervention in life or after death have been and are the chief means of moral influence. . . . Of the four, the teacher can count only upon the second to the extent that he himself wins the position of a friend and upon the third to the extent that he can by the selection of pupils, by wise legislation and by personal influence modify the tone of the school or class. Finally, many of the desirable traits of character can get exercise only in the duties and temptations of real life. The special morality of employer and employee, of buyer and seller, of husband and wife, of parents and children or of ruler and ruled requires in each case more than a school-room full of children as its adequate stimulus.

The answer to the question, 'How can a teacher make his pupils all good and efficient?', is, 'He cannot.' To expect school education to determine moral development is like expecting a city water-supply to abolish all sickness.

E. L. THORNDIKE, *The Principles of Teaching Based on Psychology*, pp. 180–1, Seiler, 1906

For discussion
In Thorndike's opinion, so far as moral training is concerned, the means at the disposal of the teacher in a day school are very limited indeed. Does this mean that he can do little about it? Is this a realistic position? Are the cards stacked against him from the start – and does this explain why most schools have preferred to concentrate on *intellectual* training?

6 Spiritual and moral development

'It shall be the duty of the local education authority for every area to contribute towards the spiritual, moral, mental and physical development of the community.'

Education Act, 1944

The nearer we got to the boys and girls on whose education we have to advise, the more it was brought home to us that Parliament gave the schools a difficult but not impossible task when it told them to foster their spiritual and moral development. We learned that those who tried with sincerity and ability to do this found that they were not only fulfilling a statutory obligation, or discharging a social responsibility; they were meeting a felt personal need of their pupils. Most boys and girls want to be what they call 'being good' and they want to know what this really implies in the personal situations which confront them. This is difficult enough, but it is not sufficient. They want also to know what kind of animal a man is, and whether ultimately each one of them matters – and, if so, why and to whom. And they want to be told the truth – 'it is no use', we were told in discussion, 'putting up a smoke screen and retiring in flight behind it'. The teacher who is not prepared to expose himself in honestly grappling with these ultimate problems had better leave them alone. His lessons must carry conviction. This is not the same as trying to convert his pupils. Above all, they don't want to be 'got at'.

Half our Future, (The Newsom Report)

For discussion

1 'Difficult, if not impossible,' said Aristotle. 'Difficult but not impossible,' the Newsom Committee affirm. Do you share their optimism – and how do you justify it?
2 Should *every* teacher 'expose himself in honestly grappling with these ultimate problems'? Can any teacher be absolved from this moral obligation?

7

Some examples of their awareness of moral conflict come from their response to the unfinished sentence, 'It's hard to ...' for example:

'. . . be perfect in this day and age.'
'. . . live up to the standards that some people think we should.'
'. . . believe in something you don't really understand.'
'. . . listen to something that you know is wrong and not being able to say anything.'
'. . . do anything good in this world for people are always looking for something bad in you.'
'. . . get on in life when there is always someone who dislikes you and tries to keep you down.'
'. . . say who's right and wrong these days about anything.'

Further evidence of their concern with moral questions and indeed of an implicit desire for non-patronizing help with them comes from many sources, including their responses to the Unfinished Sentence, 'The most important thing to teach children ...' Of the 300 items mentioned, over 80 per cent were concerned with codes of behaviour and manners. These included such things as 'unselfishness', 'tolerance', 'honesty', 'respect', 'responsibility'. Only three references were made to religion, and about 12 per cent to such practical matters as more English and Current Affairs. This response from a generation widely accused of being unconcerned with moral matters is well worth reflection.

E. M. EPPEL, 'The Adolescent and Changing Moral
Standards', pp. 131–2 in *Moral Education in a
Changing Society*, Faber, 1963

For discussion

1 Over 80 per cent of the responses to the inquiry, 'What is the most important thing to teach children?' were concerned with codes of behaviour and manners. Is it a case of 'The hungry sheep look up and are not fed'?
2 Only three references were made to religion. Comment on this finding.

8

The only way to prepare for social life is to engage in social life. To form habits of social usefulness and serviceableness apart from any direct social need and motive, apart from any existing social situation, is, to the letter, teaching the child to swim by going through motions outside of the water. The most indispensable condition is left out of the account, and the results are correspondingly partial.

The much lamented separation in the schools of intellectual and moral training, of acquiring information and growing in character, is simply one expression of the failure to conceive and construct the school as a social institution, having social life and value within itself. Except so far as the school is an embryonic typical community life, moral training must be partly pathological and partly formal. Training is pathological when stress is laid upon correcting wrong-doing instead of upon forming habits of positive service. Too often the teacher's concern with the moral life of pupils takes the form of alertness for failures to conform to school rules and routine. These regulations, judged from the standpoint of the development of the child at the time, are more or less conventional and arbitrary. They are rules which have to be made in order that the existing modes of school work can go on; but the lack of inherent necessity in these school modes reflects itself in a feeling, on the part of the child, that the moral discipline of the school is arbitrary.

Any conditions that compel the teacher to take note of failures rather than of healthy growth give false standards and result in distortion and perversion. Attending to wrong-doing ought to be an incident rather than a principle. The child ought to have a positive consciousness of what he is about, so as to judge his acts from the standpoint of reference to the work which he has to do. Only in this way does he have a vital standard, one that enables him to turn failures to account for the future.

By saying that the moral training of the school is formal, I mean that the moral habits currently emphasized by the school are habits which are created, as it were, *ad hoc*. Even the habits of promptness, regularity, industry, non-interference with the work of others, faithfulness to tasks imposed, which are specially inculcated in the school, are habits that are necessary simply because the school system is what it is, and must be preserved intact. If we grant the inviolability of the school system as it is, these habits represent permanent and necessary moral ideas; but just in so far as the school system is itself isolated and mechanical, insistence upon these moral habits is more or less unreal, because the ideal to which they relate is not itself necessary. The duties, in other words, are distinctly school duties, not life duties.

JOHN DEWEY, *Moral Principles in Education*,
pp. 15–16, Philosophical Library (New York), 1959

For discussion
1 How far is the school's indifferent success in the field of moral training due to its failure to conceive of itself as a social institution.
2 How far are the habits inculcated in school 'necessary simply because the school system is what it is'? What *are* these habits – and how, if at all, do they differ from those fostered (*a*) in the home, (*b*) in church, (*c*) in the world of work, and (*d*) in the world of entertainment?

9

Education in the classroom – and in the university lecture room too – offers by tradition less scope than it might for a frank and open discussion of values and morals and conduct. The majority of subjects are taught, pretty safely, as matters of fact or non-fact, or simply of an opinion which is to be accepted; at the sixth form stage we may go as far as saying that so and so's view is this, but such and such's view is that. But the training of personal judgment is usually a poor second to an insistence that the young should get hold of facts and opinions, an insistence aided by the temptation of securing for them just a bit better a result in a public examination than they deserve. Is it moral to confine ourselves to teaching chemistry, say, or geography as a subject in itself and say easily that it just isn't relevant to deal with wider issues? In a timetable divided up into subjects, so much that is of moral importance falls between the cracks. At any rate is there not a tendency in some schools and even colleges to give comparatively little practice to our children in making up their own minds? The emphasis is very much on their acquiring technical knowledge and competence. But that may be good equipment only if we have a personal policy and know where we are going. A technical knowledge of, say, navigation can be immensely interesting in itself. But the course the ship is to take is chosen for quite other reasons than the navigator's skill in plotting it. The educated man needs to discuss his direction of progress and the 'whys' of conduct as well as to build up knowledge and skills. Children should be given plenty of practice in making choices, including moral choices.

> W. R. NIBLETT, 'Some Problems in Moral Education Today', p. 27, in *Moral Education in a Changing Society*, (ed.) W. R. NIBLETT, Faber, 1963

For discussion
'Is it moral to confine ourselves to teaching chemistry, say, or geography as a subject in itself and say easily that it just isn't relevant to deal with wider issues?'
  Is not this precisely what is happening in most schools most of the time?

10

Moral elementary education is nothing else than the pure development of the human will, by the higher sentiments of love, gratitude, and faith, in the perfection in which they are expressed in their first blossomings in the pure relations between mother and child.
  The aim of this education is the moral perfection of our nature; its means are exercises in striving after perfection in moral thought, sentiment, and action. Applied to the visible, it reveals itself as morality in action; to the invisible, as religion in sentiment or vision.
  As we can only conceive the perfection of morality in a higher being, only in God, the first moral aspiration connects itself with the belief in God, which so simply and so naturally results from the truth of the child's love, gratitude, and faith.

> PESTALOZZI, *On the Idea of Elementary Education*, 1809

For discussion
If it is to mean 'exercises in striving after perfection', moral education must be based on religious faith, argues Pestalozzi. Is this opinion widely shared among teachers and parents nowadays?

11

Take a key question: intercourse before marriage. Only a quite exceptional teacher, willing to risk all sorts of difficulties when it became known would be willing to say anything except that it was always wrong. Then these fourteen- and fifteen-year-olds ask why. If the reply, after a bow or two to liberal views, is simply, 'Because it is against the will of God' or something to that effect, what is the result? Some of the class will agree and support the teacher. Some will think, but probably not say, 'Fiddlesticks' or something more up to date and even less elegant. The majority will listen in silence and shrug it all off afterwards, and for one or two related reasons: either because the teacher has been pushed into taking the period and has not spoken with any depth of personal conviction, or because they tacitly reject the supernatural sanction.

There simply is no future for moral education in our multi-belief society if it is tied to religious instruction and not taken in its own right. This is a hard thing for sincere Christians who would be honest in moral education to understand and accept. But I am convinced that it is so. You cannot force teachers enthusiastically to advocate doctrines and standards about which a great number of them will at least have important reservations. You cannot force young people to assent to beliefs that they know their parents do not hold in any active or serious way. You can only get serious and honest discussion of moral matters if in the class you accept the humanist criterion as the only one that will work, the test of good or evil consequences of our actions in terms of our experience and as others have lived it and reflected upon it.

> LIONEL ELVIN, 'Moral Values in a Mixed Society',
> p. 22, in *Morality and Education*, Aspects of
> Education No. 1, Journal of the Institute of
> Education, University of Hull, July 1964

For discussion

'You can only get serious and honest discussion of moral matters if in the class you accept the humanist criterion as the only one that will work.' It seems that proponents of the 'morals without religion' can be just as dogmatic as professed Christians who insist that the two go hand in hand! Where do you stand on this issue?

12

The old belief was that virtue depended on the will. Man was filled with original sin, and this needed to be controlled by the abstract faculty of volition. It was, and still is, regarded by some as impossible to root out this original nature; all that can be done is to control it. But modern science put an end to this idea. Children seem to want to be liked by their elders and their companions. This fortunately provides an avenue for educational efforts. The impulses of children can, through parental approval or disapproval, be developed in either a desirable or an undesirable direction. The old method of controlling bad conduct by means of the watchful eye of the will forced desires underground which eventually emerged elsewhere. The man who hated his father flogs his son, under the impression that he is chastising moral evil. Thus, Russell's ethical theory causes him to reject the will and religion as the bases of morality and to replace them with love and knowledge. These have bases in scientific fact. Both can be developed by means of scientifically designed education. The designing of this kind of education necessitates a thorough understanding of psychology.

J. PARK, *Bertrand Russell on Education*, p. 45,
Allen & Unwin, 1964

For discussion

1 If the doctrine of original sin is dismissed as 'unscientific' what is to take its place – Rousseau's doctrine of original goodness, or the doctrine of original neutrality?
2 How far does an understanding of psychology help to bring about a deeper understanding of problems of morality?

13

In some sense or other justification is the basis of all religion. Your character is developed according to your faith. This is the primarily religious truth from which no one can escape. Religion is force of belief cleansing the inward parts. For this reason the primary religious virtue is sincerity, a penetrating sincerity.

A religion, on its doctrinal side, can thus be defined as a system of general truths which have the effect of transforming character when they are sincerely held and vividly apprehended. . . . Religion is the art and the theory of the internal life of man, so far as it depends on the man himself and on what is permanent in the nature of things.

This doctrine is the direct negation of the theory that religion is primarily a social fact. Social facts are of great importance to religion, because there is no such thing as absolutely independent existence. You cannot abstract society from man; most psychology is herd psychology. But all collective emotions leave untouched the awful ultimate fact, which is the human being, consciously alone with itself, for its own sake.

Religion is what a man does with his own solitariness; . . . Religion is solitariness; and if you are never solitary you are never religious. . . . Accordingly, what should emerge from religion is individual worth of character. But worth is positive or negative, good or bad. Religion is by no means necessarily good. It may be very evil. . . . In your religious experience the God whom you have made terms with may be the God of destruction, the God who leaves in his wake the loss of the greater reality.

A. N. WHITEHEAD, *Religion in the Making*,
Cambridge University Press

For discussion

'Religion is what a man does with his own solitariness,' says Whitehead. 'Your character is developed according to your faith.'

Are such pronouncements acceptable to the avowed atheist, the agnostic and the rational humanist?

14

It is . . . absurd and even immoral to wish to impose upon the child a fully worked-out system of discipline when the social life of children among themselves is sufficiently developed to give rise to a discipline infinitely nearer to that inner submission which is the mark of adult morality. It is idle, again, to try and transform the child's mind from outside, when his own taste for activity research and his desire for cooperation suffice to ensure a normal intellectual development. The adult must therefore be a collaborator and not a master, from this point of view, moral and rational. But conversely, it would be unwise to rely upon biological 'nature' alone to ensure the dual progress of conscience and intelligence, when we realize to what extent all moral as all logical norms are the result of cooperation. Let us therefore try to create in the school a place where individual experimentation and reflection carried out in common come to each other's aid and balance one another.

If, then, we had to choose from among the totality of existing educational systems those which would best correspond with our psychological results, we would turn our methods in the direction of what has been called 'Group Work' and 'Self-Government'. Advocated by Dewey, Sanderson, Cousinet, and by most of the promoters of the 'Activity School', the method of work by groups consists in allowing the children to follow their pursuits in common, either in organized 'teams' or simply according to their spontaneous groupings. Traditional schools, whose ideal has gradually come to be the preparation of pupils for competitive examinations rather than for life, have found themselves obliged to shut the child up in work that is strictly individual: the class listens in common, but the pupils do their home work separately. This procedure, which helps more than all the family situations put together to reinforce the child's spontaneous egocentrism, seems to be contrary to the most obvious requirements of intellectual and moral development.

JEAN PIAGET, *The Moral Judgment of the Child*,
pp. 411–12, Routledge & Kegan Paul, 1932

For discussion

1 Like Dewey, Piaget objects to the organization of the traditional school on the grounds that it is absurd and immoral to impose adult rules and standards

at a stage of development when these are more effectively established through the activities of children's peer groups. Does this objection stop short at the primary school?

2 Piaget assigns great importance to the social life of children in promoting inner self-discipline. Can you suggest an aspect of the child's social life which is possibly even more important?

15

Imagine the following two conversations on a bus. A mother has a child sitting on her lap.

MOTHER: Hold on tight.
CHILD: Why?
MOTHER: Hold on tight.
CHILD: Why?
MOTHER: You'll fall.
CHILD: Why?
MOTHER: I told you to hold on tight, didn't I?

MOTHER: Hold on tightly, darling.
CHILD: Why?
MOTHER: If you don't you'll be thrown forwards and then you'll fall.
CHILD: Why?
MOTHER: Now hold on tightly, darling, and don't make such a fuss.

In the first example a whole range of potential learning and connections have been cut out by the categoric statement. The natural curiosity of the child has been blunted. There is no causal chain between the mother's request and the child's expected response. The change in behaviour has been brought about by a process akin to verbal conditioning rather than through instrumental learning. If the child challenges the statement then in a short period he is challenging the *right* of the mother to issue the request, that is, he is challenging the authority which inheres in the status of the mother. The potential social power in the form of the relation is revealed very quickly. In the second example the child is exposed to an area of connections and sequence. If this is challanged then another set of reasons are elicited. Of course, after a time the categoric statement is applied, but an order of learning has been made available in between. It should be noted that as a result of the linguistically elaborated relationship the initial challenges are of the reasons given to support the request. The challenge of the mother comes much *later* in the relationship and the latent social power is revealed later *and* under different conditions. If the categoric statement is used frequently in a public language then it limits learning and curiosity and induces a sensitivity towards a particular type of authority in which social power is quickly and nakedly revealed. The categoric statement becomes part of a language which narrows the range of stimuli to which the child responds.

> BASIL BERNSTEIN, 'Social Structure, Language and Learning', pp. 94–6, in *Linking Home and School*, (ed.) MAURICE CROFT *et al.*, Longmans, 1967

For discussion

We trust that the point here is clear enough, even though the passage has been lifted from its context and excludes any explanation of Bernstein's theory concerning the intimate connexion between language, learning, and educability. Very briefly, the theory is that in lower working-class families the language used tends to be a restricted code, characterized by:

(1) Short, grammatically simple, often unfinished sentences with a poor syntactical form stressing the active voice.
(2) Simple and repetitive use of conjunctions (so, then, because).
(3) Little use of subordinate clauses to break down the initial categories of the dominant subject.

This he calls a 'public' language. By contrast, the 'formal' language current among the middle classes answers to an elaborated code which permits of a much wider range of conceptual thought.

In this connexion there are three questions we should like you to consider:

(1) If morality begins at home is not the mother–child relationship crucially important?
(2) If the relationship described in the second of these examples is the one to be preferred can we hope for any improvement in moral education until *all* parents possess a 'formal' language and are capable of giving articulate reasons when the child asks 'Why'?
(3) In the first conversation the change brought about in the child's behaviour is the result of a 'process akin to verbal conditioning', thinks Bernstein. What does he mean?

16 The power of suggestion

In recent experiments, 120 college students were given a pill and then had to do a written performance test. One group were told that the pill was dexedrine, a well-known stimulant and energiser. Another group were told that they had been given a sleeping pill. In fact, however, *all* the students were given either dexedrine or placebos – dummy pills. The results of the test showed that the group who thought they had swallowed a pep-pill were full of pep, and the group who thought they had swallowed a sleeping pill became sluggish and sleepy.

ARTHUR KOESTLER, 'Pavlov in Retreat', Observer

For discussion

It is not only the very young who are wide open to the hidden persuaders of language, we are reminded. How legitimate is the use of *suggestion* in the teaching of morality?

17

Suppose, for example, that one of my children is going through a phase of telling a lot of lies. It may be that its age is such that no rational discussion of the evil consequences of lying is much good; I may engage in such discussion as a kind of lip-service to my liberal principles, but I may know that what will really influence the child to stop lying is not the discussion, but the tone in which it is conducted. Psychologists can perhaps advise on the best method of getting young children out of the habit of lying; but we can be sure that the method will not be . . . a rational one. Let us suppose that what happens is that the child senses that I disapprove very strongly of lying, and therefore stops doing it – let us ignore the question of whether this is a psychologically desirable method or not. Have I, by using this non-rational method of affecting the child's behaviour been *indoctrinating* the child? I do not think so. For I do not *want* the child to remain such that non-rational persuasion is the only kind of moral communication I can have with him. The difference lies in the aim.

There is a German rhyme that I was once taught which goes

> *Was der Vater will,*
> *Was die Mutter spricht*
> *Das befolge still.*
> *Warum? Frage nicht.*

> *What your father wishes,*
> *What your mother says,*
> *Do it in silence.*
> *Why? Don't ask questions.*

Now if I wanted my children to *keep* this sort of attitude to me, or to what I was teaching them, then I should be indoctrinating. But I do not want this. I may have *now* to use non-rational methods of teaching, but my wish is that as soon as possible they may become unnecessary. So, though on occasion I may use the very same methods of teaching as the German who wrote this rhyme, and though my teaching may have exactly the same content, that it is wrong to lie, he is indoctrinating and I am not, because he wants the child always to go on taking its morality from its elders, even after they are dead, whereas I want the child as soon as possible to learn to think morally for itself.

R. M. HARA, 'Adolescents into Adults', pp. 50–1, in *Aims in Education*, (ed.) T. H. B. HOLLINS, Manchester University Press, 1964

For discussion

1 Whatever the parent or teacher does in the way of moral education, it seems that he is liable to leave himself open to the accusation that he is taking advantage of the young either (*a*) by verbal conditioning – cf. 15, (*b*) by resorting to the power of suggestion – cf. 16, or (*c*) by conditioning. How seriously do we need to take these scruples?
2 Implicit in all of them is the belief that it is wrong to infringe the learner's free will. How would you define free will? Is it innate or is it acquired through the process of learning? If the latter, at what stage can it be said to become 'free'?

18

What then is the paradox of moral education as I conceive it? It is this: given that it is desirable to develop people who conduct themselves rationally, intelligently and with a fair degree of spontaneity, the brute facts of child development reveal that at the most formative years of a child's development he is incapable of this form of life and impervious to the proper manner of passing it on. Let me spell out these facts in a little more detail.

Firstly, a fair amount of evidence has accumulated to demonstrate the decisive importance of early learning on later development. . . .

Secondly, both the Freudian theory of the super-ego and Piaget's theory of the transcendental stage of the child's development converge to suggest that up to a certain age rules appear to a child as something external and unalterable, often sacred. . . .

Thirdly, there is evidence to suggest . . . that the giving of reasons has very little educative effect before a certain age. The explanations given by adults bite very little into the child's behaviour, though commands do have an effect at an earlier age.

Nevertheless, in spite of the fact that a rational code of behaviour and the 'language' of a variety of activities is beyond the grasp of young children, they can and must enter the palace of Reason through the courtyard of Habit and Tradition. This is the paradox of moral education which was first put so well by Aristotle in Book 2 of his Nicomachean Ethics.

R. S. PETERS, 'Reason and Habit: The Paradox of Moral Education', pp. 54–5, in *Moral Education in a Changing Society*, Faber, 1963

L

For discussion

1 We are back where we started, apparently! Moral education turns out to be not so much a problem as a paradox, thinks Peters. Is he right?

2 Do you agree that 'giving reasons has little educative effect below a certain age'? In this connexion, what *is* 'a certain age'?

19

Accordingly, it should be the aim of an ideally constructed education that the discipline should be the voluntary issue of free choice, and that the freedom should gain an enrichment of possibility as the issue of discipline. The two principles, freedom and discipline, are not antagonists, but should be so adjusted in the child's life that they correspond to a natural sway, to and fro, of the developing personality. It is this adaptation of freedom and discipline to the natural sway of development that I have elsewhere called the Rhythm of Education. I am convinced that much disappointing failure in the past has been due to neglect of attention to the importance of this rhythm. My main position is that the dominant note of education at its beginning and at its end is freedom, but that there is an intermediate stage of discipline with freedom in subordination: Furthermore, that there is not one unique threefold cycle of freedom, discipline, and freedom; but that all mental development is composed of such cycles, and of cycles of such cycles. Such a cycle is a unit cell, or brick; and the complete stage of growth is an organic structure of such cells. In analysing any one such cell, I call the first period of freedom the 'stage of Romance', the intermediate period of discipline I call the 'stage of Precision', and the final period of freedom is the 'stage of Generalization'.

A. N. WHITEHEAD, *The Aims of Education*,
pp. 47–8, in paperback edition, Benn, 1962

For discussion

No paradox at all, Whitehead assures us: provided the learning process is geared to the Rhythm of Education there is no problem. Easier said than done, no doubt, unless and until we fully understand what is involved in the 'Romance', 'Precision', 'Generalization' sequence. Do we?

For a start, how would you set about inducing 'romance' in the teaching of, say, mathematics? (It can be done!)

Scoring of the test
'For each set of three adjectives a score of 2, 1, or 0 points was given, depending on whether the moral adjective was ranked first, second, or third. These scores were summed over the twenty sets of adjectives to provide a total score.'

Getzels and Jackson do not say which of the twenty were the 'moral' adjectives, but it is fairly plain that these were:

1 honest *a*	6 dutiful *b*	11 just *c*	16 impartial *b*
2 loyal *c*	7 modest *c*	12 honorable *a*	17 faithful *a*
3 truthful *a*	8 courageous *c*	13 moral (!) *c*	18 ethical (!) *a*
4 helpful *b*	9 conscientious *a*	14 responsible *b*	19 consistent *c*
5 good *a*	10 fair-minded *b*	15 unselfish *b*	20 understanding *a*

not genuine.

You scored 40 out of 40? Fine. But how are we (or you) to know that your responses were not merely say-so? You scored 0 and want to argue about some of the 'non-moral' adjectives for which you received no credit? We don't blame you.

IO

Character Training

'Every man must carve his own statue,' wrote the Greek poet Pindar. 'Man is the creature of circumstances,' Robert Owen insisted. At the outset we are presented with a crucial question: Is the individual a free agent, in some measure responsible for shaping his own character, or is he not? Among the host of influences which are brought to bear on the growing child, what part does the school play? Easy enough to say that it serves as an initiation into social mores and community life, that it 'promotes the type' while allowing for 'growth beyond the type': the trouble about answers of this sort is that they are so highly generalized. The truth is that that aspect of moral education which we normally have in mind when we speak of character training is singularly elusive and ill-defined. Before it can become tolerably well-defined it seems that some model of the type of character which the educational process is supposed to produce is needed. Thomas Arnold's idea of the Christian gentleman provided such a model for the English Public Schools during the nineteenth century – and their success in the realm of character training was largely attributable to this fact, that they had made up their minds about the *particular personal characteristics* they wanted to encourage. To that extent they knew what they were trying to do.

Can the same be said of our State secondary schools today? Do they have a model? (The 'Common Man' perhaps?) In any case, can a day school hope to accomplish very much in this direction, bearing in mind the massive influences over which it has no control? If not, is its relative impotence altogether regrettable? What about the dangers of social engineering? In the final analysis, is not character best thought of as 'that sacred and hidden identity which no techniques can reach', and is not respect for the learner as a *person* imperative at all stages of his development?

I

One of the things about Socrates which irritated the sensible, practical Athenian was that he would insist on turning the talk to such humble and apparently irrelevant people as shoemakers and carpenters, when what they wanted to learn about was what constituted political ability or whether there was such a thing as moral obligation. If you want to be a good shoemaker, he said, the first thing necessary is to know what a shoe is and what it is meant for. It is no use trying to decide on the best sort of tools and material to use and the best methods of using them unless you have first formed in your mind a clear and detailed idea of what it is you are setting out to produce and what function it will have to perform. To use the Greek word, the *arete* of a shoemaker depended first and foremost on the possession of this knowledge. He ought to be able to describe in clear terms the nature of the thing he intended to make, and his definition should include a statement of the use to which it was to be put. It was quite natural to speak of the *arete* of a shoemaker, just as one could also speak of the *arete* of a general or statesman. In no such case did the word have any necessary connexion with the moral aspect of their activities as our word 'virtue' would suggest. It meant that in them which made good at their particular job, and by taking first the humble examples of the useful crafts, it was not difficult for Socrates to show that in each case the acquisition of this capacity depended on knowledge and that the first and most necessary knowledge was knowledge in each case of the end in view – what the man was setting out to do. Given a proper understanding of the end, the understanding of the means to be adopted could follow, but not otherwise. In every instance, therefore *arete* depended first on having a definite job to do, and secondly on a thorough knowledge of what the job was and what it aimed at effecting. If then (he proceeded) there is any legitimate sense in which we can talk about *arete* unqualified, as the Sophists were professing to teach it – that is, efficiency in living for any man as such – it follows that there must be an end or function which all alike, as human beings, have to perform. *The first task therefore, if we are to acquire this universal human virtue, is to discover what the function of man is.*

W. K. C. GUTHRIE, *The Greek Philosophers from Thales to Aristotle*, pp. 72–3, Methuen, 1950

For discussion

1 To paraphrase the Socratic argument: it is no use embarking on a course of character training unless you first have a clear and definite notion of the kind of character you hope to produce. Do we have such a notion?

2 There is a reminder here of Kerschensteiner's claim that vocational training leads to character training. (Cf. section on General and Special Education *supra*.) Does this claim deserve to be taken seriously?

3 What are we to make of the fact that the world's greatest teachers all had some conspicuous failures among their disciples? Jesus spoke 'as one having authority', yet this did not prevent Judas from betraying him. Socrates' favourite student was Alcibiades, who turned out to be a ne'er-do-well.

2

Picture to yourselves a very ugly man, with hair sticking up all over his head, his face deeply pitted by smallpox and covered with red spots, his beard ragged and in disorder, no cravat, trousers half unbuttoned, falling in folds over wrinkled stockings, which also fell over enormous slippers; his walk hurried and jerky; then eyes which sometimes expanded as they darted forth lightning, sometimes shut to lend themselves to inner contemplation; features which sometimes expressed deep sadness, sometimes happiness full of benignity; a voice which spoke now slowly, now precipitately, and was now tender and melodious, now loud as thunder: such was he whom we used to call *Father Pestalozzi*.

Although he was just as I have here described him, we all loved him, for he loved us all; we loved him so dearly that when we had not seen him for some time we were quite sad, and once he appeared we could not turn our eyes away from him. . . .

What was so emphatically called Pestalozzi's *method* was, it is true, an enigma to us. So it was to our teachers. Like the disciples of Socrates, every one of them interpreted the master's doctrines in his own fashion.

> VULLIEMIN, *Souvenirs*, quoted in A. PINLOCHE,
> *Pestalozzi*, pp. 71–3, Heinemann, 1902

For discussion

Despite their occasional failures, it seems that there is no substitute for personal example, and that if we are ever to track down the secret of character training we might do worse than begin by looking at the master spirits of the teaching profession. In the case of Pestalozzi, evidently, the magnetism of the man transcended his method.

3

Here lies

HEINRICH PESTALOZZI

Born in Zürich 12th January, 1746.
Died at Brugg 17th February, 1827.
Saviour of the poor at Neuhof,
Preacher to the people in 'Leonard and Gertrude',
Father of the fatherless at Stanz,
Founder of the new Volkschule at Burgdorf and Munchenbuchsee,
Teacher of mankind at Yverdon.

MAN, CHRISTIAN, CITIZEN

Everything for others, nothing for himself!
Blessed be his name!

Because 'they (teachers) make their effect more by what they are than what they do';[1] because knowledge is not the sole end of education; because it is *how* pupils master their subjects and utilize knowledge that matters; because a teacher needs ability to invent, to treat knowledge imaginatively, to enlist his pupils' help to explore ideas with him, and to search for wisdom, truth and beauty, it is not *so much* what he knows that is the most important thing (though in all conscience that is important enough), but what he *is*! The kind of person he is, his outlook, his modes of thought and feeling, his tastes, interests and judgments and also, his energies, his perseverance, his equanimity and especially his humour and aliveness. Therefore the main task of the training colleges must surely be to *develop the person.*

P. GURREY, *Education and the Training of Teachers,* p. 47, Longmans, 1963

For discussion

'Teachers make their effect more by what they are than what they do.' It's a worthy sentiment, no doubt, but just how should courses of training set about the task of *developing the person*? Is this their main task? Is it feasible?

4

'Keate has as lower master acquired a rooted distrust in the honour of boys in general, and he used to make point blank charges at random. . . . The effect of this was to encourage the very evil which he wished to check.'

(History of Eton College)

'There grew up a general feeling that it was a shame to tell Arnold a lie; he always believes you.'

(Life of Thomas Arnold)

For discussion

Any clues here as to how personal example makes itself felt?

5

Any character, from the best to the worst, from the most ignorant to the most enlightened, may be given to any community, even to the world at large, by applying certain means; which are to a great extent at the command and under the control, or easily made so, of those who possess the government of nations.

ROBERT OWEN, *A New View of Society: or, Essays on the Principle of the Formation of the Human Character,* 1813

[1] W. McDougall.

It may be stated, without fear of contradiction from any party who is master of the subject, that the whole success of these arrangements will depend upon the manner in which the infants and children shall be trained and educated in these schools. Men are, and ever will be, what they are and shall be made in infancy and childhood. The apparent exceptions to this law are the effects of the same causes, combined with subsequent impressions, arising from the new circumstances in which the individuals showing these exceptions have been placed.

One of the most general sources of error and evil to the world is the notion *that infants, children, and men, are agents governed by a will formed by themselves and fashioned after their own choice*. It is, however, as evident as any fact can be made to man, that he does not possess the smallest control over the formation of any of his own faculties or powers, or over the peculiar and ever-varying manner in which those powers and faculties, physical and mental, are combined in each individual.

Such being the case, it follows that human nature up to this period has been misunderstood, vilified, and savagely treated; and that, in consequence, the language and conduct of mankind respecting it form a compound of all that is inconsistent and incongruous and most injurious to themselves, from the greatest to the least. All at this moment suffer grievously in consequence of this fundamental error.

To those who possess any knowledge of this subject it is known that 'man is the creature of circumstances', and that he really is, at every moment of his existence, precisely what the circumstances in which he has been placed, combined with his natural qualities, make him.

ROBERT OWEN, *Report to the County of Lanark*, 1820
(*A New View of Society and Other Writings*,
Everyman's Library 799)

For discussion
1 Robert Owen denies the existence of free will. It is tempting to dismiss his philosophy as pure determinism, but in view of what happened at New Lanark is it not the case that its practical applications were beneficial?
2 How far do Owen's ideas underlie those of modern social planners? For example, is the Plowden recommendation that there should be a greater provision of nursery school services inspired by the conviction that, 'Men are, and ever will be, what they are made in infancy'?

6

Educators, sociologists, and lawmakers have begun to act as though man were absolutely incapable of choice, of self-determination, or of any autonomous activity. The man they have in mind when they describe their principles, plan their societies, or draw up their codes is something significantly, perhaps fatally, different from any creature who could possibly escape the catastrophe which many formerly confident 'engineers' have now begun to predict.

Moreover and merely by being treated as though he could do nothing for himself man is, perhaps actually becoming less capable of doing so. Any society which not merely tells its members that they are automata but also treats them as though they were, runs the risk of becoming a society in which human capacities atrophy because they are less and less rewarded, or even tolerated, as well as less and less acknowledged.

As the individual becomes, either in theory or in fact, less capable of doing anything for himself the question what may be *done to him* inevitably comes to seem more and more interesting. If he is so much the product of his environment that neither spontaneously nor as the result of moral adjuration can his own will make effective decisions, then it seems to follow – not that he must be simply abandoned to evolution, the dialectic of matter, or the obscure workings of the unconscious mind – but that he may be reached indirectly through the manipulation of that total environment of which he is the product. Thus sociology begins to promise to achieve by scientific methods all that which religion and moral philosophy, proceeding on false assumptions, failed to accomplish.

JOSEPH WOOD KRUTCH, *The Measure of Man*,
pp. 40–1, Redman, 1956

For discussion
Is there a growing tendency to engage in social engineering? For example, is the *shaping* of the learner's *terminal behaviour* in programmed learning part of it? The skilful (and unscrupulous) use of hidden persuaders, for example, in advertising may not go wholly undetected, but it is worth asking how far, if at all, they exist in schools?

7

We do not know much about the education of recent innovators. During the industrial revolution many were self-taught, but this is no longer common in industry, if only because of the extensive knowledge needed to understand present-day techniques. Recent research in the field of psychology has, however, revealed a disturbing possibility. Our teaching methods, certainly up to the age of sixteen, tend to demand the one right answer and throughout are marked by examinations which encourage standard answers. It may be that we turn children who are potentially creative into adults whose only wish is to succeed through conformity. Psychologists now believe that some people have an innate mode of thinking such that they tend to give the expected answer or follow the usual line of thought, whilst others have a mode that enables them to diverge easily from the conventional. It is suspected that the emphasis in our schools may teach the 'diverger' to think in a more conformist manner and thereby crush potential creativity.

We may not know the educational background of our innovators, but recent work in the U.S.A. has revealed two facts that we may suspect to be true in Britain. Despite the growth of research in large teams about half of industrial innovations still seem to be made by individuals. This emphasizes that, if the schools do stunt the creative potential of individuals, they are acting in a dys- functional way in that they are stopping the flow of innovators. Secondly, there seems to be no difference in the quality of the output of American scientists from schools or colleges in which the expenditure per pupil is high and those where it is low. Anyone with experience of British education might go as far as saying that the correlation in Britain was inverse!

P. W. MUSGRAVE, *The Sociology of Education,*
pp. 138–9, Methuen, 1965

For discussion
The researches of Getzels and Jackson in the U.S.A. (reported in *Creativity and Intelligence*) and of Dr Liam Hudson in this country (*Contrary Imaginations*) suggest that there may be two types of learner, *convergent* and *divergent*. The typology is by no means clear-cut, of course. Nevertheless, there is little doubt that, of the two, the diverger tends to be regarded as a misfit in most schools and is often actively disliked by teachers. Why? Was J. S. Mill right in fearing that a State system of education would turn out to be a 'mere contrivance for moulding everyone to be like everyone else'?

8 Two Grammar school 'characters'

A]

Christ, no, I didn't like Marbuton College. Too fast, they just got me there and they crammed my nut from the moment I arrived. That school doesn't turn out human beings, it turns out people to read and write, that's all. Look at the facts they rammed into me. School Cert. in four years. All these facts, Christ, just think of them! All that geography I did period after period, and now I hardly know where America is, and I've been to the place! Yes, I worked quite hard, I'd be about fifth or sixth in class. You do a day's work at school, you go home and you've got two and a half hours' homework because you've got to keep up to schedule, kid, and then you do another two and a half hours. You don't play out any more, and you don't see anybody except on a Friday night. Christ, what a way to grow up! You go back to school next morning, and perhaps some kid hasn't done his homework, because he's been out! What, you'd think he was a bloody communist the way they carry on. Christ, kid, they don't believe in leisure. Leisure means laziness for them. It means sitting around and loafing with your feet up, that's what leisure means. No time for all those other things like reading serious books (not that I read any serious books, not after having all that crap about Shakespeare rammed down my throat. I wouldn't read a word of it now). But leisure, that's what you need in growing up and, Christ, you don't have any leisure.

> BRIAN JACKSON and DENIS MARSDEN, *Education and the Working Class*, Routledge & Kegan Paul (p. 119, Pelican edition, 1966),
> © Institute of Community Studies

B]

I would say that I didn't become intelligent until the sixth form. Up till then I hadn't really thought about anything – I wasn't what you would call intelligent! A master called Daye had a lot to do with it. He was just utterly different. He taught you in a completely different kind of way. After we'd had a few lessons from him, he stood in front of the class one morning and said he was shocked at our knowledge of English. Absolutely shocked that boys could have learned so much literature off parrot-like and understood so very little of it. . . . It was with him that I began to understand.

> BRIAN JACKSON and DENIS MARSDEN, *Education and the Working Class*, Routledge & Kegan Paul (p. 147, Pelican edition, 1966),
> © Institute of Community Studies

For discussion
We'd say that one of these boys was a 'strong' character and that the other was a 'desirable' character. But maybe we don't see eye to eye on this particular value judgement.
1 Which of these two boys would you prefer to have in your class?
2 Which of the two would you say had the 'stronger' character?
3 We are not suggesting for a moment that the first boy is potentially 'creative' – whatever that means – but clearly he is in some sense a 'diverger'. Why does he reject a grammar-school type of education and all that it stands for?

9

Roback, in his classic on 'The Psychology of Character', defines 'character' as 'an enduring psycho-physical disposition to inhibit instinctive impulses in accordance with a regulative principle'. These principles may be limited in scope, like those of Colonel Nicholson in 'The Bridge on the River Kwai', whose principles were that an officer should care for his men, obey a superior officer, and honour international conventions. Or they might be more general ones, such as one ought not to exploit others to further one's own interest or that one ought to minimise avoidable misery. Or they might be morally suspect principles, such as that one ought always to further the interests of one's country, church, or party. A man would have 'character' to the extent to which he was impervious to temptation or to social pressure in applying particular rules intelligently in the light of such supreme principles. But, of course, he might have character – and be bad.

It is difficult to determine what educational procedures lead to the development of character which a child has to rules at different stages of his development. It is not, he claims, till about the age of seven or so that children begin to see the point of rules and to modify their behaviour accordingly. Before that age they tend to accept standards as transcendentally imposed and unalterable. And, I suppose, children start to develop character only when they are presented with conflicting standards and have to choose their own. But this does not come about only in the manner beloved of the progressives – by learning through experience in the performance of common tasks. It also develops if adults are at hand who themselves have character and who can give practical reasons for their principles. This is different from 'pep talks'. Practical wisdom is not passed on by preaching.

R. S. PETERS, *Authority, Responsibility and Education*,
pp. 114–15, Allen & Unwin, 1959

For discussion

1 How would you rephrase Roback's definition of character in everyday language?
2 'Children start to develop character only when they are presented with conflicting standards,' we are told. Consider the practical implications of this statement (*a*) for the parents in the home, (*b*) for the teacher in the classroom.

10 Outward Bound

The major appeal to the boys themselves has been to their natural love of adventure. Aspects of character can be exposed to the boy and to his companions most vividly by facing the challenge of Nature. In meeting and surmounting difficulties and dangers 'self-confidence can be greatly strengthened by the exercise of self-control and by the realization of improvement in physical and mental agility'.

The physical bias of the course, often criticized, is an intentional response to the desire of most adolescents to prove themselves. Physical endeavour offers the readiest means of satisfying this longing, but the effect on each boy goes deeper than improvement in physique, so noticeable during the course.

Individual improvement is looked for, not superiority over others. The opponents, if any, are wind and wave, hunger and cold, Nature deceptively tame one moment and ferocious the next – to be faced up to calmly, without bravado.

The aim of the Outward Bound movement might be summarized as follows:

To produce fit youngsters, enjoying 'a new conception of physical well-being . . . by living under training conditions for one month with carefully graduated exercise under competent supervision'. . . .

To produce good citizens, responsive to 'the obligation of service to others, which can best be inspired by the experience of subordinating self to a greater cause'. . . .

To produce dedicated leaders, 'with strengthened moral fibre and Christian ideals . . . in an atmosphere charged with high and Christian purpose . . . free from sectarian bias'.

A. ARNOLD-BROWN, *Unfolding Character*, p. 122, Routledge & Kegan Paul, 1962

For discussion
1 Is physical training the first step on the road to character training?
2 Can you discern any differences between the aims and methods of Outward Bound and those of organized sport in schools?

II

In the Secondary Modern school where I work we discovered that pupils had very much more physical energy and endurance than any of us had imagined. Pupils under fourteen, for example, made a record crossing of the Mamore Mountains, knocking two hours off the previous (adult) time, and then after supper in Glen Nevis hostel played hide and seek. We wondered if their other abilities had been similarly under-estimated. In a subject like art, where the confidence hadn't been knocked out of them by primary school experience, they created outstanding work. In English, they lacked confidence. There are some indications that if we could give to them the confidence in the use of a pen that they have in the use of a brush, they could produce creative written work. Is it possible that the curriculum has been deliberately designed to give the majority of pupils a poor opinion of themselves and thereby to encourage them to take no active, responsible part in the running of the country, but to leave it to the minority élite? It would be difficult to prove that. But it is not difficult to prove that, at any rate, the Establishment isn't taking any very determined steps radically to alter this scheme of things. It is content to leave things very much as they are.

Orwell pointed out that ultimately our science and technology would suffer 'because scientific and technical progress depended on the empirical habit of thought, which could not survive in a strictly regimented society'. Thus we can expect that only when the present school regimentation affects our technical progress will there be official support for some limited educational experiment.

R. F. MACKENZIE, 'On Our Way – to 1984' in *New Education*, January 1967

For discussion

1 A headmaster who has tried to organize his school on Outward Bound lines complains bitterly that he has been frustrated by the Establishment – we leave it to you to decide what he means by that – all along the line. His school is now threatened with closure. Is his complaint justified? Is our schools system so enslaved by the need to gain examination results that it cares little or nothing for character training? Are we underestimating the capacities of the mass of children for 'adventure', 'discovery', 'leadership', 'resourcefulness', etc.?

2 'Is it possible that the curriculum has been deliberately designed to give the majority of pupils a poor opinion of themselves?' Well, *is* it?

12

Mental tests, as the term is generally understood, are concerned . . . entirely with cognitive abilities. But nature does more for a child than provide him with an intellect of a particular pattern, there are also his emotional and hormic characteristics. Circumstances no doubt produce effects – favourable or un-favourable – upon these, just as they influence the history of his cognitive powers; but in so far as they are part of his endowment at birth, they constitute what is spoken of as his 'temperament'. Temperament is too often confused with character, but the two names should be kept for different ideas. Character is largely what a person makes of his temperament, just as the learning he may acquire is what he makes out of his cognitive abilities.

SIR PERCY NUNN, *Education. Its Data and First Principles*, pp. 131–2, Arnold, 1930

For discussion

'Character is largely what a person makes of his temperament.' Is this another way of saying that, 'Every man must carve his own statue'?

13

Wisdom and Spirit of the universe!
Thou Soul that art the eternity of thought,
That givest to forms and images a breath
And everlasting motion, not in vain
By day or star-light thus from my first dawn
Of childhood didst thou intertwine for me
The passions that build up our human soul;
Not with the mean and vulgar works of man,
But with high objects, with enduring things –
With life and nature – purifying thus
The elements of feeling and of thought,
And sanctifying, by such discipline,
Both pain and fear, until we recognise
A grandeur in the beatings of the heart.
Nor was this fellowship vouchsafed to me
With stinted kindness. In November days
When vapours rolling down the valley made
A lonely scene more lonesome, among woods
At noon and 'mid the calm of summer nights,
When, by the margin of the trembling lake,
Beneath the gloomy hills homeward I went
In solitude, such intercourse was mine;
Mine was it in the fields both day and night,
And by the waters all the summer long,
And in the frosty season, when the sun
Was set, and visibly for many a mile
The cottage windows blazed through twilight gloom,
I heeded not their summons: happy time
It was indeed for all of us – for me
It was a time of rapture! Clear and loud
The village clock tolled six – I wheeled about,
Proud and exulting like an untired horse
That cares not for his home. All shod with steel,
We hissed along the polished ice in games
Confederate, imitative of the chase
And woodland pleasures, – the resounding horn,
The pack loud chiming, and the hunted hare.
So through the darkness and the cold we flew,
And not a voice was idle; with the din
Smitten, the precipices rang aloud;
The leafless trees and every icy crag
Tinkled like iron; while far distant hills
Into the tumult sent an alien sound
Of melancholy not unnoticed, while the stars
Eastward were sparkling clear, and in the west
The orange sky of evening died away.

WILLIAM WORSDWORTH, 'The Prelude', Book 1,
lines 401–46

For discussion

As a romantic poet, Wordsworth's character was shaped by boyhood experiences in a Lake Country setting – 'with high objects, with enduring things'. Today, most children grow up surrounded by 'the mean and vulgar works of man'. What, then, of 'the passions that built up our human soul'?

14

It would be remarkable for anyone who ever learnt from Budge to forget the experience. He usually taught, not from the dais, but from the floor of the class-room and with an un-English amount of sweeping gesture and personal involvement. To deviate from his subject, by way of illustrating it, was his rule. Again and again he would recur to certain characters whom he specially admired. There was Queen Victoria, saying to the timid girl at the dinner-table: 'When you've *quite* finished your grapes, shall we retire to the drawing-room?' 'Wasn't it terrible?' he would ask, passionately seeking our identification with his own awestruck admiration for the Queen. Or there was 'old Jesse Boot, the first Lord Trent', a fellow Nottinghamian, 'who built up Boots the Chemists while lying on his back in a darkened room'. Few of Budge's pupils, probably, have ever verified this information but it is impossible for them to forget it.

c. DILKE, *Dr Moberley's Mint-Mark, A Study of
Winchester College*, pp. 140–1, Heinemann, 1965

For discussion

Can it be that the teacher who is most likely to influence the character of his pupils is the one who is himself a 'bit of a character'? And what does this memorable attribute involve – eccentricity – style – panache – histrionics?

15 Discipline and moral character

Lack of discipline, in the sense of inconsistent parental control, produces only poor character, whether that discipline be lenient or severe. Severe, autocratic discipline, consistently applied, produces children who 'toe the mark', but in a blind, unthinking way; and they usually end up feeling more hostile than friendly toward people in general, even if they do not allow themselves to act in an openly antagonistic manner.

By contrast, parental control which is at once consistent, trustful of the child, and allows him to practice making decisions together with the rest of his family – this produces mature, genuinely self-disciplined moral behavior. The parents who use this kind of discipline are rarely or never severe about it, and some of them are very lenient in their control without adverse effect on the child's behavior. This, in short, appears to be the best kind of discipline, and appears to be the only effective way to produce children of wholly mature, rational, self-disciplined morality.

In short, love and discipline are *both* essential, joint determinants of good character. From the present evidence, it appears that the only sure way to rear children with the best kind of character is by a combination of mature love and mature, permissive, but consistently guiding discipline.

R. F. PECK and R. J. HAVIGHURST, *The Psychology of Character Development*, p. 124, Wiley, 1960

For discussion
'It appears that the only way to rear children with the best kind of character is by a combination of mature love and mature, permissive, but consistently guiding discipline.' Is this a question-begging statement?

16

As an example of 'mature love' and 'permissive but consistently guiding discipline' you may like to consider the following incident which occurred in Homer Lane's 'Little Commonwealth', a reformatory for delinquent children:

I was sitting beside (Jason) at tea on the day following one of his attempts to run away. He was surly and unhappy and did not respond to my efforts to cheer him up.

'What's the matter, Jason?' I asked.

'Ugh! Rotten hole, this,' he replied sulkily.

'What's wrong with it?'

'I dunno'. Everything!'

'Well – why don't you get out – run away again?'

'No use. I always get caught,' he replied hopelessly.

'Why not try something new, then?' I asked. 'You've got fellows behind you. Why don't you organize them and get control of the next election of officers and reorganize things so you will like the Commonwealth?'

Jason glanced suspiciously at me. Was I chipping him?

'I'd just like to run this place, I would,' he declared aggressively.

Here was my chance. He had expressed a wish! 'Just what would you do first?' I asked. This I knew would be a poser for him, as regressive unhappiness has its source in the unconscious. Jason flushed with the exertion of trying to find an answer to my question, and he looked about the room desperately to find some inspiration, while his admiring friends at the table gaped with interest in the conversation. Finally his eyes dropped in confusion and his cup and saucer furnished inspiration.

'I'd smash up these fussy dishes,' he declared.

'Why?' I asked mildly.

M

'Oh, they're for women and la-de-da boys. Who wants pretty things like this?' he sneered, holding up his gaily coloured leadless glazed cup.

'Well, that's easy enough,' I declared cheerfully. 'Why not smash them up?'

Jason was angry, feeling cornered.

'D'yer dare me to smash my cup?' he demanded threateningly.

'Certainly,' I replied cordially. 'I want you to be happy here in the Commonwealth. If smashing dishes will bring that about, go ahead!'

'Don't you dare me,' he threatened, 'or I'll do it.'

Taking the poker from the hearth I laid it on the table.

'It's up to you,' I said.

'Go on, Jason, smash it,' cried a boy across the table, excitedly.

Jason seized the poker and struck the cup, shattering it to pieces.

His friends cheered.

'Now that's a sensible thing to do,' I said cordially. 'It's no good grousing about things you don't like. Always try to improve them by doing something,' and I placed my cup and saucer in front of him.

'Here's another.'

Again the poker descended.

'And another.'

Crash! But now Jason looked distressed. He had shattered a constellation[1] as well as the dishes. Murmurs of disapproval were heard from the other citizens, addressed to me.

'You're making him do it,' they accused.

'Oh, yes,' I agreed, 'I'm helping Jason improve the Commonwealth so he will like being here.' I pushed a plate towards Jason. 'Go ahead, old man, don't mind those chaps.'

Half-heartedly he again struck the dish, saying weakly, 'It ain't the dishes, but you dared me to smash them!' His authority-dishes constellation was now dissolved. The pile of broken crockery on the table was symbolic of one of the ideals which he had cherished from childhood, and which had made him a nuisance to society.

Jason was in evident distress, having unconsciously learned a great truth that there is no fun in destroying things if one is allowed to do so. Primitive curiosity supplies the motive for destruction.

Jason's friends now came to the rescue. They took the poker away from him and pulled him away from the table. In spite of my remonstrance they held him protectingly while they accused me of inciting him to make a fool of himself. 'Besides,' they said, 'the dishes belong to the family. You've no right to dare him to smash them.'

This was true. But, now to my dismay, Jason had recovered his nerve. In the

[1] Constellation. Lane seems to have used this word when he wished to refer to a complex, of a sentiment, or indeed any group of affect-charged associated ideas, whether conscious or unconscious.

midst of his sympathetic friends his communal instincts came to his rescue, and he now stood triumphant, a hero in his own eyes and in those of his followers. The situation was critical and much more complicated than I had foreseen. I now had a more difficult psychological problem to solve, because a new constellation had appeared in which the group ideal played a very important part. Jason was now a hero – a leader of men by reason of his reckless daring, and if matters had been left at that point the results would have been serious.

I accepted the situation. 'You are right. I am sorry about those dishes. I'll replace them,' I said, as I rose from the table. 'I thought Jason disliked the Commonwealth because of nice dishes.'

'It wasn't that, but you dared me,' said he, 'I always take a dare. I'm no coward.'

'Hear, hear!' approved the group.

I realized that this was one of the most dangerous sentiments that society can be affected with; the foundation upon which great conflicts between nations are developed.

'I'd like to see that worked out, old man,' said I, pleasantly. 'I had never thought of cowardice in that sense. It's interesting. Here's my watch, Jason. I dare you to smash it.' I placed the watch in his hand.

The lad looked at the watch and glanced round the room at the anxious faces of his friends in indecision. After a moment's hesitation his expression changed to one of desperation. He raised the watch as if to dash it into the hearth, and glanced at me hoping that I should at the last moment exercise authority and thereby leave him falsely victorious in the possession of his cherished constellations. The moment's hesitation brought the real Jason to the surface. He lowered his hand and placed the watch on the table safe. 'No, I won't smash your watch,' he said, with an attempt at good-natured generosity to cover his embarrassment. The tensity of the group relaxed with relief.

'But I dare you,' I challenged.

'No, I won't do it,' he snapped.

'But you're no coward,' I encouraged.

Jason realized that he was in a tight corner. His expression disclosed the conflict that raged within him between his old ideal of braggart boastfulness imposed upon him by unsympathetic surroundings and the real nature of boyhood gentleness.

'Come on out of here, Jas,' urged one of his friends, taking his arm and leading the distressed boy away.

As they left the room an impressive silence pervaded the group of citizens who had taken part in the scene, broken firmly by Bill the wag, who remarked with finality, 'That's done it . . .' And it had! The next morning Jason presented himself at the office and asked sheepishly if he could have work in the carpenter's shop. 'Why, what's happened, Jason, that you now wish to learn carpentry?' I asked.

The lad flushed with embarrassment. Then he smiled, and with a humorous twinkle in his eyes said confidently, 'Oh, I've just got to earn extra money to pay for them dishes you bust last night.' Jason became the best carpenter in the Community, and finally was elected Judge of the Citizen's Court, over which he presided with unusual ability. He enlisted in the Army when old enough, and spent all his leave at the Commonwealth. A valuable member of society was lost when he was killed in France.

W. DAVID WILLS, *Homer Lane*, pp. 141–4,
Allen & Unwin, 1964

For discussion

1 'Here was my chance,' says Lane. How far does the teacher's success in training character depend upon recognizing the 'psychological moment' and acting upon it? How can this recognition best be fostered? – through courses on developmental psychology – through case studies – through contacts with 'difficult' children – or what?

2 'I accepted the situation,' says Lane. What do you think of the way he handled it?

3 A. S. Neill, himself a disciple of Homer Lane, makes the following comment on the incident described in the above extract:

'He made things too simple. When he encouraged Jabez (*sic*) to smash cups and saucers and then his gold watch, Jabez threw down the poker and rushed off in tears. Lane claimed that this incident released the boy's inhibitions, that they came stumbling out in a rush. I don't believe it. There is no such thing as a dramatic cure; every cure takes a long time.'

A. S. NEILL, *Talking of Summerhill*, p. 129,
Gollancz, 1967

Do you agree?

4 Is all character training a form of therapy? – and is the average teacher equipped to undertake it?

17 The character types as a scale of psychosocial maturation

Anyone familiar with the Freudian theory of personality development will recognize the close parallel of the present typology with that theory of stages in psychosocial maturation (Rickman, 1951). When one is dealing with adolescents or adults, the use of a genetic sequence of stages to account for present behavior is, of course, an analogy. It has some real truth in it, but it also involves an oversimplification of the facts. To begin with, though, it may be useful to talk as if the types really do correspond to developmental stages.

The *Amoral* type is a person with infantile, inaccurate perceptions; infantlike emotional lability; and infantile inability to control himself in a way adequate to the demands of ordinary social living. Since he has not accepted the basic premise of human society that one must consider other people, he is infantlike in his lack of effectual moral principles. He is contradictory, inconsistent, antagonistic, and often openly hostile in his behavior.

The *Expedient* type is one who has come to terms with society in a way; but his way is that of the young child who conforms in order to avoid adult punishment or disapproval. He has no more accepted the premise of active regard for others than the Amoral person. If the punishments have been impressive enough, he may have internalized a few 'Don't's'; but he has few or no positive moral directives within him. Like a child, he is short-sighted, does not look ahead to foresee the long-range consequences of his behavior, even though this omission may thwart the very purpose of self-gratification he has in mind. He is not so well in control of himself, either, nor so well-integrated, that he can always do the 'smart thing' even if intellectually he knows what it is. While he keeps his impulses in check in order to get along without trouble, his inner emotional reactions are frequently as inappropriate as a child's, though they are not the overwhelming elations and rages of the infant. He does not always succeed in maintaining consistent adaptation even in his surface behavior, since at times, his negativistic, basically hostile feelings toward society break through his rather weak self-control.

The *Conforming* type is like a child who has come to accept the dictates of his family and society in a placid, uncritical way. He goes along passively with the social and moral rules in a rather literal way. His acceptance is positive, if mild, for he has more liking than resentment in his general outlook on the world. He is not capable of very complicated, rational thought, or at least has never learned to exercise it. He has intrinsically rather weak powers of self-direction, depending instead on the guidance of the people and the rules of the world he knows. He has incorporated many of these rules. He lives with and by them rather comfortably, for he does not have too many contrary impulses to occasion guilt or distrust of himself. Like the older child, he knows how to live peacefully in his familiar world, does not ask too many questions about its fundamental traditions, and more or less takes them for granted as absolutes. He lives in the heteronomous stage which Piaget ascribed to the years of middle childhood.

The *Irrational–Conscientious* type is as much like a child in his own way. He, too, lives by absolute rules. However, he has found himself forced to internalize them much more completely than the Conformer. He has a good deal of active hostility to be controlled, and since he accepts the dominance of society, he feels bound to control himself. His principles seem mainly to consist of 'Don'ts' (at least in the subjects in this study, and perhaps necessarily, in any such dynamic pattern). They are firmly organized, however, and rule his behavior. He is not emotionally capable of questioning his conscience or asking if it always serves a genuinely moral purpose. He does not have the freedom to perceive life whole, nor to act on rational assessment of particular situations, even if he wanted to. His superego is much stronger than the rest of his wishes and drives. It controls him, and there is not much he can do to modify or change it. In any case, it is not possible for him to seriously consider doing this. In his own way, he is no more autonomous than the Conformer. In a real sense his parents are still running his life almost completely, for he carries their injunctions around within him and heeds them constantly.

The *Rational–Altruistic* type is a continuously maturing person. He has not reached a level and stopped there for life. Instead, all his capacities are constantly and effectively at work to improve his own well-being and to promote the interests of his society, in which he takes a lively interest. He is in as full, rational control of himself as it is possible for a human to be. There is no particular age level which he represents, except that he is what is hoped for in the genuinely mature adult. As an adolescent, he does not have the wisdom of an adult; but he shows the certain promise of attaining it.

R. F. PECK and R. J. HAVIGHURST, *The Psychology of Character Development*, pp. 98–9, Wiley, 1960

For discussion

1 Broadly speaking, the five types of character outlined correspond to the stages of growth from birth to maturity. The suggestion is that many people never reach the fifth stage. 'His behaviour is quite childish,' we often say. 'Fifty-year-old adolescents' is another phrase you will recall.

Does this mean that many are incapable of 'intellectual virtue' (as Aristotle thought) or are their personal inadequacies due to faulty upbringing?

II

Examinations, Tests, Evaluation

Just as questions about aims ('What ought I to do?') carry with them questions of method ('How can I do it?') so, in turn, we are faced with questions of evaluation – 'How am I and my pupils doing?' Whether we call it examining, testing, or evaluating, teaching necessitates some form of regular feedback from the learner.

The unexamined life is not worth living – or so Socrates maintained. Harassed students may well feel tempted to retort that the examined life, at any rate as it is lived nowadays, is not worth living either! Education, they say, has become an obstacle race – 11-plus, O-levels, A-levels, and all that – in which the art of passing examinations increasingly tends to become an end in itself. For their part, teachers are often made to feel that the success of their efforts is gauged solely by the examination results they obtain. Many complain bitterly that examination requirements leave them too little room for manoeuvre, that they are tied hand and foot to a prescribed syllabus. At the same time, the demand for all kinds of paper qualifications continues to escalate; and in the Educated Society, we are told, only the qualified person can expect to achieve status.

In this situation, inevitably, most discussions of the pros and cons lead only to a conclusion in which nothing much is concluded: examinations are a necessary evil, apparently, and there is really nothing we can do about them. In an attempt to avoid such fence-sitting, the following readings have been arranged so as to form a sequence, beginning with frankly destructive criticism and leading on to viewpoints which indicate that the function of examinations is, in fact, changing – and that any discussion about them is bound to be unsatisfactory unless it takes into consideration the whole field of educational assessment.

We suggest that you should read each extract in turn and discuss the appended questions before going on to the next one. In this way you may be led to agree that Socrates was right after all. With luck you may even go farther and decide that for teacher and pupil alike the unexamined life is an educational impossibility!

Examinations: the end of education?

I

Criticism, it is said, should be constructive. The following criticisms are not constructive at all: I can think of no sovereign remedy for the evil I propose to attack – the examination system as at present practised in England. Not only do people have to pass more and more examinations than ever before, but more and more value is set on their results. This does more and more harm.

I notice it most at the University of Oxford, for it is there that I live and work. Of course, examinations always did bulk large in Oxford life, and students to worry about them too much. But in my young days they were not encouraged to do so by the wiser among their teachers. A distinguished professor once said to a pupil about his final examinations: 'Remember that there are two days of judgement and that that of the Oxford final examination is the less important of the two.' His sternest and most distinguished fellow teachers took the same view.

Now this has changed. Most modern university teachers think that a colleague who does not teach with his eye on the examination is irresponsible. University magazines publish tables comparing the results obtained by different colleges, by public and State schoolboys, by men and by women.

The effect is wholly bad. For one thing it undermines the student's morale. Every year a number break down. On the larger number who remain sane, the effect is different, but almost as deleterious. For they learn to be permanently bored by the subject they have studied. Naturally so; during three years they have been taught to approach it from the wrong angle. A subject is interesting only if it is studied for its own sake. And a teacher who is aware of this will make it his first aim to stir his pupils' genuine interest. He will therefore vary his approach to the subject to suit each pupil's particular mind and temperament, so that each may be inspired to explore the subject on his own. But a teacher cannot do this if he is thinking all the time of future examinations papers. He has to make the pupil concentrate on the aspects of his subject about which he is likely to get questions, even if these do not appeal to him; and to neglect those that do so appeal, if they are unlikely to figure largely in the papers. No wonder the pupil gets bored.

But worse. He is corrupted too. At a crucial phase in his development he is encouraged to think that nothing is quality that best achieves it. The consequence is to make him cynical about university education. The present generation of undergraduates are just as intelligent and well-intentioned as those of the past. But I notice that they are more disillusioned about the value of education. This is because they have not cultivated the faculty of disinterested study. Over 50 years ago Thomas Huxley said of some of his pupils: 'They work to pass, not to know; and outraged science takes her revenge. They do pass and they don't know.' If this was true then, it is truer now. . . .

The modern stress on examination results not only discourages and corrupts:

it is also inefficient in achieving its aim, namely to see that the most gifted gets the best chance. I must refer once more to Oxford; for it is the place I know best. In the past 50 years it has produced an enormous proportion of distinguished persons in different walks of life; statesmen, lawyers, diplomats, poets, novelists. All bear the mark of their university and most would say that they owe a great deal to her. But not more than a third of them at most did outstandingly well in examinations. Their interests were too varied and they had too much independent initiative to concentrate exclusively on their studies. The type of pupil that did tended to have less original energy: with the result that though they did well in the examinations, their subsequent careers have been an uninspiring spectacle. Worthy academics and civil servants, they are not among those who have made Oxford famous. If Oxford concentrates on producing more and more of them and fewer and fewer of the intelligent but less examination-minded, it will lose its eminence. If the process goes on all over England, England will lose its eminence, too.

The odd thing is that this trend is against the trend of modern educational theory, which is opposed to trial by examination. We are always hearing of the harm done by the 11-plus examination, of the dreadful way it strains a child's nerves and weakens his natural interests. But the same thing is true of examinations at 15-plus and 18-plus and 21-plus. It is time educationists began campaigning against them.

LORD DAVID CECIL,
Weekend Telegraph, November 1966

For discussion
No doubt you will be thinking that Lord David Cecil has overstated his case, possibly deliberately.

Do you agree that examinations are in danger of becoming a cult, and that the present system is in need of radical reform? If so, you may like to indicate some of the forms which such a reform might profitably take.

2

The intentions of the new CSE, which arose out of the report of the Beloe Committee of 1960, are honourable. The exam is aimed at 16-year-olds who at present leave school without any kind of nationally-approved testimonial, to show their prospective employers what they have achieved. At the same time, the opportunity is being taken to make these examinations the outcome of more exciting and relevant curriculums.

What is most remarkable about this month's inauguration, however, is that it marks a radical departure by the teachers themselves from the spirit of the 1944 Education Act, which sought to abolish examinations for at least all those who were not concerned with a university career, as well as Sir David Eccles' strongly-worded circular 289 eleven years later, in which the Minister said emphatically: 'all examinations restrict to some extent the teacher's freedom'.

The justifications for this, highly expensive, operation (with teachers to-ing and fro-ing all over the country on subject panel groups) are flimsy. It is claimed that employers are demanding a national measure of competence. Yet there is no evidence that in the CSE, their alleged demands are being met. Quite the contrary. The regional boards are spending a good deal of time 'selling' the CSE to employers, and explaining its intricacies to them.

It is also claimed that parental pressures demanded some piece of paper for their children to wave upon leaving school. This sort of pressure, if it existed, ought to have been resisted if it could not be justified on educational grounds. And there are ample reasons for believing that, on those grounds, the CSE will prove a dangerous innovation.

By being based on subject examinations (some schools are offering as little as one subject in the Certificate), it introduces specialisation into schools which until now have been free from these false pressures. By once again sub-dividing education in this way, it virtually ensures that all-round education will be discarded in favour of individual grades. Worst of all, it sets up yet another artificial barrier in the education system.

By 1970, between four and five million children will be involved to some degree in the CSE. Above them will be the GCE O Level students. Above these the GCE A Level scholars, and beyond these the undergraduates. At the bottom of this pyramid there will emerge a large body of children who, already labelled Eleven Plus failures, can now also assume the tag of 'unexaminables'.

As the elaborate juggernaut of the CSE begins to bundle forward this month, it may seem too late to protest at its creation. The fact remains that it represents a false god. Another hurdle has been created in an education system that already resembles a Grand National course. And unlike horses, who may be shot if seriously injured, children carry the scars of combat all their lives.

New Education (Editorial), December 1965

For discussion

1 Is the Certificate of Secondary Education merely a piece of paper for children to wave upon leaving school?
2 Is it true that the Certificate marks 'a radical departure by the teachers themselves from the spirit of the 1944 Education Act'? Are they guilty of following false gods?

3

The VALIDITY of an examination or test may be defined as the degree to which it measures what it is intended to measure. Its RELIABILITY may be defined as the consistency with which it does this.

A common criticism is that most examinations fall short of both these desiderata. Being so subjective, the marks awarded by individual examiners, particularly in subjects like essay-writing, are liable to the wildest fluctuations. Not only that, but the assessments made by different examining boards sometimes fail to average-out these discrepancies, with the result that the assessments fail to agree. Hartog and Rhodes ('The Examination of Examination') report the case of an experiment in which two experienced and distinguished boards of examiners were asked to adjudicate among candidates for the Civil Service and award a prize of £100 to the best one. This was done *viva voce*, the aim being to test 'alertness, intelligence and general outlook'. The maximum mark was 300.

The order in which the candidates were placed is shown below:

Candidate	Board 1 marks	Board 2 marks	Board 1 order	Board 2 order
1	120	212	15	11
2	260	190	1	13
3	130	175	14	$15\frac{1}{2}$
4	230	255	4*	2
5	210	232	$8\frac{1}{2}$	$7\frac{1}{2}$
6	180	250	12	3
7	200	270	11	1
8	240	224	2	9
9	230	220	4*	10
10	210	235	$8\frac{1}{2}$	6
11	210	236	$8\frac{1}{2}$	5
12	230	232	4*	$7\frac{1}{2}$
13	120	177	$15\frac{1}{2}$	14
14	210	247	$8\frac{1}{2}$	4
15	220	193	6	12
16	170	175	13	$15\frac{1}{2}$

* Three candidates bracketed equal.

For discussion
Study the two sets of marks and the two orders of merit and say which candidate, in your opinion, should have been awarded the prize.

In general, what conclusions would you draw as regards (*a*) the validity and (*b*) the reliability of this examination?

Note that the candidate placed first by Board 1 is placed 13th by Board 2, and the candidate placed first by Board 2 is placed 11th by Board 1.

The prize was awarded to candidate No. 4.

4

In another experiment the examiners were asked to assign numerical marks with a maximum of 100, and also to assign a class to each candidate in accordance with the following scheme:

Class 1 – 67 marks and over
Class 2 – 50 marks to 66 marks
Class 3 – 33 marks to 49 marks
Class 4 – under 33 marks

The numerical marks varied considerably. The range of the marks allotted to candidates varied from 7 to 36, and the average range was 19·6 per cent. The extreme cases are shown below:

	Examiners					
	A	B	C	D	E	
Candidate			Marks awarded			Range
No. 25	60	32	65	50	68	36
No. 1	45	38	20	55	20	35
No. 40	40	44	70	75	50	35

The averages of the marks awarded by the different examiners, on the other hand, were close together. They were as follows:

A, 51·9,   B, 52·7,   C, 54·8,   D, 54·0,   E, 50·6.

The following table shows the statistical distribution of classes by the various examiners:

Examiner	1st Class	2nd Class	3rd Class	4th Class
A	7	24	15	4
B	8	23	14	5
C	5	29	15	1
D	2	34	12	2
E	5	26	14	5

HARTOG and RHODES, *The Examination of Examination,*
Macmillan

For discussion
Comment on these 'results' (*a*) as regards the reliance to be placed on any of the individual examiners' assessment, (*b*) as regards the validity of *qualitative* ('Class') assessments as compared with quantitative (numerical) assessments.

5

Another criticism is that the marks awarded in examinations are often quite meaningless.

When the teacher has finished marking a set of examination papers he has a clear idea of the mark 60. If he puts the papers in order of merit and counts down to find the mark of the middle pupil he is only making explicit what was implicit in his mind before. If he goes further and finds the mark of the pupil who is one quarter from the top and bottom respectively, he will get a still clearer picture of the value of 60. In the teacher's marks book the marks retain, at least for a time, their full meaning. Later on they may be transferred to the class teacher's marks register, to a head-teacher's record card and to a parent's progress card. All that is usually entered on the pupil's permanent record is the entry 'English 60'. The collateral information that gave 60 its meaning is thrown away and the head-teacher is left to wonder if a pupil who has scored 60 in English and 60 in history has done equally well in both subjects. He has to go on the assumption that the two marks are equal, although only by chance will this be true. It is a serious matter that marks in the files of the head-teacher, on which the final assessment of the pupils for educational and vocational guidance or other external purposes is based, should be so lacking in exact specification.

In some secondary schools, in addition to the pupil's mark, the class average or the pupil's place in the order of merit is given against each subject in the report to parents. Even so, it will not be an easy task for the parent to decide how much better or worse 60 in English is than 60 in history. Here is a term report for a pupil from a secondary school:

Subject	Mark	Class average
English	61	58
History	70	52
Geography	70	52
Arithmetic	46	48
Algebra	55	56
Geometry	71	63
Science	62	63
French	50	40
Latin	72	68
Art	58	57

What is the parent to make of the fact that in this report the class average mark in French is 40 and in Latin 68? The teacher of Latin knows that he has set a comparatively easy paper and the French teacher recognises that his paper has been too stiff; the head-teacher may come to the conclusion (quite unwarrantedly) that the class is better at Latin than at French or that it is a way these two teachers have of marking which he must keep in mind when forming a judgment. The parent, however, taking the figures at their face value, will come to the conclusion that the French teacher is a poor teacher.'

> D. M. MCINTOSH *et al.*, *The Scaling of Teachers' Marks and Estimates*, pp. 5–7, Oliver & Boyd, 1949

For discussion
What practical precautions can the teacher take to ensure that the marks he awards are reasonably fair to all concerned?

6

It seems that differences in opinion as to relative merit are bound to arise no matter how carefully designed the examination procedure is.

The most important source of unreliability . . . is the personal element which enters into every examiner's evaluation of a script. We will first summarise some of the evidence regarding this subjectivity. The classical experiments were carried out in America as far back as 1912. Starch and Elliott (1913) sent copies of a single geometry paper to the chief geometry teachers of 116 high schools, with the request that they should mark it in accordance with their usual practice. The marks awarded varied all the way from 28% to 92%. Two of the teachers gave it more than 90%, 18 gave it between 80% and 90%, 18 gave it between 60% and 30% and 2 under 30%. Similar results were obtained with papers in English and history. Equally striking is the anecdote related by Wood (1921) of the papers which were marked in the usual way by six examiners. The first examiner, for his own guidance, wrote out a set of (what he regarded as) model answers to the questions; but he unfortunately left this among the candidates' papers. He was subsequently awarded marks varying from 40% to 90% by the five other examiners! Many experiments, conducted under far more strictly controlled conditions than these, have substantially confirmed their findings.

Another example will be quoted which better illustrates the subjectivity of marking under ordinary school conditions. Boyd (1924) collected large numbers of essays on 'A Day at the Seaside' from 11-year Scottish school-children (i.e. children at the qualifying stage). From these he selected 26 as representing the whole range of merit, and had them marked independently by 271 teachers. The marks were not numerical, but consisted of seven grades, ranging from Excellent to Unsatisfactory. On comparing the results of the different markers, it was found that almost every essay received at least 6 of the 7 possible grades. The following instance is typical: 3 teachers marked it Excellent; 31 VG plus; 80 VG; 125 G plus; and 4 marked it moderate (the lowest grade but one). Boyd shows that part of the discrepancy was due to differing standards. But even when the 20% most lenient markers and the 20% most severe were excluded, the average essay was still awarded at least 4 out of the 7 grades.

P. E. VERNON, *The Measurement of Abilities*, pp. 203–5,
University of London Press, 2nd edition 1956

For discussion

At this point we have an interesting experiment which members of the group can easily carry out for themselves. Each student has to write a short paragraph on a selected topic, say the Comprehensive school – a class essay will do equally well if time does not allow of the writing being done on the spot. Each paragraph or essay is then read quickly and given a mark by all the other members in the group, taking care to see that the marks remain concealed. The scripts are handed round from one to another until each has been marked several times. The game can be played out within the hour and can be very revealing, especially when (as sometimes happens) the writer finds that the assessments of his 'effort' made by fellow students vary from A to D on a five-point scale.

How unreliable can we teachers get?

7

Towards the end of last term the Head suddenly asked for the examination marks of 12 Fourth Form boys who came from the parish of Hardgrind.

Hardgrind's greatest son, for many years the chairman of our school governors, had endowed a prize to be awarded to the Fourth Form boy from his parish who showed the best academic promise. 'I want these boys to take the same eight subjects; I want all the subjects to be given equal esteem, and I want them all marked out of a 100.' The staff were agreed that this was a reasonable idea, and were full of admiration at this evidence of perspicacity in their late chairman.

The marks were collected and totted up as follows:

					Subject					
	Boy	A	B	C	D	E	F	G	H	
1	Smith	80	50	80	50	25	60	32	42	= 419
2	Baxter	95	70	15	80	40	40	30	48	= 418
3	Crawford	50	80	65	20	70	55	34	40	= 414
4	Adams	81	60	30	60	60	36	44	42	= 413
5	Jones	94	20	75	50	50	30	47	46	= 412
6	Brown	60	90	20	75	30	45	45	46	= 411
7	Green	100	40	40	70	20	40	52	48	= 410
8	Tinker	10	75	50	55	30	60	56	45	= 381
9	Hardy	31	30	60	70	48	35	55	50	= 379
10	James	80	10	50	25	30	70	50	55	= 370
11	Lloyd	20	80	30	30	40	55	60	52	= 367
12	Samson	70	25	10	50	40	50	55	60	= 360

Everyone agreed that justice had been done and that Samson, like his more famous predecessor, deserved his crushing defeat. Suddenly, however, Snowball, the Head of the Science Department, said that he had read or heard somewhere about the effects of the spread of marks. 'Haven't we here a spread of 90 marks in one subject and 20 in another? Can we justly say that we are holding the subjects in equal esteem when we allow such discrepancies to happen! I've no idea how to adjust the marks, but Stoutfellow should be able to help us. I've little doubt, however, that it will make no worthwhile difference in the result.'

That night Stoutfellow, the head of the Maths Department, adjusted the marks so as to give all subjects the same spread, and the order came out as follows:

Boy	Subject								
	A	B	C	D	E	F	G	H	
1 Samson	67	19	0	50	40	50	83	100	= 409
2 Lloyd	11	88	29	17	40	63	100	60	= 408
3 James	78	9	57	8	20	100	67	75	= 405
4 Hardy	23	25	71	83	56	13	83	50	= 404
5 Tinker	0	81	57	58	20	75	87	25	= 403
6 Green	100	38	43	83	0	25	73	40	= 402
7 Brown	56	100	14	92	20	38	50	30	= 400
8 Jones	93	13	93	50	60	0	57	30	= 396
9 Adams	79	63	29	67	80	15	47	10	= 390
10 Crawford	44	88	79	0	100	63	13	0	= 387
11 Baxter	94	75	7	100	40	25	0	40	= 381
12 Smith	78	50	100	50	10	75	7	10	= 380

'Why!' exclaimed the head of the Modern Languages Department, 'this exactly inverts the order in the first place. My utter faith in the efficacy and the reliability of marks is thoroughly shaken. To think that I was once responsible for getting the Head to give a boy a sharp thrashing because he was bottom of my form. I have become a sheep without a shepherd.'

'This will shake to its foundation the very basis of all assessment of academic progress from the 11+ exam to the award of state scholarships. Never again will I believe a mark list,' muttered sadly the usually ebullient head of the English Department.

'The fundamental Law of Indeterminacy of subatomic Physics seems to apply to mark lists. Chaos has once again come back to its own,' learnedly commented our Physics expert.

The A.M.A., Journal of the Incorporated Association of Assistant Masters in Secondary Schools, November 1958, quoted in R. L. BOWLEY, Teaching Without Tears, Centaur Press, 1967

For discussion

This is a hypothetical case, of course, and an extreme one. Allowing for this, are there any reasons for thinking that the second order of merit is to be preferred?

8

Commenting on attempts to shock the public conscience with regards to examinations, Professor P. E. Vernon has this to say:

The present writer is more impressed by the smallness than by the largeness of the discrepancies, and would conclude from his study of the results that important public examinations, like the School Certificate and university honours, are marked much more consistently than is usually the case. Instead of laying their chief emphasis on the extreme discrepancies, the authors might have pointed out that the median disagreement between any two examiners is not more than 3% in the best-conducted examinations. Since this figure represents the Probable Error of an examinee's mark a few examinees will naturally show discrepancies four or five times as large. It represents an average correlation between different examiners of 0·80, when the standard deviation of their marks is 10%. And decidedly lower figures have been obtained by other investigators.

Nevertheless . . . it indicates that many less thorough examinations are deplorably unreliable; that in the absence of a scheme of instructions drawn up and applied by experienced examiners, much worse discrepancies may arise; that when the average and the dispersion of marks are not standardised, gross differences may appear in the proportions of Credits, Passes, Fails, etc., which are awarded; and that even a P.E. of 3% may frequently make all the difference between a Pass and a Fail, or a First and a Second Class.

P. E. VERNON, *The Measurement of Abilities*,
University of London Press, 1956

For discussion

Do you agree that a knowledge of statistical procedures plays an essential part in the training of teachers? In what ways can it be helpful? For a start, how about taking the first set of school (or College) examination results and scrutinizing the dispersion of marks.

9

The main complaint made against the baccalaureat system is that far too much 'cramming' is necessary in order to pass. *Le bachotage* is almost the normal occupation of the bright young 17-year-old. The examination has become the

N

necessary passport to success, particularly in the bourgeois family, where failure is seen as a major disaster. Thus school becomes a place for intensive work, with the examination the main obsession.

Accusations of unfairness are as rare as in England, and the pass rate – some 60 per cent of all candidates – hardly varies from one year to another, or from one jury to another. This high percentage of failure – slightly higher than at A-level in England – is surely, however, a massive indictment of the examining system on both sides of the Channel. In Germany, Luxembourg and Holland, to name three neighbouring countries, the rate of failure in the equivalent examinations is only about 10 per cent. This is surely more reasonable: one does not give a young person an expensive secondary education up to the age of 18 only to tell him at the end of it that he has failed to reach a reasonable level of attainment. It is surely more enlightened to see that he abandons a course before it is too late to start another more within his capabilities. This is a line of thought that is becoming more and more prevalent in France, and one that might profitably be pursued in England as well.

The present French system of examination, however, appears to be no more arbitrary in practice than that of the eight English examining boards, whose syllabuses and examining papers must necessarily differ slightly in emphasis and marking, despite their strict regard for accuracy and scrupulous fairness.

The trend in France, as elsewhere on the Continent, is increasingly to regard examinations as tests of verification. Personal confrontation of examiners and candidate, coupled with information about his past performance in school, is becoming increasingly important. The examination will enable the candidate to be 'oriented' correctly towards the next stage of his career, whether this be in employment or in further education. The principle of guidance is being substituted, in fact, for the principle of selection and elimination.

W. D. HALLS, *Society Schools and Progress in France*,
pp. 126, 130–1, Pergamon Press, 1966

For discussion

1 The French authorities, we gather, are now more inclined to take the pupil's past performance into account. What is there to be said in favour of a system of *continuous assessment*? How can teachers' estimates be made more reliable?
2 The baccalaureat, as an external, public examination, is conducted with a strict regard for accuracy and its assessments are generally accepted as fair. Is this confidence misplaced?

10

Particularly striking was a study of the philosophy examination in the Baccalaureat. One hundred scripts were marked by six examiners. Only 10 of the candidates were passed by all the examiners, only 9 failed by all of them. The remaining 71 were passed by some, failed by others.

P. E. VERNON, *The Measurement of Abilities*,
pp. 205-6, University of London Press, 1956

For discussion
Are you still happy about the accuracy of the assessments made in external, public examinations?

II

The general principle for testing the results of teaching may be illustrated further by some of the prohibitions it implies: Distrust the repetition of words as a test of anything more than verbal memory.

Use definitions but never as a sole test; – the power to define may exist without the knowledge of the term and knowledge of a term may exist without the power to define it.

Distrust any one particular kind of problem as a test of appreciation of a law. Distrust especially problems that are familiar or of a well-known type.

Do not take it for granted that the ability to handle certain elements when isolated implies the ability to handle the same elements in complex connections.

Do not test the ability to do one thing by the ability to do something else if a direct test is practicable.

SUMMARY
Testing the results of teaching and study is for the teacher what verification of theories is to the scientist, – the *sine qua non* of sure progress. It is the chief means to fitting teaching to the previous experience and individual capacities of pupils, and to arousing in them the instinct for achievement and the capacity for self-criticism. The test for knowledge, skill, appreciation and morality is in each case appropriate action. A valid test is one in which the response in question (knowledge, or skill or ideal or whatever it may be) and only that response will produce a certain observable result.

E. L. THORNDIKE, *The Principles of Teaching
Based on Psychology*, pp. 263–4, Seiler, 1906

For discussion
1 'Distrust the repetition of words as a test of anything more than verbal memory.' But isn't it a fact that most examinations rely exclusively on repetition of words?
2 'Testing the results of teaching is for the teacher what the verification of

theories is to the scientist.' Tests are used in schools for a wide variety of purposes, as we all know. How would you enumerate these purposes? How do they differ from those of a conventional written examination?

12

We need to distinguish between organizing the curriculum with information or knowledge as the educational objective; between using repetition or discovery as the instructional method; between measuring the number of facts or evaluating the quality of wisdom as the criterion of achievement. We have perhaps already said enough to point to the issues with respect to the curriculum and instructional problem. We have suggested that we may take a sense-perception or an intuitive-perception point of view, we may construct a curriculum focusing on information or on knowledge, we may teach through emphasizing description or inquiry. We should like to say something in addition about the problem of evaluating educational achievement.

The most widely used measure is the so-called objective, standardized, short-answer test. There is no doubt that these tests have had value; but the fact remains that no matter what the curriculum or the objective of instruction, the typical instrument of this kind tends to be overladen with sense-perception and information criteria. To be sure, it can quickly and effectively measure the information a student has acquired. But is this all we need to measure? The issue is not, as it is too often stated, short answers *versus* essay question, objective *versus* subjective tests. Of course we want objective, that is, consistently scored, tests. The issue is not one of method but of substance – not what kind of test but a test of *what*.

If we are to encourage divergent thinking as well as convergent thinking reward discovery as well as memory, we need achievement tests that are appropriate to these outcomes. And if the best we can do is essay tests, then essay tests that can be scored consistently it must be. The alternative is to say that since we cannot measure these educational objectives by short-answer tests, we will avoid the measurement dilemma by not worrying about these objectives, however desirable. We would agree with Guilford, who suggests that if we are to educate for creativity, 'It almost goes without saying that the assessment of achievement should be different from those provided by most current marking practices'.

J. W. GETZELS and P. W. JACKSON, *Creativity and Intelligence*, p. 130, Wiley, 1962

For discussion

1 In the U.S.A. so-called objective tests virtually replace the essay-type examinations which are customary in Britain. What are their advantages? The writers indicate some of the disadvantages of objective tests, but are they insuperable?

2 Read the first sentence in the extract very carefully, with particular reference to the distinction drawn between organizing the curriculum with 'information' or 'knowledge' as the educational objective, and between methods aiming at 'repetition' or 'discovery'. This raises the fundamental question of the *function* of examining and testing.

If the purpose of teaching is to help pupils to 'pass an examination' is it not likely that the emphasis will be on 'information' and 'repetition'? Is there, then, to be no place for methods which encourage 'discovery'?

13

Examinations have many purposes and uses:

to measure pupils' knowledge of facts, principles, definitions, laws, experimental methods, etc.

to measure pupils' understanding of the work of the course.

to show pupils what they have learnt.

to provide pupils with landmarks in their study and checks on their progress.

to make comparisons among pupils, or among teachers, or among schools.

to act as prognostic tests for directing pupils in fast or slow streams in school.

as an incentive to spur, to encourage diligent study.

to encourage study by promoting competition among pupils.

to certify a necessary level for employment in jobs after pupils leave school.

to certify a general educational background for jobs.

to act as a test for general intelligence for jobs.

to award scholarships, university entrance, etc. . . .

There is one more function of examinations:

to exhibit our aims to our pupils, so that examinations become a vehicle to aid in achieving our aims.

This is an overall function that pervades all other uses and aims – but it is a function that is often left unmentioned.

Nuffield Physics, Teachers Guide 1, p. 79,
Longmans/Penguin Books, 1966

For discussion

The overall function of examinations is to exhibit our aims to our pupils. How can we be satisfied that the aims are worthy ones?

14

At this point you may find it useful to refresh your memory by referring back to R. F. Mager's advice about specifying objectives in the section on Aims in Education. Teaching, needless to say, is a dialogue in which each of the partners is constantly receiving information from, and asking questions of, the other partner. Unremitting cross-questioning is the hallmark of the Socratic method, and the same is true of programmed instruction. Quite apart from any pre-test (to find out what he knows and does not know) or post-test (to find out what he has learned) the learner who works his way through a programme is being tested (questioned, examined, evaluated, assessed) *all the time.* At each step in the learning process he has to answer a question or do something to show that he is carrying out the instructions, and is immediately informed of the correctness or incorrectness of his response.

It is perhaps significant that the invention of teaching machines owes something to the excessive burden of marking examination scripts!

'Initially, Pressey was chiefly concerned to find a way of saving time in the scoring of objective-type tests which he had to administer weekly to large number of college students. In these tests, which largely replace essay-type examinations in many American schools and colleges, the student selects his answers from a series of multiple-choice questions. Pressey estimated that in the course of a year he spent something like 1,000 hours in scoring such tests. His aim was to reduce the burden of marking and free himself from the drudgery of a necessary but unrewarding clerical test.

'He began by designing various forms of simple apparatus, using mechanisms no more complicated than those found in an ordinary alarm clock. One of his first test-giving and test-scoring machines was about the size of an ordinary portable typewriter, only much simpler in its construction. On the left-hand side was a small aperture in which the multiple-choice questions were presented on a typewritten sheet; for example:

'In evolutionary terms, one of these animals is more highly developed than the others:

    (1) spider   (2) trout   (3) frog   (4) crow

'On the right-hand side were four keys. All the student had to do was to read each question as it appeared and press whichever of the keys seemed to him to correspond with the correct answer. The number of his correct responses was recorded on an automatic counter at the back of the machine. All the instructor had to do was to insert the test-sheet beforehand and note the number recorded on the counter after the student had finished.

'So far so good, but there was one further refinement which gave this labour-saving gadget an advantage which even Pressey had not anticipated. By shifting a lever inside the mechanism it was possible to control the presentation of the test items so that the next question did not appear until the student got the answer right. The student might make two, three, or even four attempts before finally selecting the appropriate key. Once again, the automatic counter recorded the number of his attempts. In this way the student was instantly made aware of any mistakes *and* was given the right answer in the process.

'It turned out that the progress of students using these gadgets was measurably superior to that of students whose tests were marked in the usual way by the teacher. The inference was that besides being a labour-saving device, this test-scoring machine was a teaching aid in its own right.'

W. KENNETH RICHMOND, Teachers and Machines,
Collins

For discussion

1 Pressey concluded that immediate 'knowledge of results' was an important ingredient in successful learning; and this is now a recognized principle of programming – you make your responses and are at once told whether it is right or wrong. So teaching and testing are combined. How essential is immediate 'knowledge of results' do you think? In working through the various sequences of READINGS IN EDUCATION you have been presented with a series of questions, but the answers you gave have been left entirely to you. Except very obliquely, you have not been told what answers to make. Would it have been better if you *had* been told?
2 Broadly, the method we have followed has been to present a bit of evidence and ask, 'What do you deduce from this?', and then to present another bit (either in support or in flat contradiction of the first) and ask again, 'If you deduced *that* what do you deduce from this?', and so on. Is this if-then procedure effective? Is it not this kind of procedure which distinguishes the new methods of teaching mathematics, physics, chemistry and biology from those in vogue in the past?

15 A look at the future

MG What of examination procedure of the future? Is this a problem of verification by the various teaching techniques?

GP Examination procedure of the future? What are the examination procedures of the present?

MG Official procedures of pencil and paper examinations.

GP Either you ask me to write an essay on the details of acetaldehyde or to discuss paramecium, or something of this sort? Or, alternatively, you ask is paramecium the name of a unicellular organism, a tea kettle, a multicellular object, or a rock? I am required to tick one of these as being right, and some mark is awarded according to the tick. Both alternatives strike me as being a little non-sensical, although the first is perhaps capable of examining something. But what do you want to examine? Surely an examination procedure must be related to a method of control, not merely to a criterion. If you like, one entails the other. You cannot control without experimenting to find out about behaviour, and you cannot experiment without exercising some degree of control. In the special and formalised control of learning which we call 'teaching', our 'experiments' will 'examine' the student. So examining is part and parcel of the teaching. Any training routine involves various kinds of test. These may, of course, be multi-choice response tests or they may assume any other form, but there is no question here of a formal examination day with an outcome that brands a student for life.

It seems to me that a proper examination procedure is one which is optimal for gleaning the information needed to achieve a specified form of control over a system, in particular, control of some kind of learning. We examine a system in order to control it, just as we continually examine the child if we interact with him personally in order to teach him. Private instructors are continually examining the child. The current obsession with formal end-of-term examinations, therefore, is a little curious. These procedures may be expedient but their objectives are obviously quite distinct from those of a control examination, which is a necessary part of teaching. I am not at all sure these sort of formal tests of ability will ever be used in the future, and I doubt if they have any useful purpose at the moment.

One optimum form of examination would measure how much effort the teacher must make in order to persuade the student to adapt in a certain direction, or to control the child's learning as a whole. Given this we have as much information as we can obtain. But this data is approximated within the teaching procedure itself. So the end-of-term examination, either with the essay or the multiple choice questionnaire is redundant; if only the available data is recorded and analysed throughout instruction. If you only have a limited contact with a man, as in job selection, then the best alternative to a continual recording of the effort that a real life teacher or an adaptive machine must make in order to teach will be obtained through an interview. Once again the applicant can either be interviewed in conversation with a real life individual or a suitable adaptive machine.

MG Are you saying then that the abolition of the examination systems as we know them today would be a necessary thing in the future, once we have the kind of co-operative machines of this kind in existence?

GP Yes. If you have co-operative systems the classical examination procedure is redundant. The whole co-operative business involves an examination. We need

not take the child on a given day and put him on his mettle because his characteristics are being continually examined.

MG What we need to substitute for today's examination system is an intimate
relationship between an individual teacher and an individual student, and we
cannot get that.

GP You can approximate it pretty well with these co-operative systems. Further,
although a teacher can adapt to a student even better than a machine, he may be
biased by issues that are irrelevant to the learning process. A machine is obviously
unbiased in its approach.

MG Would it be an oversimplification to say the emphasis is moving from the
acquisition to the availability of knowledge?

GP This is probably very true. Mere factual knowledge, for example, the knowledge of the engineering student who can achieve parrot-like repetition of the
formulae used in bridge building, is not of much value. You can argue that
parrot-like repetition *is* required, but I believe the argument is false. The need is
partly an artefact due to the existing method of examination. Surely a tape
recorder would beat any man at mere *repetition*, and in a sensibly oriented society
tape recorders or computer memories or reference books would be used for this
purpose, and human beings for a purpose for which they are better adapted.
The kind of continual examination we have considered is ideally suited to testing
the *use* rather than the possession of knowledge. Furthermore, this continual
examination is far more objective. I do not want to go into great detail on this
subject, but I would like to point out that when we talk of measurement, it is
generally assumed that the measured system is quasi-stationary, or in a meta-
stable state. This is far from the truth when we post an examination to a child. I
can conceive no worse method of achieving a meta-stable or stationary state in a
system to be measured than to take a child and say, 'Now it's your eleven-plus
today.' In the first place there is the emotional tension induced by this absurd
procedure. I become virtually hysterical upon the day I am required to do the
examinations, and this is true of many people. So none of us is in a stationary
state. It seems to me that the only faculty tested by the eleven-plus is the special
training the children are given to precondition them for the experience of being
examined. On the other hand, the co-operative systems that we have been discussing, continually change the sort of test they apply in order to maintain the
invariant relationship between the student and the machine. This leads to a
stationary measuring condition and, if we admit the student himself learns and
changes his characteristics as a result of being tested, then it is the *only* procedure
that *will* achieve a stationary measuring condition. Next, any system like this has
the further virtue that it can be shown to maximise the information available
from the test results about chosen features of the student's behaviour. This is a

provable consequence of their design and we can regard a suitably organised system as a kind of experimental examiner.

GORDON PASK, 'A look at the Future', in
Mechanisation in the Classroom, GOLDSMITH (ed.),
Souvenir Press

For discussion

1 Would you say that the main purpose of examinations is to provide the feedback of information necessary for the control of the learner's progress?
2 Will data-processing equipment and computer-assisted instruction pave the way to a more efficient system of testing and examining than the one we have today?
3 Is the end-of-term examination redundant?
4 Does teaching mean testing as you go? If so, how do you react to Pask's assertion that a 'stationary measuring condition' can only be provided by some kind of adaptive teaching machine which continuously monitors and responds to the learner's responses?

16

It has been our painfully achieved conclusion that if evaluation is to be of help it must be carried out to provide feedback at a time and in a form that can be useful in the design of materials and exercises.

But it is not obvious what the 'right time' is or what form of information is the most helpful. I found myself sufficiently puzzled after a year or two of curriculum work to feel the need for setting down guidelines or a 'philosophy' of evaluation. I quote directly from a memorandum that followed a first intensive workshop given over to exploring the problem of evaluating a course of study.

1 *Evaluation is best looked at as a form of educational intelligence for the guidance of curriculum construction and pedagogy.* The earlier in the curricular effort intelligence operations begin, the more likely are they to be of use. Effective evaluation should provide corrective information, but it should also provide informative hypotheses about how to proceed. Indeed, the sensible plan is to start gathering useful information as a *guide to the planning* of a curriculum. To design a course in American history, one would be aided by knowing the historical conceptions of children of the age to be instructed: what are their conceptions of historical cause and effect, their concepts of historical time, their ideas about revolution, and so on. In no sense can such 'scouting' determine the specific materials to be used; but it can pose the instructional problems to be solved.

2 *Evaluation, to be effective, must at some point be combined with an effort to teach so that the child's response to a particular process of teaching can be evaluated.*

Evaluation should examine not only the product or content of learning but also the process by which the child gets or fails to get to mastery of materials, for only in that way can the efficacy of pedagogy be examined. Content cannot be divorced from pedagogy. For it is the pedagogy that leads the child to treat content in critical ways that develop and express his skills and values. The 'instructional interview', of which more will be said later, was designed precisely to assess how a child makes materials his own and how he puts the materials to use in his thinking.

3 *Evaluation can be of use only when there is a full company on board, a full curriculum-building team consisting of the scholar, the curriculum maker, the teacher, the evaluator and the students.* Its effectiveness is drastically reduced when it is used for the single purpose, say, of editing a chapter, making a film, devising a text. For a curriculum is a thing in balance that cannot be developed first for content, then for teaching method, then for visual aids, then for some other particular feature. The essence of evaluation is that it permits a general shaping of the materials and methods of instruction in a fashion that meets the needs of the student, the criteria of the scholar from whose discipline materials have been derived, and the needs of the teacher who seeks to stimulate certain ways of thought in his or her pupils.

> Reprinted by permission of the publishers from
> JEROME S. BRUNER, *Toward a Theory of Instruction*,
> pp. 163-5 (The Belknap Press), Harvard University
> Press. Copyright © 1966 by the President and
> Fellows of Harvard College

For discussion
Strictly speaking, this carries us forward to the next section which deals with the curriculum, but it has been inserted here because it raises a number of important issues.

First, what is implied by the statement that, 'Evaluation is best looked at as a form of educational intelligence for the guidance of curriculum construction and pedagogy'? Are there any signs to indicate that the examinations and tests used in British schools are being used in this way? Second, 'Evaluation ... must ... be combined with an effort to teach so that the child's response to a particular process of teaching can be evaluated'. Programmed learning is one technique which attempts to do this. Are there any others?

12

Curriculum

Properly understood, the concept of the curriculum involves far more than the content of education: it is not to be identified with subject-matter or with syllabuses and schemes of work. How we teach is as much a part of it as what we teach. Curricular problems, in other words, cannot be dissociated from problems of methodology.

Teachers may feel that they have little or no effective say in deciding *what* they teach – more often than not their course of action is prescribed for them by headmasters, by local authority regulations and, not least, by examination requirements – but when it comes to the question of *how* they teach teachers in Britain enjoy a degree of freedom which their colleagues in other countries may well envy.

No doubt this explains the jocular remark of the first Minister of Education to hold office: 'Minister knows nowt about t' curriculum.' Twenty years ago such an acknowledgement could be made openly, almost boastfully. The position today is very different: a Minister charged with the duty of promoting and direction of national policy can no longer afford to profess blithe unconcern about what is taught and how and why it is taught in schools and colleges. The work of the Schools Council, the Nuffield Science Project and similar ventures represent a significant departure from the easy-going acceptance of traditional ways of doing things. As yet, curriculum study and reform has not been tackled in Britain with anything like the same energy and determination as it has been, for example, in the U.S.A. Since 1957, prompted by the post-Sputnik scare (and with the assistance of generous grants from the Federal Government) American teachers and academics have joined forces as never before in working out new curricula, and in the fields of mathematics, physics, chemistry and biology some notable advances have been made. Certain common features are beginning to emerge. There is, first, the importance attached to *structure* – the need for providing a clear conceptual framework within which the pupil can fit all the complicated and multifarious factual details he is expected to learn. Next, there is the recognition of the importance of *sequence* (*a*) in the sense of ensuring that the inherent 'logic' of the subject matter, task, or discipline is followed and (*b*) in the sense of ensuring that both the teaching and learning processes keep step with the psychological stages of development.

These are only two aspects of contemporary curriculum study which demand serious attention from teachers. In any case, the accelerating pace of social and technological change is so dizzy that those who prefer to cling to well-tried ways in the spirit of leave-well-alone may soon find that they are appealing, not to tradition, but only to a dead convention. Whatever the subject we teach, be it mathematics or English, modern languages or Classics, molecular biology or Education, each of us nowadays finds himself on shifting ground!

I

It is clear then that there should be legislation about education and that it should be conducted on a public system. But consideration must be given to the question, what constitutes education and what is the proper way to be educated. At present there are differences of opinion as to the proper tasks to be set; for all peoples do not agree as to the things that the young ought to learn, either with a view to virtue or with a view to the best life, nor is it clear whether their studies should be regulated more with regard to intellect or with regard to character. And confusing questions arise out of the education that actually prevails, and it is not at all clear whether the pupils should practise pursuits that are practically useful, or morally edifying, or higher accomplishments – for all these views have won the support of some judges; and nothing is agreed as regards the exercise conducive to virtue, for, to start with, all men do not honour the same virtue, so that they naturally hold different opinions in regard to training in virtue.

It is therefore not difficult to see that the young must be taught those useful arts that are indispensably necessary; but it is clear that they should not be taught all the useful arts, those pursuits that are liberal being kept distinct from those that are illiberal, and that they must participate in such among the useful arts as will not render the person who participates in them vulgar. A task and also an art or science must be deemed vulgar if it renders the body or soul or mind of free men useless for the employments and actions of virtue. Hence we entitle vulgar all such arts as deteriorate the condition of the body, and also the industries that earn wages; for they make the mind preoccupied and degraded. And even with the liberal sciences, although it is not illiberal to take part in some of them up to a point, to devote oneself to them too assiduously and carefully is liable to have the injurious result specified. Also it makes much difference what object one has in view in a pursuit or study; if one follows it for the sake of oneself or one's friends, or on moral grounds, it is not illiberal, but the man who follows the same pursuit because of other people would often appear to be acting in a menial and servile manner.

The branches of study at present established fall into both classes, as was said before. There are perhaps four customary subjects of education, reading and writing, gymnastics, music, and fourth, with some people, drawing; reading and writing and drawing being taught as being useful for the purposes of life and very serviceable, and gymnastics as contributing to manly courage; but as to music, here one might raise a question. For at present most people take part in it for the sake of pleasure; but those who originally included it in education did so because, as has often been said, nature itself seeks to be able not only to engage rightly in business but also to occupy leisure nobly; for – to speak about it yet again – this is the first principle of all things. For if although both business and leisure are necessary, yet leisure is more desirable and more fully an end than business, we must inquire what is the proper occupation of leisure.

ARISTOTLE, *Politics*, Book 8, Loeb Classical Library

For discussion

1 Even in Aristotle's day, it seems, the nature of the curriculum was in dispute. How do the 'customary subjects of education' in ancient Athens differ from those which modern schoolchildren are required to learn?

2 Aristotle draws a distinction between liberal and illiberal studies. Is the distinction still worth drawing in a society where all men are free?

3 Aristotle distinguishes between studies which enable us 'to engage rightly in business' and those which enable us to 'occupy leisure nobly'. This raises an issue which we discussed under the heading of General and Special Education. In view of the prospects of an Age of Automation the question is: Are our present courses of instruction calculated to promote the right use of leisure?

2a

If there requires further evidence of the rude, undeveloped character of our education, we have it in the fact that the comparative worths of different kinds of knowledge have been as yet scarcely even discussed – much less discussed in a methodic way with definite results. Not only is it that no standard of relative values has yet been agreed upon; but the existence of any such standard has not been conceived in a clear manner. And not only is it that the existence of such a standard has not been clearly conceived: but the need for it seems to have been scarcely even felt. Men read books on this topic, and attend lectures on that; decide that their children shall be instructed in these branches of knowledge, and shall not be instructed in those; and all under the guidance of mere custom, or liking, or prejudice; without ever considering the enormous importance of determining in some rational way what things are really most worth learning. It is true that in all circles we hear occasional remarks on the importance of this or the other order of information. But whether the degree of its importance justifies the expenditure of the time needed to acquire it; and whether there are not things of more importance to which such time might be better devoted; are queries which,

if raised at all, are disposed of quite summarily, according to personal predilec-
tions. It is true also, that now and then, we hear revived the standing controversy
respecting the comparative merits of classics and mathematics. This controversy,
however, is carried on in an empirical manner, with no reference to an ascertained
criterion; and the question at issue is insignificant when compared with the
general question of which it is part. To suppose that deciding whether a mathematical or a classical education is the best, in deciding what is the proper curriculum, is much the same thing as to suppose that the whole of dietetics lies in
ascertaining whether or not bread is more nutritive than potatoes!

The question which we contend is of such transcendent moment, is, not
whether such or such knowledge is of worth, but what is its relative worth?

2b

Our first step must obviously be to classify, in the order of their importance, the
leading kinds of activity which constitute human life. They may be naturally
arranged into: 1. those activities which directly minister to self-preservation;
2. those activities which, by securing the necessaries of life, indirectly minister to
self-preservation; 3. those activities which have for their end the rearing and
discipline of offspring; 4. those activities which are involved in the maintenance
of proper social and political relations; 5. those miscellaneous activities which fill
up the leisure part of life, devoted to the gratification of the tastes and feelings.

That these stand in something like their true order of subordination, it needs
no long consideration to show. The actions and precautions by which, from moment to moment, we secure personal safety, must clearly take precedence of all
others. Could there be a man, ignorant as an infant of surrounding objects and
movements, or how to guide himself among them, he would pretty certainly lose
his life the first time he went into the street; notwithstanding any amount of
learning he might have on other matters. And as entire ignorance in all other
directions would be less promptly fatal than entire ignorance in this direction, it
must be admitted that knowledge immediately conducive to self-preservation is
of primary importance.

That next after direct self-preservation comes the indirect self-preservation
which consists in acquiring the means of living, none will question. That a man's
industrial functions must be considered before his parental ones, is manifest from
the fact that, speaking generally, the discharge of the parental functions is made
possible only by the previous discharge of the industrial ones.

2c

If by some strange chance not a vestige of us descended to the remote future save
a pile of our school-books or some college examination-papers, we may imagine

how puzzled an antiquary of the period would be on finding in them no sign that the learners were ever likely to be parents. 'This must have been the curriculum for their celibates,' we may fancy him concluding. 'I perceive here an elaborate preparation for many things; especially for reading the books of extinct nations and of co-existing nations (from which indeed it seems clear that these people had very little worth reading in their own tongue); but I find no reference whatever to the bringing up of children. They could not have been so absurd as to omit all training for this gravest of responsibilities. Evidently then, this was the school-course of one of their monastic orders.'

Seriously, is it not an astonishing fact, that though on the treatment of offspring depend their lives or deaths, and their moral welfare or ruin; yet not one word of instruction on the treatment of offspring is ever given to those who will by and by be parents? Is it not monstrous that the fate of a new generation should be left to the chances of unreasoning custom, impulse, fancy – joined with the suggestion of ignorant nurses and the prejudiced counsel of grandmothers? If a merchant commenced business without any knowledge of arithmetic and book-keeping, we should exclaim at his folly, and look for disastrous consequences. Or if, before studying anatomy, a man set up as a surgical operator, we should wonder at his audacity and pity his patients. But that parents should begin the difficult task of rearing children, without ever having given a thought to the principles – physical, moral, or intellectual – which ought to guide them, excites neither surprise at the actors nor pity for their victims.

HERBERT SPENCER, *What Knowledge is of Most Worth?*

For discussion

1 The supremacy of the 'Liberal Arts' remained largely unchallenged until the second half of the nineteenth century. Normally they interpreted themselves in secondary schools and colleges through the Classics, failing which more modern literary studies were granted pride of place. Either way, their pre-eminence was defended on the grounds of their intrinsic value as expressions of 'the best that has been thought and said in the world'.

   In asserting the claims of science, Spencer urges the need for a different set of values – with literary studies low on the list of priorities. Was he right in doing so?

2 Spencer's classification of studies in the order of their importance reflects the influence of evolutionary theory. Can the order he suggested be approved today? Is it possible to arrange the curriculum in terms of the relative worth of different studies?

3 What do you mean by 'lumber' in the curriculum? Why is it so difficult to get rid of? Apart from 'reading the books of extinct nations' – Latin and Greek are, of course, the obvious examples which occur to mind in discussions of this

sort – can you think of subjects (or aspects of subjects) which continue to be taught for no better reason than the fact that their existence is taken for granted?

3

The monopoly, which ensured that every educated person was acquainted with Latin and Greek and which enabled everyone to share in a common literary taste, is over. Since it is vain to wish it back again, it is idle to bewail it. But the termination of a monopoly does not mean the suppression of the product or its exclusion from the market. What it is important to distinguish clearly – and it is something that has been obfuscated in both recent and former discussions about the merits of a classical education – is that the case for the study of the classics as a monopoly subject is not at all the case for the study of the classics as such. On the latter question the arguments advanced by Sir Richard Livingstone in 1916 (A Defence of Classical Education) even today promise the fullest and most cogent answer. It cannot seriously be maintained that a knowledge of Greek and Latin is not desirable. The study of the Latin language is indispensable for the understanding of modern European languages and does facilitate a sense of style in English composition. Latin and Greek literature do contain some of the finest and most influential works ever composed. Our philosophy and our religion are in large measure the products of Greek thought. The classics have for so long been a part of the English civilization that a man who is totally unacquainted with them is shut off from a whole area of experience which our forefathers knew. To deny that it is desirable that our generation should share in these things is to deny that there is any worth in any non-technological education. The literature and history of a country is a continuous thread. Break it at some arbitrary point and the proportion is destroyed and the utility impaired. The question, then, is not whether a classical education is desirable but whether in the present state of society, when the conflicting claims of a multitude of subjects vital to the country's survival and prosperity clamour for recognition, a high degree of priority can be given to a classical education. In a free society the choice of education as of profession, is, in theory, left to personal inclination and, in practice, is determined by supply and demand or by fashion. But until a boy reaches an age when examination demands and his own enthusiasm – for the superficial appeals to few adolescents – make him devote himself to the specialist pursuit of one particular line, it would be very illiberal not to encourage a system of education that gave him the entrée to as many fields as possible. This is not special pleading for the preservation of the classics in preparatory schools. It is, rather, a plea that between the ages of ten and fourteen boys of reasonable intelligence at all types of schools should be taught subjects which are the essential groundwork for later development. Too often curricula are determined not by what is likely to be ultimately useful to the pupil, however uncongenial it may seem to him to be at the time, but by what is immediately popular, because untaxing. Too often 'Current

O

Affairs' is substituted for mathematics or Latin. It is a disastrous fallacy to believe that small boys know what is good for them.

R. M. OGILVIE, *Latin and Greek*, pp. 180–1, Routledge & Kegan Paul

For discussion

1 Should a high degree of priority still be given to a classical education?
2 Current Affairs, it is suggested, is untaxing compared with Latin. Is this a good argument?
3 The study of the Latin language is indispensable for the understanding of modern European languages, says the writer. Is it?
4 It cannot seriously be maintained that a knowledge of Russian and Chinese is not desirable. How do you respond to such a statement?

4

Today, one of the main forces driving cultural and, hence, curricular change is science and its application in technology. As science improves our knowledge and mastery of the physical world, it also challenges established values and constantly adds to the vast accumulation of facts which we must take into account in order to act. Through technology science influences the economy, creating new jobs and destroying old ones, and it promises with automation to transform the whole pattern of employment. Through technology, too, as in transport and communications, science influences social arrangements, bringing the world closer together and everywhere spreading urbanism and industry.

Science and technology lead also to an increasing specialization of knowledge and function, in education as elsewhere. There are other changes, too, but most have either sprung from science and technology or been influenced by them: a growing population, increased leisure, greater affluence, fresh forms of entertainment, an expansion in the power and responsibility of governments, new methods of warfare and diplomacy (largely created by the discovery and development of nuclear power), and the growing interdependence of nations. All these factors make one thing clear: The school today must educate its pupils so that they can adapt to the unforeseeable events that are bound to occur in their lifetimes. As Margaret Mead has said, 'No one will live all his life in the world into which he was born, and no one will die in the world in which he worked in his maturity.'

G. F. KNELLER, *Educational Anthropology*, p. 137, Wiley, 1965

For discussion

1 If scientific technology leads to increasing specialization how is it going to be possible to provide a general education which will enable pupils 'to adapt to the unforeseeable events that are bound to occur in their lifetimes'?

2 If scientific technology is the pacemaker is curriculum reform moving fast enough to keep up with it? Is there a danger of cultural lag?

5

From the theoretical point of view education is the study of the organisation of knowledge. If we consider the various fields of knowledge, the so-called subject-matters, it is difficult to avoid the conclusion that they are ill-defined and largely irrelevant to the modern world, and that the relations between them are so little understood that they are not even a topic for investigation. The existing curriculum – the list of subjects studied – in our schools, colleges and universities stands in dire need of a radical revision and we must not be afraid because of our own training under this curriculum to promote the necessary changes. There are some attempts to change, it is true, but, on the whole, the curriculum in most schools, colleges and universities is antiquated. To deal with the content of some traditional school subjects first:

at a time when computers hold out the possibility of solving many of our problems and of advancing our power over nature, instead of teaching numerical analysis, probability and linear programming in mathematics, we are still solemnly solving right angled triangles by trigonometrical methods;

at a time when physicists are employing the concepts of wave and field with incredible results, the teaching of physics proceeds as if the separate study of heat, light, and sound was never to be altered;

at a time when we are concerned, desperately concerned, with the unity of mankind throughout the world, we go on teaching history as if the Establishment of the British Empire was the inevitable end to which all the past converged;

at a time when we need to understand ourselves and our fellow men as agents, that is, as men trying to achieve purposes by action, virtually the whole content of the social sciences is rigidly excluded from the secondary curriculum;

at a time when the study of structural linguistics has transformed our understanding of language, we continue to analyze and parse English sentences in terms of concepts invented by German philologists for the study of two non-spoken classical languages, Greek and Latin;

at a time when biochemistry and mathematics are transforming the old distinction between botany and zoology, botany is still concerned, all too often, with nomenclature, identification and taxonomy;

and, finally, at a time when the optimists are learning Russian and the pessimists are learning Chinese, the language teaching in our schools is predominantly in French and greatest irony of all, it has just been discovered that fluency is the aim; as if being bilingual was a mark of education.

Now, although there is much point in these criticisms they do not go far enough; but if they were paid attention to, some much needed reforms would be carried out. The problem with the curriculum is not simply that the content of the various subject-matters needs bringing up to date, it is that the very classification of subject-matter is itself out of date. One sign of this is that there has been a growth recently of subjects designed to fill in the gaps between the stones in the edifice of knowledge – biochemistry and biophysics, social psychology and social history, the history of science and the philosophy of science, and so on – and more such subjects will arise simply because the stones of the edifice of knowledge are of knowledge; there is just a collection of outhouses.

JOHN BREMER, 'Educational Education', pp. 37–8,
in *Education for Teaching*, Journal of the Association
of Teachers in Colleges and Departments of Education

For discussion
1 'On the whole, the curriculum in most schools, colleges and universities is antiquated.' It is a heavy charge. Is it libellous?
2 'The problem with the curriculum is not simply that the content of the various subject-matters needs bringing up to date, it is that the very classification of subject-matters is itself out of date.' How seriously should we take this viewpoint – and how best can the problem be tackled?

6

Hitherto the general tendency has been to take for granted the existence of certain traditional 'subjects' and to present them to the pupils as lessons to be mastered. There is, as we have said, a place for that method, but it is neither the only method, nor the method most likely to be fruitful between the ages of seven and eleven. What is required; at least so far as much of the curriculum is concerned, is to substitute for it methods which take as the starting point of the work of the primary school the experience, the curiosity, and the awakening powers and interests of the children themselves. . . .

(Introduction, p. xxix)

To put the point in a more concrete way, we must recognise the uselessness and the danger of seeking to inculcate what Professor A. N. Whitehead calls inert ideas – that is, ideas which at the time when they are imparted have no bearing upon the child's natural activities of body or mind and do nothing to illuminate or guide his experience.

There are doubtless several reasons why a principle so obviously sane should in practice be so often neglected ... In the earliest days of popular education children went to school to learn specific things which could not well be taught at home – reading, writing and cyphering. The real business of life was picked up by a child in unregulated play, in casual intercourse with contemporaries and elders, and by a gradual apprenticeship to the discipline of the house, the farm, the workshop. But as industrialization has transformed the basis of social life ... the schools ... have thus been compelled to broaden their aims until it might now be said that they have to teach children how to live. This profound change in purpose has been accepted with a certain unconscious reluctance, and a consequent slowness of adaptation. The schools, feeling that what they can do best is the old familiar business of imparting knowledge, have reached a high level of technique in that part of their functions, but have not clearly grasped its proper relation to the abstract. In short, while there is plenty of teaching which is good in the abstract, there is too little which helps children directly to strengthen and enlarge their instinctive hold on the conditions of life by enriching, illuminating and giving point to their growing experience.

Applying these considerations to the problem before us, we see that the curriculum is to be thought of in terms of activity and experience rather than of knowledge to be acquired and facts to be stored. Its aim should be to develop in a child the fundamental human powers and to awaken him to the fundamental interests of civilized life so far as these powers and interests lie within the compass of childhood. ...

The Primary School (Hadow Report, 1931)

For discussion
'The curriculum is to be thought of in terms of activity and experience rather than of knowledge to be acquired and facts to be stored.' In theory, if not always in practice, this has become a guiding principle for teachers in primary schools. What exactly does it mean? If it is a sound guiding principle in primary schools why is it not followed, say, in grammar schools?

7 School factors: progressiveness

Some of the most interesting results to be found in Dr Warburton's chapter 'Attainment and the School Environment' in the symposium Education and Environment are those for progressiveness, showing that schools adopting progressive methods have fewer backward children and more bright children. This effect is more strongly marked with reading than with arithmetic. This is a useful piece of factual evidence in a field of educational controversy where opinion is more often mediated by attitude and prejudice than by the results of actual investigation. 'Progressiveness' in school organisation and teaching methods is usually contrasted with 'formal' or traditional education. By and large, 'progressive' methods of organisation and teaching are now accepted as normal and desirable in the infant schools of England and Wales. The controversy arises over the question whether such methods are 'right' for children in junior and secondary schools. Antagonists see activity methods as dangerous to standards (and values). 'Letting children do what they like' will inevitably lead to the avoidance of difficult tasks and difficult subjects: literacy and numeracy are bound to fall. But in those primary schools which adopted this approach no catastrophic decline in standards was observed, and the outstanding improvements in the energies and enthusiasms of the children, and their attitude towards school and learning, was clearly demonstrable. There are many teachers in junior schools, and a smaller number in secondary schools, who believe that progressive methods are generally superior – in every way – to more formal methods of education. The number of junior schools organised entirely on these lines is not large, but is growing slowly.

Methods which have proved successful in infant schools with children of five and six cannot be transferred unchanged to junior and secondary schools. Much harm has been done to sound progress by the uncritical and thoughtless adoption of 'progressive methods' by teachers with little grasp of the basic philosophy behind them, or of the essential aims of such methods, motivated merely by the desire to climb on the bandwagon of fashion. Techniques in the secondary school still remain somewhat tentative and experimental, but much can be done by those teachers whose educational philosophy leads them to value the 'child-centred' school, with an active approach to learning as the main ingredient.

The schools in Dr Warburton's survey were graded on a scale 'ranging from the extremely formal, rigid, and orthodox to the most informed, free, and progressive, with a curriculum organised through activities related to the interest of the children'. The fact that such a rating was shown, unequivocally, to be associated with the results of the attainment tests, and particularly with ability in reading comprehension, is one of the most significant findings of all those reported in this book. It may give heart to the progressives in the teaching profession, and remove many of the doubts of those who see the advantages of such methods but fear some of the 'side effects'.

> S. WISEMAN, 'Education and Environment', p. 109, in
> *Linking Home and School*, (ed.) M. CROFT *et al.*,
> Longmans, 1967

For discussion

1 Are you still a doubting Thomas? If so, the onus is on you to adduce solid evidence that activity methods are dangerous to standards of attainment.
2 Incidentally, both 'standards' and 'attainments' are constantly changing. How?

8

What do we as teachers give the children? What society has given them in the past is all too evident. High windows through which they cannot look, forbidding staircases, bare, unlovely yards, smelly lavatories, dark cloakrooms – and these were not confined to maintained schools. You will find them all in the older public schools, of course being swept away as fast as money allows. We do much better than that now, though we are only just beginning to build schools which are really designed for the education, as distinct from the instruction of children. But what I really want to consider is the educational material that we, as teachers, think suitable for our children and in particular the literature. I shall begin with the grace which is almost universally said or sung before school dinner and which is presumably, therefore, thought worthy of the children.

> *Thank you for the world so sweet;*
> *Thank you for the food we eat;*
> *Thank you for the birds that sing –*
> *Thank you God, for everything.*

Let us submit this to a critical examination. It begins without any invocation to the Almighty, who is treated to a cursory nod in the last line. Thanks are offered for 'the world so sweet'. The world may be thought of as wonderful, terrible, beautiful, immense, ancient, incomprehensible but not surely as sweet which, even in a child's experience, is an inadequate epithet. Then we have 'the birds that sing'. Does this mean 'birds when they are singing but not at other times' or 'the birds that sing as distinct from the much greater number that don't' or does it mean that the writer is ornithologically uninstructed, or, as I think more probable, that he was dealing in clichés without any real or imaginative experience behind them? It passes from ornithology to theology and God is thanked 'for everything'. There is a sense in which someone who had progressed far along the road of prayer and devotion might thank God for everything and mean something real by it, but it is not something that any child ought to be asked to say, for 'everything' to a child will include, battle, murder and sudden death, and this in a context in which God is being thanked for his gifts. The prayer is a dreadful piece of work, doggerel lacking in any kind of merit, and I can only explain its popularity by supposing that prayers are not commonly studied critically at all. But why give the children this wretched rubbish when there is the whole splendid Anglican Liturgy to choose from, most of it simple and easy to understand apart from an occasional archaism as in 'Prevent us, O Lord, in all our doings' which can be very easily explained? 'Thank you for the world so sweet' is for 'the kiddies', not for children whom we love and respect.

JOHN BLACKIE, *Good Enough for the Children*,
pp. 51–3, Faber, 1963

For discussion

In ancient Greece children learned to recite Homer at an early age, presumably in the belief that only the best was good enough for them. Blackie's question is pertinent – as teachers (and parents) are we not under a moral obligation to ensure that what we offer is good enough for the children? What criteria are we to take in order to decide what is good, bad and indifferent – Aristotle's? – Spencer's? – Matthew Arnold's? – Piaget's?

9

There is a dilemma in describing a course of study. One must begin by setting forth the intellectual substance of what is to be taught, else there can be no sense of what challenges and shapes the curiosity of the student. Yet the moment one succumbs to the temptation to 'get across' the subject, at that moment the ingredient of pedagogy is in jeopardy. For it is only in a trivial sense that one gives a course to 'get something across', merely to impart information. There are better means to that end than teaching. Unless the learner also masters himself, disciplines his taste, deepens his view of the world, the 'something' that is got across is hardly worth the effort of transmission.

The more elementary a course and the younger its students, the more serious must be its pedagogical aim of forming the intellectual powers of those whom it serves. It is as important that a good mathematics course be justified by the intellectual discipline it provides or the honesty it promotes as by the mathematics it transmits. Indeed, neither can be accomplished without the other.

> Reprinted by permission of the publishers from
> JEROME S. BRUNER, *Toward a Theory of Instruction*,
> (The Belknap Press), Harvard University Press.
> Copyright © 1966 by the President and Fellows
> of Harvard College

For discussion

The content of the curriculum calls for serious consideration, we decided. But in selecting it even more fundamental considerations need to be taken into the reckoning. Do you agree that teaching is in jeopardy once it succumbs to the temptation to impart information?

10

The syllabus is a precise indication of the subject matter to be covered. It is not a scheme of work. Several factors have to be considered when expanding a syllabus to a scheme of work. They are: the subject matter; the class; the time available and the use to which each teaching period will be put.

SUBJECT MATTER

Before stating the aims in teaching a particular subject it is essential to write out unambiguously and briefly the aims of the whole course of study in relation to the needs of the student in process of building a career in a particular industry. The precise aims of a session's work in the particular subject should then be stated concisely in relation to what has been taught in previous sessions and will be taught in succeeding sessions. There should then be an exact statement of what students must learn by the end of the session. Technical teachers, responsible for a subject in a particular course, must, therefore, make an objective appraisal, under the guidance of the head of department of what is to be taught in each year of the course. Committing the information to paper helps to direct the teacher's thought clearly and objectively and to the expression of exact aims and targets.

ALEXANDER MACLENNAN, *Technical Teaching and Instruction*, pp. 80-1, Oldbourne, 1963

For discussion

1 Back to aims and objectives!
'There should be an exact statement of what students must learn by the end of the session.' How does this compare with Mager's advice? (Cf. section on Aims in Education.)
2 The passage is intended for teachers of technical subjects. Is it equally applicable to all subjects?

11 The determination of subject-matter

From 'The Requirements for Major Curriculum Revision' by Jerrold R. Zacharias and Stephen White in New Curricula *edited by Robert W. Heath (p. 71). Copyright © 1964 by Robert W. Heath. Used by permission of Harper & Row, Publishers*

Two questions must be answered in the course of determining the subject-matter that will constitute the unit under consideration. First, what is it desired that the student learn from the unit? Second, what selection of material and what ordering of that material will make it most probable that he will indeed learn?

There is never a unique answer to the first of these questions. Turning again to physics, one might wish to provide the student with an intimate knowledge of modern technology, or with an acquaintance with the manner in which physics has grown. During the early days of the Physical Science Study Committee, both of these were entered as possibilities and were warmly debated; if either had carried the day, the Committee physics course would be quite different from the course as it now exists. In fact, it was decided instead that the course would be directed toward familiarizing the student with two central notions of modern physics: the wave-particle duality and the modern concept of the atom. Behind this decision was the view that these two notions lay at the heart of the modern physicist's outlook upon his universe, and that it was this outlook that the course should convey.

This answer set boundaries upon the answer to the question of selecting and ordering. If a one-year course was to deal intelligibly with the wave-particle duality and nature of the atom, much that has been conventionally taught as physics would have to be ignored or skimped. Physics is too rich to be taught in its entirety in a single year; the criteria of selection would have to identify those portions of physics which contributed to the elucidation of the wave-particle duality and the nature of the atom.

As a consequence, the Physical Science Study Committee course contains little about sound, or electric circuitry, or relativity. They are omitted, not because they are devoid of interest, but because they are not central to the theme.

For discussion

1 More so perhaps than in other fields of human inquiry, the explosion of knowledge in the natural and applied sciences has made it impossible to cover what formerly was regarded as the essential groundwork. Even the research scientist, working at the frontier of his chosen field, cannot be expected to know everything that is going on in other sectors of the field. At the school level, therefore, some principle of selection is necessary. How would you state this principle?

2 The aim of the Physical Science Study Committee course is to convey an 'outlook'. Can the same be said of most traditional science courses – and if so, how successful were they in achieving it?

3 In an attempt to give structure and coherence to the course, the Committee fixed on two central themes. Is this a plan which could usefully be followed in Arts subjects, say, English and History?

12 Curriculum revision

From 'The Requirements for Major Curriculum Revision' by Jerrold R. Zacharias and Stephen White in New Curricula *edited by Robert W. Heath. (pp. 68–70). Copyright © 1964 by Robert W. Heath. Used by permission Harper & Row, Publishers*

Over the past six years, major curriculum revisions have been undertaken in the United States over a wide range of subjects. Early activities were restricted to mathematics and the natural sciences, but more recently revisions have been extended to the fields of modern languages, including English.

The purposes of all these activities are much the same. They reflect, in the first place, dissatisfaction with the gulf that has been permitted to open between the professional scholar or research scientist, on the one hand, and the schoolroom on the other.

This general dissatisfaction has been reinforced by a growing awareness that the capacity of children to learn has commonly been grievously underestimated. Mathematicians particularly have discovered that children by the age of ten years or even less can master extremely subtle concepts, if those concepts are properly presented to them. Investigations over the past ten years have led one psychologist to propose that 'any subject can be taught effectively in some intellectually honest form to any child at any stage of development'. Even if this statement is broadly qualified, it remains difficult to presume that the gulf between the professional practitioner and the general student is a necessary consequence of the student's incapacity or unreadiness. If any charge of incapacity or unreadiness is to be laid, it must now be upon the professional scholar himself, who has been either incapable of presenting his discipline in an appropriate manner or unwilling to divert himself from his specialized activities to make the requisite effort.

The arousal of fundamental interest in the content of elementary and secondary education is a development of profound significance. Curriculum revision has attracted the participation of professional scholars whose leadership made the recent massive efforts effective. The first such revision to be carried out as a major program on a national scale was that of the Physical Science Study Committee, which began in 1956 and entered the American school system as a complete one-year physics course in 1960. Most later revisions have been patterned to some degree upon that carried out by the Committee. Considerations set forth in this paper reflect the close association of its authors with the Physical Science Study Committee program, and consequently are likely to be drawn from the Committee's experience; they should be taken as applicable to the entire range of curriculum revision to the extent that they are general considerations arising out of general problems.

At least four distinct components can be distinguished in a program of curriculum revision: (a) the process of determining the precise boundaries of the educational unit that will be treated; (b) the process of identifying the subject-matter which is to be dealt with within that educational unit; (c) the embodiment of that subject-matter in material form, as text, laboratory or classroom materials, and other learning aids; and (d) the preparation of teachers in the new subject-matter and in the use of the materials. Of these four components, the first is likely to precede the rest; the determination of subject-matter, its embodiment, and the preparation of teachers must however be carried on to a large degree simultaneously.

For discussion

1 The writer gives two main reasons for thinking that major revisions of the existing curriculum are needed. What are they?
2 'Mathematicians . . . have discovered that children by the age of ten years or even less can master extremely subtle concepts, if these concepts are properly presented to them.' Is this in keeping with a developmental approach and the 'activity and experience' doctrine?
3 Examine the four phases of curriculum planning outlined in the passage and compare them with the strategy adopted by the Nuffield Science Project.
4 Is it possible to determine the precise boundaries of Arts subjects? We ask this because the most spectacular advances in new curricula seem to have been made in mathematics and science subjects. Is this because the need was greater in these subjects, the task somehow easier – or is it simply because Arts subject teachers tend on the whole to be conservative?

13 The structure of knowledge

Briefly stated, the hypothesis is that whatever the subject happens to be, and regardless of its 'difficulty', a way can be found of cutting it down to size, reducing it to a set of basic concepts which constitute its essential framework. Once this framework has been found the complexities and intricacies of subject-matter within the field are greatly simplified. The learner can find his way around the field more easily and see just where, how and why the bits of information he gathers fits – bits and pieces which would otherwise tend to seem trivial, irrelevant, or accidental. The framework is invaluable in clearing the ground and removing the impedimenta to learning, and for that reason alone is economic of effort. It is also productive in that it enables fresh combinations of ideas to be made and facilitates transfer of training to other fields. In setting forth the objectives at the outset it enhances the spirit of inquiry by ensuring that the learner knows where he is going.

This principle of parsimony is by no means original. It is implicit in the Comenian intention to teach 'all things to all men'. A good example of it is to be found in the 'four great novel ideas' which Whitehead listed as being characteristic of nineteenth-century theoretical science – the idea of physical activity pervading the whole of space, the idea of atomicity, the idea of the conversion of energy, the idea of evolution. Another example of its ruthless application to curriculum reform is to be seen in Chemical Bond Approach Project, which centres upon a single idea. According to this, the making and breaking of ties between atoms *is* chemistry, and everything in the course follows from, and hinges upon, an understanding of this one idea.

Preoccupation with the problem of structure has been forced upon educationists by the explosion of information. Particularly in the natural sciences, the exponential growth of knowledge has necessitated the adoption of conceptual schema which serve to make mass data more manageable and classifiable. With more and more needing to be learned and standards of attainment rising as fast as they are it is only natural that educationists should feel impelled to address themselves to the task of finding ways and means of shedding the load which the school-child has to carry in the second half of the twentieth century. On the one hand it is more obvious nowadays than ever before that not everything can be learned, on the other the demands of general education can be satisfied with nothing less than a broad grasp of essentials in a number of fields.

In this situation is it any use appealing to Turing's Theorem: 'Provided a problem is well defined its complexity can be broken down into a set of simpler operations'? Is it realistic to suppose that there is always a way of doing this, and that provided he is clear-sighted about the objectives the learner can be trusted to look after himself.

As we shall argue in another connexion, a measure of uncertainty is a necessary pre-condition for any purposeful inquiry. The point is that this uncertainty should never be associated with the task itself. The advantage of making plain the skeleton framework on which the subject-matter arranges itself is that it virtually rules out methods of presentation which create the impression that the outcome of the task is highly dubious and can only be arrived at, if at all, by hit-or-miss – an impression which is bound to be discouraging.

Once again, however, we are brought back to the objection that some subjects lack any obvious structure and that in these cases the task of instruction is singularly ill-defined. The triumph of mathematics is that it is 'thought moving in the sphere of complete abstraction', which explains why it can be reduced to a set of basic propositions which give unity and coherence to the field of study. Literary, philosophical, and aesthetic studies, on the other hand, have a way of refusing to be pinned down, emphatically not the kind of subjects which permit of the objectives being written on the back of an envelope. In any case, teachers of the humanities will ask, is it not an illusion to suppose that the elucidation of the underlying structure in a subject field, supposing that there is such a thing, will by itself make learning easier?

W. KENNETH RICHMOND, *The Teaching Revolution*, Methuen, 1967

For discussion
Sorry to keep harping on this 'elucidation of structure' theme, but it seems vital. To repeat, *is* it an illusion to suppose that, *whatever the subject*, a way can be found of cutting it down to size and reducing it to a set of basic concepts which constitute its essential framework?

14 Aims of mathematical education

It is not possible to discuss the educational implications of the work reported here without also discussing briefly the aims of mathematical education, and these are in fact far from clear. The so-called 'practical' people merely state somewhat vaguely that mathematics is necessary in practice, both in everyday life and in scientific work and industry, and so all mathematics ought to be practical – there are no other admissible reasons why children should learn mathematics. Reflection will show that extremely little mathematics is in fact necessary in everyday life. Multiplication is already largely superfluous, and the number of people who are going to need mathematics for their work is relatively small (they could easily be taught it as part of their vocational training). Yet a large proportion of school time, both in the elementary and higher grades, is spent in studying quite detailed mathematics, with admittedly rather indifferent results. It seems that we ought either to reduce the amount of mathematics learnt by children or be rather more clear about why we are making them learn it. Perhaps we have something quite different at the back of our minds when we think about mathematical education – something not entirely practical, namely a feeling that mathematics should add something to the quality of the person who has learned it by allowing him to participate in a cultural stream. But it is quite clear that things have not worked out this way. Mathematics is not used or enjoyed by people after they leave school, so that if our aim was to allow children to participate in this aspect of our culture, we have certainly largely failed. It is legitimate to ask why this is so, and what it is about the present arrangement in mathematics-learning that prevents all but a few children from appreciating the beauty of mathematical structure. There are a number of relevant suggestions we might make on the practice of mathematics-learning as a result of the observations made in these experiments.

Once we have agreed that our aims are not entirely practical, the whole question of what mathematics to teach children is immediately thrown wide open. If mathematics-learning is to be regarded honestly as a cultural activity in the way we regard the appreciation of literature, art and music, then the present syllabuses immediately lose their sanctity. Any syllabus would be suitable provided that with it most children could appreciate mathematics as a beautiful structure, irrespective of possible practical uses. Many parts of mathematics are accessible to quite young children, as our work with all the experimental groups shows. A great deal of the mathematics studied by these children has always been regarded as 'higher' mathematics, and for that reason difficult. Yet there is considerable evidence, even apart from the work reported here, that certain mathematics is often regarded as easier by the lower grades than by the higher grades. The Madison Project, for example, has been giving fourth- and fifth-grade children algebra, including 'difficult' things like quadratic equations, and progress on the same syllabus has almost invariably been more rapid in the lower than in the higher grades. Our groups D and E were able to understand what is substantially the idea of mathematical groups, and to some extent the construction of vector spaces and algebras; Group A finally achieved insight into the overall relationship between powers, logarithms and roots; and Group B were able to achieve quite complex isomorphisms on the place-value concept. All this provides additional evidence that we have seriously under-estimated what mathematics children can do and enjoy.

z. p. dienes, *An Experimental Study of Mathematics Learning*, pp. 154–5, Hutchinson, 1964

For discussion

1 Has your own education led you to think of mathematics 'as a cultural activity in the way we regard the appreciation of literature, art and music'? We'll lay ten to one that the answer is an emphatic negative! Why do you suppose that we are prepared to offer such long odds?
2 Does your mind boggle at the mere mention of vector spaces, isomorphisms and place-value concepts? These ten-year-olds took them in their stride – and enjoyed every minute of it. How do you imagine it was done – by super-efficient instruction? – by using teaching machines? – by guided play-way and activity methods?

(If you are in any doubt we suggest that you should read Dienes' account of his experiments with young children in *An Experimental Study of Mathematics Learning*, Hutchinson, 1964.)

15

From Realms of Meaning *by Philip H. Phenix (pp. 10–12). Copyright © 1964 by Philip H. Phenix. Used by permission of McGraw–Hill Book Company.*

Four principles for the selection and organization of content are suggested as means of ensuring optimum growth in meaning. The first principle is that the content of instruction should be drawn entirely from the fields of disciplined inquiry. The richness of culture and the level of understanding achieved in advanced civilization are due almost entirely to the labors of individual men of genius and of organized communities of specialists. A high level of civilization is the consequence of the dedicated service of persons with special gifts for the benefit of all. Every person is indebted for what he has and is to a great network of skilled inventors, experimenters, artists, seers, scholars, prophets, and saints, who have devoted their special talents to the well-being of all. Nobody, no matter how capable, can make any perceptible progress on his own without dependence on the experts in the various departments of life.

It follows that the teacher should draw upon the specialized discipline as the most dependable and rewarding resource for instructional materials. While he should seek to make the disciplined materials his own, he should not presume to originate the knowledge to be taught, nor should he expect the fruits of learning to come forth as if by miracle from the shared experience of the students or as the product of common sense.

The term 'discipline' is not meant to refer to an unchanging set of established fields of knowledge. New disciplines are regularly coming into being, such as cybernetics, parapsychology, theory of games, astronautics, and the like. New combinations, such as biochemistry and history of science, are forming. Also, many established disciplines are undergoing radical internal transformations: modern physics, music, history, and theology, to mention only a few. In fact, there is scarcely a field of study that is not today different in important respects from what it was only a few decades ago. Hence the present proposal to use materials from the disciplines does not constitute an argument for education to return to a traditional subject-matter curriculum. It simply argues for the exclusive use of materials that have been produced in disciplined communities of inquiry by men of knowledge who possess authority in their fields. Given the developments in disciplined inquiry, the proposal to use knowledge from the disciplines favors a modern rather than a traditional type of curriculum.

The second principle for the selection of content is that from the large resources of material in any given discipline, those items should be chosen that are particularly representative of the field as a whole. The only effective solution to the surfeit of knowledge is a drastic process of simplification. This aim can be achieved by discovering for each discipline those seminal or key ideas that provide clues to the entire discipline. If the content of instruction is carefully chosen and organized so as to emphasize these characteristic features of the disciplines, a relatively small volume of knowledge may suffice to yield effective understanding of a far larger body of material. The use of teaching materials based on representative ideas thus makes possible a radical simplification of the learner's task.

A third and related principle is that content should be chosen so as to exemplify the methods of inquiry and the modes of understanding in the disciplines studied. It is more important for the student to become skilful in the ways of knowing than to learn about any particular product of investigation. Knowledge of methods makes it possible for a person to continue learning and to undertake inquiries of his own. Furthermore, the modes of thought are far less transient than are the products of inquiry. Concentration on methods also helps to overcome the other two forms of meaninglessness earlier considered, namely, fragmentation and surfeit of material. Every discipline is unified by its methods, which are the common source of all the conclusions reached in that field of study. As this common thread, the characteristic modes of thought are included in the category of representative ideas, which, as indicated above, allow for the simplification of learning.

A fourth principle of selection is that the materials chosen should be such as to arouse imagination. Growth in meaning occurs only when the mind of the learner actively assimilates and re-creates the materials of instruction. Ordinary, prosaic, and customary considerations do not excite a vital personal engagement with ideas. One of the qualities of good teaching is the ability to impart a sense of the extraordinary and surprising so that learning becomes a continuous adventure. According to this principle, ordinary everyday life-situations and the solving of everyday problems should not be the basis for curriculum content. The life of meaning is far better served by using materials that tap the deeper levels of experience. Such materials reveal new perspectives on old problems by throwing familiar experiences into fresh combinations and showing old beliefs in novel contexts. Such imaginative use of materials generates habits of thought that enable the student to respond to rapid changes in knowledge and belief with zest instead of dismay and to experience joy in understanding rather than the dead weight of ideas to be absorbed and stored.

For discussion

1 Do you agree that 'the content of instruction should be drawn entirely from the fields of disciplined inquiry'? Is anything else good enough for the children?
2 'The only effective solution to the surfeit of knowledge is a drastic process of simplification.' How, in practice, can this simplification be achieved?
3 'The content should be chosen so as to exemplify the methods of inquiry and the modes of understanding in the disciplines studied.' Is this another way of saying that the curriculum is *not* to be conceived in terms of facts to be stored and knowledge to be acquired?

16

For the purpose of discussion let us say that the child's function in the school is to deal with the curriculum. It is then obvious that the home life of the child has nothing to do with the curriculum. While in the school it has to repeat certain lessons in language, do the prescribed sums in arithmetic, recite the bits of history or geography or science it has memorized. Does it do any of these things at home? If it wants to tell its mother something that happened on the road, it straight away launches into a narration, without any thought of idiom or syntax. When the mother sends the child to fetch small change for a coin, the child does not recall the monetary tables it learned from the arithmetic teacher. Such instances can be multiplied. While many of the things the child learns in the school are intimately connected with its activities and transactions in home life, is it not remarkable that the child carries on these activities and transactions without ever a thought about the concerned things learned in the school? So much for the really useful things learnt in the school. But what about the other things, the huge mass of information gathered and skills acquired? They have no bearing

P

whatever on the home life of the child. For all practical purposes the child lives a double life, in two separate worlds, the school world and the world of its home, its parents, friends and relatives.

That leads us to extra-curricular activities, a term meant to include a number of activities, all of recent growth, lying outside the area covered by the curriculum proper and meant to make the school world a real world and school life the real life for the child. I have to make an observation at the outset. The very argument for the inclusion of extra-curricular activities in the school programme is an admission of the cleavage between school life and home life created by the curriculum. Further, in spite of all the emphasis that has been bestowed upon extra-curriculum and curriculum proper has scarcely been disturbed and therefore even if the extra-curricular programme fulfils its purpose to perfection the curriculum will continue to operate in the direction I have already indicated.

Now to extra-curricular activities. It is of interest to note that this term has recently been displaced by another of similar sound, namely, co-curricular activities. Perhaps somebody thought that this species of school activities should be given equality of importance with the curriculum, though it is ununderstandable how a change of label will achieve this purpose. Well, extra-curricular activities generally consist of games and sports, debates and dramas, excursions and visits to places, gardening and other hobbies and, recently, social service and community work. None of these programmes has any tendency to draw together the school and the home. They serve only to expand the area of school activities, but not to integrate the child's school life with its home life. I will even go so far as to say that most of them serve only to widen the cleavage between the two.

The one common feature of all these extra-curricular activities is that none other than school children are admitted to them. Parents have no part in it. Brothers and sisters, friends and cousins are only outside spectators, if they are not enrolled as school children. Now, human society, in its natural state of existence, consists of all age groups. If persons belonging to a particular age group are isolated and gathered together to live a common life, that life cannot be called the natural life as known to human society. The features of their common life cannot be transplanted to their natural environment when they break up and return to their homes. As a course of training in a particular discipline the common life may be useful to them and they may acquire special skills and modes of thought and action which they might have occasion to utilize in their life. But these and similar advantages should not obscure our view of the truth, namely, that the common life and course of training can no more be said to be a pattern of their natural life than, say, a course of treatment in a nursing home. In the same way the extra-curricular activities of the school are very useful in many ways; but in so far as their connection with the normal life of children in their natural environment is concerned, they do not have any influence towards bridging the gulf between the curriculum-centred activities of the school and the home life of the child; but, on the contrary, being set in the background of the school system, they assume the same hue, though in a different shade, as curricular studies and therefore accentuate the difference between the home and the school.

G. RAMANATHAN, *Education from Dewey to Gandhi*,
pp. 43–4, Asia Publishing House, 1962

For discussion
We have left this to the last because it raises an awkward question. If, by the term 'curriculum' we mean the activities and experiences of school life why should extra-curricular activities be deemed necessary? If, as Dewey maintained, education is all one with living should not the curriculum include a whole range of activities which are normally excluded from the day school's routine?

13

Methods

For the conscientious teacher and parent the question, 'What ought I to do?' is invariably accompanied by another – 'How can I do it?' As to that, there is never a cut-and-dried answer. Methods which succeed admirably in the hands of one teacher with one set of pupils in a given situation often prove abortive in another. Until a genuinely prescriptive theory of instruction has been worked out, and as yet only its broad outlines can be envisaged, it seems that there is nothing for it but to recognize that the state of methodology is as confused and chaotic as that of any other sector in the field of educational theory.

Possibly the most chastening fact which emerges from the study of the history of education is that pupils have contrived to learn reasonably well not because of the methods used by teachers but in spite of them. Worth pondering, too, is the fact that many research investigations report no significant differences in the results obtained from the adoption of some of the latest and most high-powered techniques of instruction. The biggest variable in the learning situation is the learner himself.

Having said this, it is only right to add that the *conditions* for successful learning are now tolerably well known, and that because of this higher levels of attainment are accessible to an increasing number of children. Contemporary pedagogy should not rest content until the same can be said for all.

I

It appeared that as far back as the year 1798, Joseph Lancaster taught a few poor children in the Borough Road; himself and parents were in low circumstances, but he seemed to be actuated by a benevolent disposition, and to possess great talents for the education of youth; he was countenanced and supported by a few benevolent individuals; and, as the subscriptions were limited to a very small sum, he was obliged to devise the most economical plans. By a series of improvements, he at length demonstrated the possibility of instructing even a thousand children (if so many could be collected together in one room) by a single master;

he divided his school into eight classes, each of which was managed by a monitor, whose duties were exactly prescribed to him, and who was made responsible for the good order of his class; over these a monitor-general was placed, who regulated the business of the whole school, under the immediate direction of the master. Upon Lancaster's plan, a single book was found sufficient for a whole school, the different sheets being put upon pasteboard, and hung upon the walls of the school. He avoided the expense of pens and paper in the first stages of education, by substituting slates; he also introduced the plan of teaching the younger children to form the letters in sand, which plan was borrowed, I believe, from Dr Bell, who had imported it from India; he contrived to teach writing and spelling at the same time, and he made a single spelling-book serve for a whole school, however large. He taught arithmetic from lessons which he had constructed for the purpose, whereby the monitor might correctly teach the principles of it, even if he were not fully acquainted with them himself; in this case also, one book of arithmetic served for the whole school. So that the expense of teaching on this plan, consists in the salary of the master or mistress, the rent of the school-room, and from ten to twenty pounds per annum, according to the size of the school, for the necessary apparatus. I was particularly struck with the liberality upon which the system was conducted.

> Evidence of William Allen, Secretary, British and Foreign Schools Society. Report from Select Committee of the House of Commons appointed to inquire into the Education of the Lower Orders of the Metropolis. 1816

For discussion
We begin with the case of Joseph Lancaster because it underlines the point of asking, 'What can I do?' The methods used in the Monitorial schools were rudimentary and mechanical; but, given the social–economic circumstances of the time, could Lancaster have done better?

2

In the field of methodology and school organization, one of the major questions at issue is the role of class-teaching (which bears on the question of streaming and setting), the place of individual work and the value of group projects. At the university and college level there is the lecture, a mediaeval survival, which may well not be the best method of imparting knowledge (or stimulating thought) in the 1960s. To study the evolution of teaching method is to find that it has closely depended on general pedagogic ideas, the availability of teachers and their standard of training, the kind of technical aids to be drawn upon, the nature of school buildings provided and so on. Class teaching (the 'Prussian' system, as it used to be known) appears as the product of a specific set of circumstances, particularly during the past century. All this is both full of interest and a material help to getting present problems and possibilities into perspective. Do we want schools with separate classrooms in the future, as in the past, or do the new technical aids now coming into use, the methods of teaching at our disposal, and indeed our whole approach to the educational process, suggest considerable changes in the arrangement and organization of the school? It is only if such questions are well thought out, and teachers press for the facilities necessary to engage in new methods of education, that it is possible to short-circuit, as it were, the tendency of educational institutions to be rooted in yesterday's needs.

BRIAN SIMON, 'The History of Education',
pp. 101–2, in *The Study of Education*,
(ed.) J. W. TIBBLE, Routledge & Kegan Paul, 1967

For discussion

1 From the monitorial system to team-teaching is a long step. Obviously methods of teaching have changed along with the organization of schools. How would you describe the general trend of these changes?

2 Thirty years ago students training to become teachers were required to set out their notes for lessons according to the Herbartian five formal steps – Preparation, Presentation, Association, Generalization, Application. This practice appears to be dying out. Why?

3

What is important for this purpose is the role which we allot to the transmission of information, in the sense of a certain body of facts, the date of the Treaty of Utrecht, the rainfall of the Kalahari desert, the molecular structure of benzene.

The way in which the teacher helps the student to learn and remember these facts will obviously depend to some extent on the reason why it is thought desirable that the student should do so. In the case of the medical student and 'diseases' the reason is obvious, but this has not always been so in the realms of general education. In the nineteenth century, the theory underlying this kind of teaching seems to have been that there was a certain body of knowledge which should be the permanent possession of any educated man or woman, and the assumption was that once learnt it would not be forgotten. This approach is parodied in the famous skit *1066 and All That*. We all know that such 'knowledge' is not retained. One reason may be that, unlike the medical student's knowledge of diseases, it forms no part of the pupil's subsequent mental life. It does not matter to most of us operationally whether it was peasants or pheasants who were revolting in the fourteenth century. If, therefore, it was still considered necessary to impart and learn this sort of information it was also necessary to find some other reason for doing so. An early rationalization was that, although the knowledge itself was of no permanent value, the process of acquiring and memorizing it improved the faculty of memory. It was even thought that the more difficult and wearisome the act of memorizing, the more salutary the 'training' effect would be and the longer the information would be retained. Educational psychologists may suppose that this theory has been conclusively disproved by experimental evidence (as indeed it has), but the fact that many practising teachers still cling to it is well exemplified by the following quotation from the official handbook on the teaching of classics issued by the Incorporated Association of Assistant Masters:

> Many teachers maintain that a classified list of verbs, by grouping verbs of similar form together, makes as it were, the task of learning these verbs too easy, with the result that they do not stick in the memory. For this reason many prefer a casual or illogical list of verbs, or even an alphabetical list, to one arranged according to a system.

For those who accept this interpretation of the behaviour of human memory, the teaching technique for the imparting and memorization of information has usually been the analysis of the material into a series of fragmentary 'facts', the memorization of these (probably in homework), their repetition in a test the following morning, and, finally, an examination at the end of a 'term' which might be of almost any duration, to determine how much of the factual material has been retained. This pattern of teaching has stamped itself very firmly on the whole tradition of teaching and it would be hard to find any range of education from the junior school to the university where its influence is not still strong. It would be quite unjustifiable, therefore, in a book of this nature to dismiss it out of hand.

Let us first admit that whether we are concerned with the development of skills, knowledge or understanding there are certain things that simply have to be learnt either as information or as behaviour patterns. Neither the arabic numerals nor the letters of the alphabet have any intrinsic relationship with their meaning, that is their operational use. This relationship is conventional and simply has to be learnt. It is information passed on from one generation to the next, from teacher to pupil. But whereas in older methods of teaching the common method was to teach the pupil the relationship first and then let him practise the use of it, we see that teachers nowadays are reversing the order, so that children are encouraged to recognize and use written words or sentences and numerical concepts before any attempt is made to explain to them the structure of spelling or number. In the same way, in teaching a foreign language we now begin with speech patterns, heard and repeated orally, before we begin to look at the written language or attempts to analyse its grammar or syntax. For many years the process of learning by simple demonstration and practice was also the only one used in the teaching of manual skills, but there is evidence now that here, too, learning is more effective if such methods are supplemented by an attempt to bring out the principles underlying the manual skill. This reversal by which operation precedes analysis was first recommended as long ago as the sixteenth century for the teaching of Latin, but it has taken a very long time for it to be generally adopted in practice.

A. D. C. PETERSON, *Introduction to 'Techniques of Teaching'*, pp. 8–10, Pergamon Press, 1965

For discussion

1 Easy enough to agree that methods which insist on 'drumming it into them' stand condemned. But why is it that teachers have, on the whole, been slow and reluctant to admit that their main job is not simply imparting information?
2 How widespread is the attitude reflected in the quotation from the handbook of the Incorporated Association of Assistant Masters? Is there any justification for it? *Can* the task of learning be made too easy?

4

Economy, as we shall see, varies with mode of representation. But economy is also a function of the sequence in which material is presented or the manner in which it is learned. The case can be exemplified as follows (I am indebted to Dr J. Richard Hayes for this example). Suppose the domain of knowledge consists of available plane service within a twelve-hour period between five cities in the Northeast – Concord, New Hampshire, Albany, New York, Danbury, Connecticut, Elmira, New York, and Boston, Massachusetts. One of the ways in which the knowledge can be imparted is by asking the student to memorize the following list of connections:

> Boston to Concord
> Danbury to Concord
> Albany to Boston
> Concord to Elmira
> Albany to Elmira
> Concord to Danbury
> Boston to Albany
> Concord to Albany

Now we ask, 'What is the shortest way to make a round trip from Albany to Danbury?' The amount of information processing required to answer this question under such conditions is considerable. We increase economy by 'simplifying terms' in certain characteristic ways. One is to introduce an arbitrary but learned order – in this case, an alphabetical one. We rewrite the list:

> Albany to Boston
> Albany to Elmira
> Boston to Albany
> Boston to Concord
> Concord to Albany
> Concord to Danbury
> Concord to Elmira
> Danbury to Concord

Search then becomes easier, but there is still a somewhat trying sequential property to the task. Economy is further increased by using a diagrammatic notation, and again there are varying degrees of economy in such recourse to the iconic mode. Compare the diagram on the left and the one on the right.

FIG. 10

The latter contains at a glance the information that there is only one way from Albany to Danbury and return, that Elmira is a 'trap', and so on. What a difference between this diagram and the first list!

> Reprinted by permission of the publishers from
> JEROME S. BRUNER, *Toward a Theory of Instruction*,
> pp. 46–7, (The Belknap Press), Harvard University
> Press. Copyright © 1966 by the President and
> Fellows of Harvard College

For discussion

Can the task of learning be made too easy, we asked? Bruner's example is apposite. Too often the information, process or skill to be learned is presented in higgledy-piggledy fashion with the result that it can only be mastered with difficulty. Rather than rely on excessive memorization it is essential to bring out the inherent structure so that the learner can see at a glance where all the bits and pieces he has to memorize are to fit. Any other method means muddling through. Do you agree?

5

I BELIEVE THAT

The question of method is ultimately reducible to the question of the order of development of the child's powers and interests. The law for presenting and treating material is the law implicit within the child's own nature. Because this is so I believe the following statements are of supreme importance as determining the spirit in which education is carried on.

The active side precedes the passive in the development of the child-nature; that expression comes before conscious impression; that the muscular development precedes the sensory; that movements come before conscious sensations; I believe that consciousness is essentially motor or impulse; that conscious states tend to project themselves in action.

The neglect of this principle is the cause of a large part of the waste of time and strength in school work. The child is thrown into a passive, receptive, or absorbing attitude. The conditions are such that he is not permitted to follow the law of his nature; the result is friction and waste.

Ideas (intellectual and rational processes) also result from action and devolve for the sake of the better control of action. What we term reason is primarily the law of order or effective action. To attempt to develop the reasoning powers, the powers of judgment, without reference to the selection and arrangement of means in action, is the fundamental fallacy in our present methods of dealing with this matter. As a result we present the child with arbitrary symbols. Symbols are a necessity in mental development, but they have their place as tools for economizing effort; presented by themselves they are a mass of meaningless and arbitrary ideas imposed from without.

The image is the great instrument of instruction. What a child gets out of any subject presented to him is simply the images which he himself forms with regard to it.

If nine-tenths of the energy at present directed towards making the child learn certain things were spent in seeing to it that the child was forming proper images, the work of instruction would be indefinitely facilitated.

Much of the time and attention now given to the preparation and presentation of lessons might be more wisely and profitably expended in training the child's power of imagery and in seeing to it that he was continually forming definite vivid and growing images of the various subjects with which he comes in contact in his experience.

Interests are the signs and symptoms of growing power. I believe that they represent dawning capacities. Accordingly the constant and careful observation of interests is of the utmost importance for the educator.

JOHN DEWEY, 'The Nature of Method',
Article Four of *My Pedagogic Creed*

For discussion

1 Questions of method are really questions about child development, says Dewey. Must they always take as their starting-point the learner's own interests?

2 'I hear and I forget, I see and I remember. I do and it becomes part of me.' Is this the sum of Dewey's methodology?

6 Less formal methods of teaching

Informal methods are founded on active participation and learning by students. Many technical teachers assume that technological subjects can be presented only as lectures. The weakness in the lecturing method is that the teacher having thought about his technical material during preparation then expounds his thinking to the class. He assumes that because he is reasoning as he is telling the class the subject matter, that the students are also reasoning at exactly the same pace as himself, and towards the same conclusions. His approach is based on a traditional pattern of teaching method which lays far too much stress on the teacher's performance.

The established method of judging the skill of a technical teacher or a technical student-treacher still centres very largely on observation of his technique for as short a time as five minutes to as long as an hour. The 'platform performance and platform manner' combined with 'tricks of the trade' are given an exaggerated significance. Technical teaching should be concerned with the teacher's performance only in so far as he is advancing the students' knowledge of subject matter and their ability to think about it clearly. The criterion of effective technical teaching is what the students have learned not what the teacher has done or how he has done it.

ALEXANDER MACLENNAN, *Technical Teaching and Instruction*, p. 126, Oldbourne, 1963

For discussion

'Informal methods are founded on active participation.' Yet most lessons tend to be one-way affairs with the teacher doing most of the talking. The same is even truer of the university and college lecture (which the Robbins Report wanted to keep only as an 'occasion'). Why this liking of the platform manner? Why this stress on the need for verbal exposition?

7

In putting the book into a logical shape, I found I had two main difficulties to contend with.

The first was the vagueness of the word 'method' when used of various ways of teaching reading. Writers of books on reading usually classify the practice of teachers as belonging to this or that *method*. The most common labels are: alphabetic, phonic word, and sentence. But a method called alphabetic may also be called the spelling method or the A B C method; a method called phonic may sometimes be called syllabic; a word method may be referred to as the look-and-say method, and the sentence method may be labelled the global method. There are some other 'methods' too – the phrase method and even the ginger-bread method. It was not possible to solve the problem by banning the word 'method' from the pages of the book; it was too deeply entrenched in the vocabulary of reading for that. The alternative was – and it is part of the purpose of this introduction to emphasise this – to try to keep it clear in the reader's mind that each of these methods is amoebic in its power to change shape. There were alphabetic methods, but no single alphabetic method, and the same is true of all the other practices that are called methods. A subsidiary difficulty to this first main one was the fact that often writers on this subject use the term 'method' when it would have been more logical to refer to 'teaching material' as, for example, when a teacher is said to be using the 'phonic method' when she is in fact teaching by an alphabetic method though using books designed for teaching by a phonic method.

HUNTER DIACK, *In Spite of the Alphabet*,
pp. 7–8, Chatto & Windus, 1965

For discussion
Whatever the subject, the teacher has a wide variety of so-called methods from which to choose. Herbartian lessons or 'activity and experience' in informal groups, Dalton Plan, projects, programmed learning, school broadcasts and television, audio-visual aids, etc., etc. Which is it to be? The competing claims of the various methods of teaching reading may well leave him (usually her!) bewildered. Clearly there is something to be said for each of them.

Is it fair to conclude from this that 'pupils have contrived to learn reasonably well not because of the methods used by teachers but in spite of them'?

8 The importance of tests of methods

What the teacher should do with respect to each act of teaching each pupil, the leaders in education should do with respect to the general methods of teaching a subject recommended to all teachers. Expectations of results, even if based on right principles, must be corroborated by actual verification.

As a rule the best present judgment about the efficiency of a method will rest upon its harmony with the principles derived from the facts of human nature and upon its success or failure as measured by the opinion of those who try it.

The best present judgment will not be mistaken very often or very much, but there could be safer tests of the worth of methods. For when a principle derived from the facts of human nature is applied under the peculiar conditions of school life it may need modification; and the opinions of even the best teachers concerning the value of a method may be shortsighted and partial. What is needed is the comparatively sure decision of that superior variety of opinion which is called science.

E. L. THORNDIKE, *The Principles of Teaching Based on Psychology*, pp. 264-5, Seiler, 1906

For discussion

1 Are we any nearer to getting a scientific measure of the relative efficiency of different methods of teaching than Thorndike was at the beginning of the century? Why is the problem of evaluating different methods so complex?
2 Research studies of such new techniques as programmed learning, closed-circuit television, and audio-visual aids often report 'No significant differences' as compared with traditional methods. Does this mean that an L.E.A. is guilty of wasting the rate-payers' money if it decides to install an expensive closed-circuit television network or purchase teaching machines for its schools?

9

Streaming in fact . . . has been shown to be a self-validating process; the so-called 'correctness' of the initial classification is held to be 'proved' since, at the end of four years' schooling, wide differences are revealed between the level of attainment of high and low streams. The process of streaming itself must, however, ensure this result in the case of the vast majority of children. Investigations have shown that streaming tends to be rigid – transfer between streams takes place at a much lower level than teachers in the schools themselves seem to believe. The process is in itself divisive – the school, instead of being a unity, is divided internally into two or more different 'schools within a school', each with its own programme. It leads also to rigidity in teaching method – the aim being to get a homogenous 'class' which can be taught as a class, whereas the modern tendency is to rely more on group and individual work allied with class teaching. In spite of the fact that streaming is justified on the grounds of allowing for 'individual differences' it deliberately creates a situation where children can the more easily (in theory) be dealt with in the mass. The system tends also towards a certain fatalism – not much is expected from low streams, since the process of streaming reflects and crystallises the theory that these children lack 'intelligence'. Although much extremely good work goes on among low streams, the overall effect of this situation is to lower teachers' expectation, whereas, according to some recent research, the child's response is, at least in part, determined by the nature of these expectations. Finally, streaming, by separating out the more advanced children, creates a situation where low standards of intellectual and personality development among the majority of children are regarded as acceptable.

B. SIMON, *Non-Streaming in the Junior School,*
pp. 16–17, P.S.W. (Educational) Publications, 1964

For discussion

1 On the face of it, the question of whether or not to stream pupils may not seem to be a question of method. On the contrary, it is at the very heart of the question. In Britain it is probably true to say that the majority of teachers dislike the idea of handling mixed-ability groups (at any rate at the secondary stage) on the grounds that methods appropriate for bright pupils are inappropriate for the duller ones. In many Continental countries, on the other hand, teachers take mixed-ability grouping for granted and are frankly incredulous when told about the British practice. 'All our children learn at least one foreign language,' they say, 'Why don't yours?'

Why indeed?

2 Straight question: Do you believe that it is perfectly possible to teach any subject effectively in some intellectually honest fashion to any child at any stage of development?

10

A theory of instruction has four major features.

First, a theory of instruction should specify the experiences which most effectively implant in the individual a predisposition toward learning – learning in general or a particular type of learning. For example, what sorts of relationships with people and things in the pre-school environment will tend to make the child willing and able to learn when he enters school?

Second, a theory of instruction must specify the ways in which a body of knowledge should be structured so that it can most readily be grasped by the learner. 'Optimal structure' refers to a set of propositions from which a larger body of knowledge can be generated, and it is characteristic that the formulation of such structure depends upon the state of advance of a particular field of knowledge. The nature of different optimal structures will be considered in more detail shortly. Here it suffices to say that since the merit of a structure depends upon its power for *simplifying information,* for *generating new propositions,* and for *increasing the manipulability of a body of knowledge,* structure must always be related to the status and gifts of the learner. Viewed in this way, the optimal structure of a body of knowledge is not absolute but relative.

Third, a theory of instruction should specify the most effective sequences in which to present the materials to be learned. Given, for example, that one wishes to teach the structure of modern physical theory, how does one proceed? Does one present concrete materials first in such a way as to elicit questions about recurrent regularities? Or does one begin with a formalized mathematical notation that makes it simpler to present regularities later encountered? What results are in fact produced by each method? And how describe the ideal mix? The question of sequence will be treated in more detail later.

Finally, a theory of instruction should specify the nature and pacing of rewards and punishments in the process of learning and teaching. Intuitively it seems quite clear that as learning progresses there is a point at which it is better to shift away from extrinsic rewards, such as a teacher's praise, toward intrinsic rewards inherent in solving a complex problem for itself. So, too, there is a point at which immediate reward for performance should be replaced by deferred reward. The timing of the shift from extrinsic to intrinsic and from immediate to deferred reward is poorly understood and obviously important. Is it the case, for example, that wherever learning involves the integration of a long sequence of acts, the shift should be made as early as possible from immediate to deferred reward and from extrinsic to intrinsic reward?

Reprinted by permission of the publishers from
JEROME S. BRUNER, *Toward a Theory of Instruction*,
pp. 40–2 (The Belknap Press), Harvard University
Press. Copyright © 1966 by the President and
Fellows of Harvard College

For discussion

1 Note that Bruner's outline of the theory is at best putative. Even so, we suggest that it deserves the closest scrutiny. Taking each of the four features in turn:

(*a*) How would you list the pre-school influences which determine the child's approach to school learning? If they are largely or entirely beyond the teacher's control need they always be beyond his ken?

(*b*) We have touched on the importance of *structure* more than once in the course of these readings. How would you explain it, for example, to a language teacher who believed that 'a classified list of verbs . . . makes . . . the task of learning too easy' (cf. extract 3 above)?

(*c*) Similarly, as regards *sequence* we point out in the next extract that it has to be understood in a twofold sense. Would you care to anticipate the argument and say what you think we mean by this?

(*d*) As regards the nature and pacing of rewards and punishments, our own view is that much more attention should be paid to the former than has been customary. Do you agree?

2 You are now reaching the end of this book. You will have observed that each

section has been arranged as a sequence and that the various sections form a sequence of a kind. In a way, then, it resembles a programmed book, with one important difference – the questions for discussion are always left open-ended. There is no immediate reinforcement ('reward') for getting the 'right' answer. This is because we think Bruner is right in saying that 'wherever learning involves the integration of a long sequence of acts the shift should be made as early as possible from immediate to deferred reward'. In *Readings in Education* apart from the section on 'The Nature and Nurture of Human Abilities', this policy has been followed from the start. How effective has it been? Only you can decide.

11 Sequence

The notion of sequence has a twofold implication: (1) It implies that every subject has its own peculiar structure, its own internal regularities, principles, rules, laws, etc. and that these can be arranged in order so as to form a hierarchy. (2) It implies the existence of different levels of understanding appropriate to different stages of growth and mental development.

The second is the implication we have in mind when we speak of a developmental approach to teaching. In the past it has given rise to a number of tentative theories of instruction, e.g. Whitehead's three stages of Romance, Precision and Generalisation. It may be that Bruner's 'Enactive', 'Iconic', and 'Symbolic' levels of knowing are no better than a rehash of the same general theory. It may also be the case that at present no theory can hope to do more in the way of prescription than to restate the hoary old maxims about working from the concrete to the abstract, from particular instances to general conclusions, induction to deduction and so on *ad nauseam*. If so, it will earn no acclaim from anyone.

At the same time the hypothesis that any subject, no matter how abstruse, can be rendered intelligible to any child at any stage provides a clue of in-estimable worth. The fact that at the enactive level the child knows how to balance himself on a see-saw is the guarantee that, provided the teacher goes about it in the right way, he can be raised to the symbolic level of understanding Newton's Law of Moments. The secret of finding the 'right way' lies in making explicit what, initially, is implicit in the child's experience. The 'way' is dictated partly by the requirements of the internal logical structure of the subject itself, and partly by the pacing and timing of instruction to suit requirements which may be called maturational.

As regards the importance of sequence in this second sense, it seems that curriculum planning, strongly influenced by the 'child-centre' school of thought and supported by the findings of Piaget and his associates, has favoured the developmental approach, while the programmed learning movement has been more concerned to interpret sequence in terms of the systematic presentation of information and instruction. On the whole, this apparent discrepancy between the aims of the new curriculum planners and the programmers is not regrettable, for although on the face of things it may seem that they figure in the roles of the Herbatians and the Froebelians only in modern dress, the two sides are looking at the problem of sequence from different angles. The two approaches are complementary and each stands to gain from the other.

One labours to find the inherent step-by-stepness in the subject matter, the other to ascertain the 'suitable time'. Latterly, the two sides have showed signs of drawing closer together.

W. KENNETH RICHMOND, *The Teaching Revolution*, Methuen, 1967

For discussion
Take any scheme of work for which you are responsible (or, better still, a course of study which you have taken) and analyse the methods used (*a*) as regards *structure*, and (*b*) as regards *sequence*. Might it have been improved in either respect?

12

QUESTION: *What are the principal characteristics of programed instruction?*

ANSWER: The instructional material is developed by careful analysis of the behavior to be taught. All information, actions and decisions required for successful performance by the learner are carefully specified.

The subject-matter is broken down into a series of short instructional steps called frames. These are organized in a logical step-by-step sequence that leads the learner from his program behavior to the desired terminal behavior. Each frame provides one or more informational statements or illustrations and incorporates one or more questions to which the learner must make an active (verbal, written, or physical) response. Following his response to each question, the learner is immediately shown the correct response to compare with his own.

The learning session is self-paced by the learner. The presence of a teacher is not required, although, in many instances, it may be desirable.

QUESTION: *What are the psychological principles on which programed instruction is based?*

ANSWER: Programed instruction is based on the principle of 'reinforcement' – providing a reward for desired behavior so that the behavior tends to re-occur. Desired learning is automatically 'reinforced' with programed instruction by immediate confirmation of each correct response that the learner makes. The
Q

learner's self-awareness of successfully responding is inherently rewarding. Programed instruction structures the learning situation so that the learner is able to progress with minimum errors from one learning step to the next. The learner's knowledge of his capability to progress successfully is another source of reinforcement and, thereby, serves to enhance the effectiveness of the learning process.

QUESTION: *What is the instructional cycle with programed instruction?*

ANSWER: The cycle of instruction consists of the following steps:

1 The learner reads a small unit of instructional material (an instruction, a fill-in-the-blank question, a multiple-choice question, an essay question, or an incomplete diagram).
2 He makes a response by carrying out the instruction, filling in the blank, making a selection from the multiple choice, answering yes-or-no, or completing the diagram.
3 He is shown the correct answer and advances to the diagram.

S. MARGULIES and L. D. EIGEN, *Applied Programed Instruction*, p. 16, Wiley, 1962

For discussion
1 Whatever else may be said for or against it, programmed learning at least represents a systematic attempt to analyze the structure and sequence of the learning process. It has been heralded as a technology of instruction. With what justification?
2 It is often said that if a subject can be taught it can be programmed. How valid is this claim?

13

Our job involves people – and it's a big job. Last year we trained over 362,000 airmen at a cost of approximately 700 million dollars. As new command and control systems approach operational status, our training requirements will become more complex. We have made many improvements in our training procedures and management techniques, but we are constantly concerned with the Command's ability to meet the Air Force training job in the future. We must constantly revise our training concepts, methods, and procedures to meet tomorrow's mission in terms of cost.

Since November 1961, the Air Training Command, through contract with outside agencies, has trained more than 300 personnel throughout the Air Force in the techniques of developing programmed materials. Although it has been said that this effort more than doubled the number of instructional programmers in this country, our capability is still minimal when one considers that we have more than 2,400 training courses. My advisors inform me that, were we to exploit our present capability to its maximum, we could not program more than 5% of the Air Training Command effort within the next three years.

In addition, realizing that we would encounter the usual resistance experienced by those introducing a relatively new instructional methodology, we provided orientation and indoctrination in programmed instruction to more than 1,500 supervisors and training managers. This effort was very important in producing the cooperation and support necessary to an evaluation of this effort.

At present, we have more than 100 programmed instructional packages in use or in the process of being developed. These materials cover subjects ranging from 'T-37 Emergency Procedures' in flying training, to 'Precision Measuring Equipment' in technical training.

Our general objective is to determine whether a programmed instructional package in lieu of, or as a supplement to, conventional methods of training will substantially improve the quality of our graduates and materially decrease the costs. Concretely, we have specified that for a program to be acceptable, 90% of the students must score 90% or above on a comprehensive test covering all of the course objectives.

Our preliminary results show that we are on our way to reaching our 90/90 objective, with reductions in training time of 25–50%. One of our programs has reduced our training time as much as 83%.

> J. E. BRIGGS, 'Programmed Instruction: Breakthrough in Air Force Training?', pp. 131–2 in *Trends in Programmed Instruction*, (eds.) G. D. OFIESH and W. C. MEIERHENRY, Department of Audiovisual Instruction, National Education Association of the U.S.A. and National Society for Programmed Instruction, 1964

For discussion

Ninety per cent success with 90 per cent of the population may strike us as a tall order, and no one need pretend that anything like this degree of success has yet been achieved by using programmed materials in schools. Is this because the subjects taught in school are more difficult than those in military training – or is it because the methods used (including the kinds of programme available so far) are relatively inefficient? Is 90 per cent success with 90 per cent of the population unattainable?

14

Even our best schools are under criticism for their inefficiency in the training of drill subjects such as arithmetic. The condition in the average school is a matter of widespread national concern. Modern children simply do not learn arithmetic quickly or well. Nor is the result simply incompetence. The very subjects in which modern techniques are weakest are those in which failure is most conspicuous, and in the wake of an ever-growing incompetence come the anxieties, uncertainties, and aggressions which, in their turn, present other problems to the school. Most pupils soon claim the asylum of not being 'ready' for arithmetic at a given level, or, eventually, of not having a mathematical mind. Such explanations are readily seized upon by defensive teachers and parents. Few pupils ever reach the stage at which automatic reinforcements follow as the natural consequences of mathematical behaviour. On the contrary, the figures and symbols of mathematics have become standard emotional stimuli. The glimpse of a column of figures, not to say an algebraic symbol or an integral sign, is likely to set off, not mathematical behavior – but a reaction of anxiety, guilt or fear.

The teacher is usually no happier about this than the pupil. Denied the opportunity to control via the birch rod, quite at sea as to the mode of operation of the few techniques at her disposal, she spends as little time as possible on drill subjects and eagerly subscribes to philosophies of education which emphasize material of greater inherent interest. A confession of weakness is her extraordinary concern lest the child be taught something unnecessary. The repertoire to be imparted is carefully reduced to an essential minimum. In the field of spelling, for example, a great deal of time and energy has gone into discovering just those words which the young child is going to use, as if it were a crime to waste one's educational power in teaching an unnecessary word. Eventually, weakness of technique emerges in the disguise of a reformulation of the aims of education. Skills are minimized in favor of vague achievements – educating for democracy, educating the whole child, educating for life, and so on. And there the matter ends, for, unfortunately, these philosophies do not in turn suggest improvements in techniques. They offer little or no help in the design of better classroom practices.

Will machines replace teachers? On the contrary, they are capital equipment to be used by teachers to save time and labor. In assigning certain mechanizable functions to machines, the teacher emerges in his proper role as an indispensable human being. He may teach more students than heretofore – this is probably inevitable if the world-wide demand for education is to be satisfied – but he will do so in fewer hours and with fewer burdensome chores. In return for his greater productivity he can ask society to improve his economic condition.

The role of the teacher may well be changed, for machine instruction will affect several traditional practices. Students may continue to be grouped in 'grades' or 'classes', but it will be possible for each to proceed at his own level, advancing as rapidly as he can. The other kind of 'grade' will also change its meaning. In traditional practice a C means that a student has a smattering of a whole course. But if machine instruction assures mastery at every stage, a grade will be useful only in showing how far a student has gone; C might mean that he is halfway through a course. Given enough time he will be able to get an A; and since A is no longer a motivating device, this is fair enough. The quick student will meanwhile have picked up A's in other subjects.

Differences in ability raise other questions. A program designed for the slowest student in the school system will probably not seriously delay the fast student, who will be free to progress at his own speed. (He may profit from the full coverage by filling in unsuspected gaps in his repertoire.) If this does not prove to be the case, programs can be constructed at two or more levels, and students can be shifted from one to the other as performances dictate. If there are also differences in 'types of thinking' the extra time available for machine instruction may be used to present a subject in ways appropriate to many types. Each student will presumably retain and use those ways which he finds most useful. The kind of individual difference which arises simply because a student has missed part of an essential sequence (compare the child who has no 'mathematical ability' because he was out with the measles when fractions were first taken up) will simply be eliminated.

B. F. SKINNER, 'The Science of Learning and the Art of Teaching', *Harvard Educational Review*, 24:2 (Spring 1954), pp. 86–97. Copyright © 1954 by President and Fellows of Harvard College

For discussion
Skinner contends that much of the drudgery could be taken out of teaching by using mechanical devices which often do the job much more effectively than the 'flesh and blood' teacher. Does their usefulness stop short at this?

15

Between them, the blacksmith, the machinist and the metallurgist may be taken as typifying three stages in industrial development. The teacher's role similarly, though less obviously, may be thought of as passing through the three same stages. Like the blacksmith's, it remained for centuries at the level of craftsmanship, not greatly concerned with theory, using only the simplest of tools, and content to carry on in much the same way from generation to generation. Like the factory worker, the teacher during the last hundred years has taken to using machines of one sort or another and become more specialised in his techniques in the process, but still one who is more concerned with the practical rather than the theoretical aspects of his work. The difference between the two stages of development is brought out more clearly if we consider, first, the close resemblance between the activities that went on in the old-time school-room and the village forge, and, second, the resemblance between the organisation of the contemporary school and the factory. As things are, it may be stretching the analogy too far to claim that the teacher, like the metallurgist, has reached the stage of technology, but the signs are that this will be his future role.

What, precisely, does the word 'technology' imply? Compared with a 'technique', its characteristics are: (1) that it is capable of dealing with a much wider range of processes, (2) that it is 'science-based', grounded on a thorough grasp of the theory and principles behind the processes with which it deals, and (3) that because of this, it is able to initiate new processes. By definition, technology is implicated in the process of social change. It is no accident that whereas the stage of craftsmanship covered thousands of years and the stage of technicianship a century or so, the pace of events has stepped up to racing pitch during the last decade. New communication systems are developing so rapidly that teacher–pupil relationships, methods of presentation, planning of courses, etc., look like being affected, many would say revolutionised, as never before. Since 1960, a number of instructional devices which preserve at least some of the best features of private tuition have been widely publicised. Closed circuit television, the language laboratory, and the teaching machine are three examples which immediately come to mind. Each in its different way promises to change the conventional role of the teacher almost beyond recognition. To the extent that *direct* human controls are replaced by mechanical controls, this is the first move towards automation in the educational process, and in the long run its implications are certain to be as far-reaching in the school as they have already been in the factory and the office. Although the ultimate consequences cannot as yet be foreseen, the chances are that they will lead to a more rational deployment of staff, enhance professional status, and increase the individual teacher's output. In much the same way that an engineer sitting at a console can, at the touch of a switch, control the power which energises an industrial plant, tomorrow's teacher will be in a position to control a vastly greater flow of knowledge and ideas than was once thought possible. Before he can do so, however, he will need to master the basic principles of these latest technologies of instruction. At the moment it is a euphemism to say that these principles have still to be worked out fully and that they are imperfectly understood even by those who have made names for themselves by being first in the field.

W. KENNETH RICHMOND,
Teachers and Machines, Collins

For discussion
That machine technology is affecting the teacher's role is not in dispute. Do you agree that in the long run the widespread use of mechanical devices will 'lead to a more rational deployment of staff, enhance professional status, and increase the individual teacher's output'?

16

How diverse and divergent are the teaching devices which have been, and are being invented! In a way this is excellent, for it allows all sorts of experimental teaching techniques to be applied, and both teachers and students can discover what works for them. But, for reasons of efficiency and economy, the time must come for us to settle upon something definitive. Is it not possible to conceive of some composite device which might combine the advantages and surmount the limitations of individual devices?

I read recently of how a school (in France, I think) has placed the classroom TV set in the centre of the ceiling. Pupils viewed the image reflected in desk top mirrors. The idea was simply to give each pupil an optimum view of the screen. It appears that this could be developed in connection with other techniques. Imagine a large classroom or hall, large enough to take a whole form of perhaps 250–300 'comprehensive' children. Give the hall a dome-shaped ceiling with, inset at various points, a number of rear-projection screens. Beyond each screen would be a loop projector. These projectors would run simultaneously and continuously showing loop films of identical lengths. Each film would represent a section of the total lesson, and these sections would be in sequence.

Desk top mirrors could be adjustable so that each pupil could see any one of the screens reflected. A taped sound track for each film could be heard by the pupil through ear-phones. The mirror would, in fact, be part of a teaching machine set into each 'desk' and the adjustment of the mirror would automatically select the appropriate tape.

On the teaching machines, a moving roll of paper could be automatically numbered by the mirror adjustment and on this the pupil could write answers to questions incorporated in, or arising from, the film/commentary. Or he might press answer buttons or tape record or telephone an answer or comment. That is to say, the visual material in the film and the audio material on the tape would be programmed.

On the nature and quality of the answers given by the student to the questions on Film No. 1 would depend the type of mirror adjustment at the end of the films. If the answers were satisfactory, the adjustment (automatic or teacher controlled) would be to Film 2. If not, they would re-view No. 1. The teacher could cut out the taped commentary and substitute his own, if he wished, or he might adjust mirrors away from all screens and simply discuss difficulties during one run of the film and let the pupils see the next viewing.

It cannot be denied that such lavish use of film as is suggested above would not at present be economically viable. But there are already signs that cheap film stock and cheap video tape are on the way.

DAVID ANGUS, 'A View of the Top',
Letter in *New Education*, November 1966

For discussion

Is this a pipe dream or an Orwellian nightmare?

Is it not likely that the foreseeable future will see the adoption of methods of teaching which at present are not dreamed of in our educational philosophy?

Index

(Italic numbers indicate quotations)

A.M.A., The, 181–2
ability, 230, 235; measurement of, 185, *see also* intelligence tests; Nature and Nurture of, 68–98; pool of, 55, 89–93
activity methods, 202–4, 213; *see also* schools
Adams, Sir John, *17, 18, 39*, 40
'Adolescent and Changing Moral Standards, The', E. M. Eppel, *141–2*
'Adolescents into Adults', R. M. Hara, *150–1*
Aims of Education, The, A. N. Whitehead, *52–3, 152*
Allen, A. B., *108–9, 114*
Allen, William, *218–19*
alphabet, 7–9
Angus, David, *237–8*
Applied Programed Instruction, S. Margulies and L. D. Eigen, *231–2*
arete, 155
Aristotle, 5, 17, *136–7*, 141, 151, 172, *195–6*
Arnold, Matthew, 37
Arnold, Thomas, 154, 157
Arts: division from Sciences, 45, 48–53, 210, 211; Liberal, 49, 53, 198
Ascham, Roger, *60*
Ashby, Sir Eric, *45*
assessment: of ability, 184–5; *see also* evaluation and examinations
Association of Head Teachers, *113*
audio-visual aids, 227, 236–8
authority, 119, 124–5, 128–30, 148
Authority, Responsibility and Education, R. S. Peters, *33–4, 161–2*
Autobiography, Charles Darwin, *133*

Baccalaureat, *see* examinations, French
Bantock, G. H., *66–7*
Barker, Ernest, 38
Being a Headmaster, Norman Tosh, *59–60*
Beloe Committee, 175
Bernstein, Basil, 103, *148–9*
Berufs- oder Allgemeinbildung? Kerschensteiner, 41
Best, Edward, *19–21*
Bertrand Russell on Education, J. Park, *145–6*
Blackie, John, *103–4, 205*, 206
Boas, Guy, *120*
books, 4–6
Borders and Beyond, The, Abel Chapman, *11–12*
Bowley, R. L., *181–2*
Boyd, 180
Branch Street, Marie Paneth, *124*
Bremer, John, *201–2*
Briggs, J. E., *232–3*
Brogan, Colm, *35–6*
Brown boys, 83–4, 86
Bruner, Jerome S., 24, 55, 57, 58, *192–3, 206, 222–3, 228–9*, 230
Brunton Report (*From School to Further Education*), 46–8
Budge, 166

Cecil, Lord David, *174–5*
Certificate of Secondary Education, 175–6
Chapman, Abel, *11–12*
character: definitions of, 161–2; of the teacher, 156–7, 166–7; influences on,

158–9, 162–6; training, 40, 41–2, 43, 130, 154–72, 195, see also education, moral; types of, 159–61
Cheetham, A., 107–8
Chemical Bond Approach Project, 210
Children and their Primary Schools, see Plowden Report
Christianity, 2, 3–4, 17, 134, 137, 145, 154
chromosomes, 69–70
Clarke, Sir Fred, 53–4
class: effects of social, 78, 80–6, 91–2, 102–3, 121–2, see also language; -teaching ('Prussian' system), 219–20, 227–8
Classics, 38, 198–200, 201
colour-blindness, 70–1
Comenius, 4–5, 48, 210
communication, 42
Comprehensive School, The, R. Pedley, 95
Concept of Mind, The, Gilbert Ryle, 21–2
conditioning, 151
conformity, 159–61
Contrary Imaginations, Liam Hudson, 12–13, 160
control: aversive, 116–17; moral, 114; parental, 166–7; see also discipline
courses: planning of, 207–8; work-based, 46–8; see also curriculum
Cousinet, 147
creativity, 159–60, 186
Creativity and Intelligence, J. W. Getzels and P. W. Jackson, 135–6, 160, 186
Cubberley, E. P., 105–6
Culture and General Education, W. Kenneth Richmond, 48–51
Current Affairs, 199–200
curriculum: classical, 38; organization of, 46–8, 53, 163–4, 192–3, 230–1; structure and sequence, 194–217

Dalton plan, 15
Darwin, Charles, 133; family pedigree of, 72, 74
De Magistro, St Augustine, 3–4
'Defence of Classical Education, A', Sir Richard Livingstone, 199
delinquency: causes of, 59–60; treatment of, 167–70

democracy: education for, 44; in education, 127–8
detention system, 107
determinism, 158
'Development of Current Ideas about Intelligence Tests'. Philip E. Vernon, 65–6
Dewey, John, 15, 30, 128, 142–3, 147, 217, 224, 225
Diack, Hunter, 225–6
Dickens, Charles, 102–3
Die drei Grundlagen für die Organisation des Fortbildungs-Schulwesens, Kerschensteiner, 42
Dienes, Z. P., 212–13
Dilke, C., 166
discipline, 119–33; definitions of, 114–15, 119–20; free, 125, 152; intellectual, 213–14; lack of, 121, 124, 166–7; moral, 142–3, 147–8, 166–70; Public School, 107–8; self-, 125, 134, 147–8; Spartan, 108–9
Discipline without Punishment, Oskar Spiel, 14
disobedience, 104–5
Dr Moberley's Mink-Mark, C. Dilke, 166
Drever, Professor J., 93

educability: concept of, 55–67; factors determining, 73–98, 149
education: aims and objectives, 25–36, 126–7, 138, 144, 195–6, 202–3, 206–7; general and special, 37–54; German, 105–6; liberal–cultural, 37–40, 45, 49–54; moral, 41, 46, 131, 134–53, 154, see also character training; opportunities for higher, 81–2, 87–9; principles of, 11–24; progressive, 117, 203–4; Russian, 63, 66; state, 160; university, 88–9, 93, 174–5; vocational–technical, 37, 39–54
Education Act 1944, 140, 175, 176
Education and Environment, S. Wiseman, 75, 76, 128, 203–4
Education and the Working Class, Marsden and Jackson, 86, 160–1
Education and Training of Teachers, P. Gurrey, 156–7
Education and Values, G. H. Bantock, 66–7

Education for Tomorrow, John Vaizey, *63–4*

Education from Dewey to Gandhi, G. Ramanathan, *215–17*

Education: Its Data and First Principles, Sir Percy Nunn, *126–7, 164*

Educational Anthropology, G. F. Kneller, *200*

'Educational Education', John Bremer, *201–2*

educators: aims of, 33–4; past, 14–18; *see also* teachers

Effects of Federal Programs on Higher Education, The, H. Orlans, *91*

Eigen, L. D., *231–2*

electric age, the, 7–9

Elliott, 180

Elvin, Lionel, *144–5*

Emile, Rousseau, *5, 6, 138–9*

environment, *see* 'Nurture'

Eppel, E. M., *141–2*

Establishment, the, 42, 163, 164

ethics, 136–7; *see also* education, moral, and character training

Ethics and Education, R. S. Peters, *114–15*

Eton College, 76, 77, 157

Eton Microcosm, A. Cheetham and E. Parfit, *107–8*

evaluation, 173, 186, 192–3; *see also* examinations

Evolution of Educational Theory, The, Sir John Adams, *17, 18, 39, 40*

Examination of Examination, The, Hartog and Rhodes, *177, 178*

examinations, 173–93; 'A' level, 77, 79, 80, 85; degree, 79, 80, 174–5; eleven-plus, 77, 78, 85; French, 183–5; 'O' level, 77, 79, 80; *see also* Certificate of Secondary Education

Experimental Study of Mathematics Learning, An, Z. P. Dienes, *212–13*

Farley, Richard, *121–2*

Fraser, the Rev. James, *58–9*

free will, 151–2, 154, 158

freedom, 119, 152

Freud, 170

Froebel, 14, 15, 29

From School to Further Education, *see* Brunton Report

General Education in a Free Society, Harvard Committee, *42–5*

genetics, 69–74

genotype, 73–4

Georg Kerschensteiner, Diane Simons, *41*

Getzels, J. W., *135–6*, 153, 160, *186*

Gillett, A. N., *121*

Gladstone, 38–9

Glaucon, 18–19, 56–7

glaucoma, 71–2

Good Enough for the Children, John Blackie, *103–4, 205*

Great Didactic, The, Comenius, *4–5*

Greek Philosophers from Thales to Aristotle, The, W. K. C. Guthrie, *154–5*

Groundwork of Educational Theory, J. S. Ross, *126*

Guerry, 96

Gurrey, P., *156–7*

Guthrie, W. K. C., *154–5*

H.M.S.O., *90*

Hadow Report (*The Primary School*), *202–3*

'Half our Future', *see* Newsom Report

Halls, W. D., *183–4*

Hara, R. M., *150–1*

Hard Times, Charles Dickens, *102–3*

Harding, D. W., *97*

Hartog, 177, *178*

Harvard Committee, *42–5*, 49

Haüberle, 105–6

Havighurst, R. J., *166–7, 170–2*

Hayes, J. Richard, 222

Herbart, 15, *40–1*, 42, 126, 220

heredity, *see* 'Nature'

Highfield, M. E., *110–12*

History of Education, E. P. Cubberley, *105–6*

'History of Education, The', Brian Simon, *219–20*

History of Eton College, *157*

home background, 78–86, 91, 215–17

Homer Lane, W. David Wills, *167–70*

Hudson, Liam, *12–13*, 160

Hughes, A. G. and E. H., *124–5*

Hull, 12–13
humanism: as basis of moral education, 145; technological, 45
Huxley, Thomas, 37, 174

identical twins, 75–6, 79
Imaginary Conversations, Walter Lippman, *56*
Incorporated Association of Assistant Masters, 221
In Spite of the Alphabet, Hunter Diack, *225–6*
indiscipline, *see* discipline, lack of,
indoctrination, 150–1
inert ideas, 202–3
inheritance, laws of, 69–74
instruction: programmed, *see* programmed learning; theory of, 228–9; technology of, 232; *see also* teaching
intelligence: and class, 78–86; and delinquency, 59–60; definition of, 55–67; inheritance of, 72–6; tests, 65–6, 75, 90–3, 164
Introduction to Modern Genetics, C. H. Waddington, *70, 72*
Introduction to 'Techniques of Teaching', A. D. C. Peterson, *220–2*
Introduction to the Philosophy of Education, An, D. J. O'Connor, *14–16*

Jackson, Brian, 86, *160–1*
Jackson, P. W., *135–6*, 153, 160, *186*
James, Walter, *106–7*
James, William, 43
Jarman, T. L., *38*
Johnson, Dr, 17

Kalton, G., *77*, 129
Keate, 157
Kerschensteiner, Georg, *41–2*, 46, 155
Kneller, G. F., *200*
knowledge: fragmentation of modern, 37, 49–52; information and, 186–7; place in education, 220–2; scientific, 11–14; 200–1; structure of, 210–11; technical, 143–4; use of, 191, 196–8; virtue and, 134
Koestler, Arthur, *149–50*
Krutch, Joseph Wood, *158–9*

Lambert, Royston, *129*
Lancaster, Joseph, 218–19

Landmarks in the History of Education, T. L. Jarman, *38*
language: meaning and, 1–4, 6–7; of different classes, 148–9
Larwood, H. J. C., *93*
Latin and Greek, R. M. Ogilvie, *199–200*
leadership, 93–4, 95, 163–4
learning: children's capacity for, 209–10, 224–5; convergent and divergent, 159–61, 186; imagination and, 214–15
Learning and Teaching, A. G. and E. H. Hughes, *124–5*
Leavis, 37
lectures, as method of teaching, 219, 225
leisure, 160–1, 195–6, 200
Letter to James Mill, Francis Place, *57, 58*
Letters, Plato, *1–2*
liberal studies, 195–6; *see also* Arts, Liberal
Life of Thomas Arnold, 157
Ligon, Ernest M., *130*
Lippman, Walter, *56*
literacy, 7–9; crime and, 96–7
Little Commonwealth (reformatory), 167–70
Livingstone, Sir Richard, 199
Local Education Authorities, 110–12, 140
Locke, John, 5, 20, *57, 58, 138*, 139
'Look at the Future, A', Gordon Pask, *189–92*
Lowe, Robert, *37–8*, 48

Macaulay, 62
MacDougall, 114
Mackenzie, R. F., *163–4*
Maclennan, Alexander, *206–7, 225*
Madison Project, 212–13
Mager, R. F., *28–9, 30, 31–2*, 207
Margulies, S., *231–2*
marking, 177–83, 188–9
Marsden, Denis, 86, *160–1*
Marx, 21, 63
mathematics, 201, 208–11, 212–13, 234–5
Mcintosh, D. M., *179–80*
McLuhan, Marshall, 7–9
Measure of Man, The, Joseph Wood Krutch, *158–9*

Measurement of Abilities, The, P. E. Vernon, *180–1, 183, 184–5*
memory, 221–3
Mendel, 69–70
methodology, 194, 218, 219
methods, 218–38; progressive and activity, 203–4
Mill, J. S., 160
Moberley, Sir Walter, 48
Modern Languages, 199–200
Montessori, 14, 15
Moral Judgement of the Child, The, J. Piaget, *127–8, 147*
Moral Principles in Education, John Dewey, *142–3*
'Moral Values in a Mixed Society', Lionel Elvin, *144–5*
morality: test of, 135–6, 152–3; *see also* education, moral
mother, role of, 148–9
Murray, Gilbert, 38
Myth of the Four Metals, Plato, 55–8, 95

National Foundation for Educational Research in England and Wales, *110–12*
Nature: challenge of, 162–3; Rousseau and, 5, 139
'Nature' (heredity), 55, 56–8, 63–6, 68–98
Nature of Education, The, Colm Brogan, *35–6*
'Nature of Method, The', John Dewey, *224*
Neill, A. S., *170*
New Education, *176*
New View of Society, A, Robert Owen, *57, 58, 157–8*
Newcastle Commission Report, *58–9*
Newsom Report ('Half our Future'), 55, *62–3*, 83, *84, 122–3, 140–1*
Niblett, W. R., *143–4*
Nicomachean Ethics, Aristotle, *136–7, 151*
Nisbet, S., *26–7*
Non-Streaming in the Junior School, B. Simon, *227–8*
Norwood Report, 55, *60–2*, 63
Nuffield Physics, Teachers Guide, *30–1, 187*

Nuffield Science Project, 194, 210
Nunn, Sir Percy, *126–7, 164*
'Nurture' (environment), 57–8, 62–6, 68–98

O'Connor, D. J., *14–16*, 17, 18, 22
Ogilvie, R. M., *199–200*
'On Our Way – to 1984', R. F. Mackenzie, *163–4*
On the Idea of Elementary Education, Pestalozzi, *144*
'One Rat in Twenty is a Leader', Colin Wilson, *93–4*
Open Society and its Enemies, The, Karl Popper, 58
opportunity, equality of, 64, 83, 85
Order, and discipline, 124–7
organization: school, 219–20; tripartite, 60–2, 63
Orlans, H., *91*
Orwell, George, 163, 238
Outline of History, H. G. Wells, 38
Outward Bound movement, 162–4
Owen, Robert, *57*, 58, 154, *157–8*
Oxford, 174–5

Paneth, Marie, *124*
parenthood: training for, 197–8; *see also* control, parental
Parfit, E., *107–8*
Park, J., *145–6*
Pask, Gordon, *189–92*
'Pavlov in Retreat', Arthur Koestler, *149–50*
Peck, R. F., *166–7, 170–2*
Pedley, R., *95*
perception, 3–4
personality, *170–2*
Pestalozzi, 14, 15, *144*, 156
Peter the Great, 109
Peters, R. S., *9–10, 33–4, 114–15*, 116, *151*, 152, *161–2*
Peterson, A. D. C., *220–2*
Phenix, Philip H., *213–15*
phenotype, 69, 73–4
Philosophical Analysis and Education, Edward Best, *19–21*
Philosophies of Education, Ernest M. Ligon, *130*
philosophy, 9–10

'Philosophy of Education, The', R. S. Peters, 9–10

Physical Science Study Committee, 207–8, 209

physics, 201, 207–8

Piaget, Jean, 65, *127–8*, *147*, 148, 151, 171, 230

Pinsent, A., *110–12*

Place, Francis, *57*, 58, 65

Plato, *1–2*, 17, *18–19*, 55, *56–7*, 58, 94, 95

Plowden Report (*Children and their Primary Schools*), *30*, 65, *113*, *124*, 128, 158

Politics, Aristotle, *195–6*

poor, education of, 37–8, 58–9

Popper, Karl, 58

practice, and theory, 11–24, 27, 52–3, 68

'Prelude, The', Wordsworth, *165*

Preparing Objectives for Programmed Instruction, R. F. Mager, *28–9*

Pressey, 188–9

Primary and Classical Education, Robert Lowe, *37–8*

Primary School, The, see Hadow Report

Primary School, The, Scottish Education Department, 128

Principles of Teaching Based on Psychology, The, E. L. Thorndike, *131*, *132*, *140*, *185*, *226–7*

Process of Education, The, Jerome Bruner, *57*, 58

'Programmed Instruction', J. E. Briggs, *232–3*

programmed learning, 31–2, 34–5, 117, 159, 188–93, 230–4; see also teaching programme

psychology, 12–13, 16; morality and, 146

Psychology of Character Development, The, R. F. Peck and R. J. Havighurst, *166–7*, *170–2*

'Psychology of Character, The', Roback, 161

Psychology of Punishment, The, A. B. Allen, *108–9*, *114*

Public Schools, The, G. Kalton, 77, *129*

punishment, 99–118

Purpose in the Curriculum, S. Nisbet, *26–7*

Ramanathan, G., *215–17*

Realms of Meaning, Philip H. Phenix, *213–15*

'Reason and Habit', R. S. Peters, *151*

religion, 139, 142, 144–5, 146, 159

Religion in the Making, A. N. Whitehead, *146*

Report to the County of Lanark, Robert Owen, *158*

'Republic, The', Plato, *18–19*, *56–7*, 58

'Requirements for Major Curriculum Revision, The', Jerrold R. Zacharias, *207–9*

rewards, 229–30, 231–2

Rhodes, 177, *178*

Rhythm of Education, 152

Richmond, W. Kenneth, *22–4*, *48–51*, *188–9*, *210–11*, *230–1*

Riesman, 134

Roback, 161–2

Robbins Report, *78*, 79, *80*, 81, *89*, 225

Robinson boys, 83–4, 86

Robinson Crusoe, Daniel Defoe, 5

Ross, J. S., *126*

Rousseau, *5*, 6, 15, *138–9*, 146

Russell, Bertrand, *125*, 146

Ryle, Gilbert, *212*

Sadler, J. E., *121*

Sanderson, 116, 128, 147

Scaling of Teachers Marks, The, D. M. McIntosh, 179–80

Scholemaster, The, Roger Ascham, *60*

school-leaving age, 58–9, 87–90

schools: Activity, 128, 147; as social institutions, 142–3, 147–8; boarding, 107–8; Comprehensive, 36, 53, 65, 67, 85, 95; day, 140, 154; Grammar, 61, 63, 77, 78, 80, 83, 85, 88–9, 94, 95, 160–1; infant, 30; Jesuit, 107; junior, 30; Monitorial, 218–19; Primary, 30, 113, 163, 202–3; Public, 77, 107–8, 129, 154; Scottish secondary, 46–8; secondary, 53, 60–2, 89, 95, 96, 179; Secondary Modern, 36, 61, 63, 77, 78, 83, 85–6, 94; state, 34–6, 129, 154, 160; technical, 61, 63

Schools Council, The, 194

science, 11–14, 163–4; place in curriculum, 38, 198, 200, 210; teaching of, 30–1
Sciences: division from Arts, 45, 48–52, 210, 211; Liberal, 195–6
'Science of Education, The', Herbart, 40–1
'Science of Learning and the Art of Teaching, The', B. F. Skinner, 116–17, 234–5
Secondary Modern Discipline, Richard Farley, 121–2
self-preservation, 197–8
sequence, 8, 33–4, 222–3, 228–32; see also curriculum
Simon, Brian, 219–20, 227–8
Simons, Diane, 41
Skinner, B. F., 116–17, 234–5
Snow, C. P., 8, 37, 42, 50
social engineering, 154, 158–9
Social Psychology and Individual Values, D. W. Harding, 97
'Social Structure, Language and Learning', Basil Bernstein, 148–9
Social Studies, 45
Society, Schools and Progress in France, W. D. Halls, 183–4
sociology, 14, 159
Sociology of Education, The, P. W. Musgrave, 159–60
Socrates, 18–19, 56, 134, 154–5, 156, 173, 188
'Some Problems in Moral Education Today', W. R. Niblett, 143–4
Some Thoughts Concerning Education, John Locke, 20, 57, 58, 138
Souvenirs, Vulliemin, 156
specialism, 45–6, 49
specialization, 37, 39, 45, 48–51, 200; CSE and, 176
Spencer, Herbert, 17, 196–8
Spiel, Oskar, 14
St Augustine, 3–4
St Paul, 134
Staatsbürgerliche Erziehung der deutschen Jugend, Kerschensteiner, 41
Starch, 180
statistics, 97, 183
Statistics of Education, H.M.S.O., 90
Stones, E., 34–5
streaming, 227–8

structure, 228–9, 231–2; see also curriculum suggestion, 149–50
Survey of Rewards and Punishments, A, M. E. Highfield and A. Pinsent, 110–12

Talking of Summerhill, A. S. Neill, 170
Teacher and his World, The, Walter James, 106–7
teaching: class-, 219–20, 227–8; examinations as a part of, 190–3; machines, 188–92, 227, 234–8; methods of, 24, 218–38; programme, example of, 68–98; see also instruction
'Teaching of Programming Techniques in Teacher Education, The,' E. Stones, 34–5
Teaching Revolution, The, W. Kenneth Richmond, 22–4, 210–11, 230–1
Teaching without Tears, R. L. Bowley, 181–2
teachers: 'born', 14; character of, 156–7, 166–7; problems of, 112, 121–3, 141; role of, 234–7; technical, 207, 225; training of, 14, 19
Teacher's Story, A, Guy Boas, 120
Teachers and Machines, W. Kenneth Richmond, 188–9, 235–6
Technical Teaching and Instruction, Alexander Maclennan, 206–7, 225
technologists, 42, 45
technology, 9, 45, 46–8, 200–1; the electric, 8–9; of education, 235–6
Technology and the Academics, Sir Eric Ashby, 45
temperament, 164
tests, 173, 185–93; see also intelligence tests
theory: and practice, 11–24, 27, 52–3, 68; -building, 12–14, 21–2
Thorndike, E. L., 131, 132, 140, 185, 226–7
Tosh, Norman D. F., 59–60
Toward a Theory of Instruction, Jerome S. Bruner, 192–3, 206, 222–3, 228–9
Tozer, A. H. D., 93
Tractatus, Ludwig Wittgenstein, 6–7
training: Air Force, 232–3; character, see character training; intellectual,

132-3, 140, 142; of judgement, 42-5, 143-4
training colleges, 14, 157
Training for Teaching, J. E. Sadler and A. N. Gillett, *121*
Turing's Theorem, 211
Two Cultures, the, 37, 48-53
type, movable, 4-5, 9

Understanding Media, Marshall McLuhan, *7-9*

Vaizey, John, *63-4*, 65
Vernon, Philip E., *65-66*, *180-1*, *183*, *184-5*
'View of the Top, A', David Angus, *237-8*
virtue, 134, 136-7, 172, 195-6; *see also arete*
' "Vocational" and "Cultural" ', Sir Fred Clarke, *53-4*

vocationalism, *see* education, vocational–technical
Vulliemin, *156*

Waddington, C. H., *70*, *72*
Warburton, Dr, 203, 204
Welfare State, 122
Wellard, 108
What Knowledge is of Most Worth? Herbert Spencer, *196-8*
White, Stephen, *207-9*
Whitehead, A. N., 29, 49, *52-3*, 94, *146*, 147, *152*, 202, 210, 230
Wills, W. David, *167-70*
Wilson, Colin, *93-4*
Wiseman, S., *75*, *76*, 128, *203-4*
Wittgenstein, Ludwig, *6-7*, 119
Wood, 180
words, and meanings, 1-10
Wordsworth, William, *165*, 166

Zacharias, Jerrold R., *207-9*